Hacking in the Humanities

Bloomsbury Studies in Digital Cultures

Series Editors
Anthony Mandal and Jenny Kidd

This series responds to a rapidly changing digital world, one which permeates both our everyday lives and the broader philosophical challenges that accrue in its wake. It is inter- and trans-disciplinary, situated at the meeting points of the digital humanities, digital media and cultural studies, and research into digital ethics.

While the series will tackle the "digital humanities" in its broadest sense, its ambition is to broaden focus beyond areas typically associated with the digital humanities to encompass a range of approaches to the digital, whether these be digital humanities, digital media studies or digital arts practice.

Titles in the series
Queer Data, Kevin Guyan
The Trouble With Big Data, Jennifer Edmond, Nicola Horsley,
Jörg Lehmann and Mike Priddy

Forthcoming titles
Ambient Stories in Practice and Research, Edited by Amy Spencer
Metamodernism and the Postdigital in the Contemporary Novel,
Spencer Jordan
Questioning Google's Search Engine, Rosie Graham

Hacking in the Humanities

Cybersecurity, Speculative Fiction, and Navigating a Digital Future

AARON MAURO

BLOOMSBURY ACADEMIC
LONDON • NEW YORK • OXFORD • NEW DELHI • SYDNEY

BLOOMSBURY ACADEMIC
Bloomsbury Publishing Plc
50 Bedford Square, London, WC1B 3DP, UK
1385 Broadway, New York, NY 10018, USA
29 Earlsfort Terrace, Dublin 2, Ireland

BLOOMSBURY, BLOOMSBURY ACADEMIC and the Diana logo
are trademarks of Bloomsbury Publishing Plc

First published in Great Britain 2022

Cover design: Rebecca Heselton
Cover image: Trojan horse by Delapouite / games-icons.net

A catalogue record for this book is available from the British Library.

A catalog record for this book is available from the Library of Congress.

ISBN: HB: 978-1-3502-3098-9
       PB: 978-1-3502-3102-3
       ePDF: 978-1-3502-3099-6
       eBook: 978-1-3502-3100-9

Series: Bloomsbury Studies in the Digital Humanities

Typeset by Integra Software Services Pvt. Ltd.

To find out more about our authors and books visit www.bloomsbury.com
and sign up for our newsletters.

For Catherine

Contents

Acknowledgments

The land that made this book possible is the traditional territory of the Haudenosaunee and Anishinaabe peoples. This land is covered by the Upper Canada Treaties and is within the land protected by the Dish with One Spoon Wampum Agreement. The friendship and generosity of Indigenous people is the foundation that makes possible our security now and in the future.

I wrote this book in the winter of 2020–1, during the worst of the Covid-19 pandemic lockdowns. "Social distancing" was the public health euphemism for our collective isolation, even as frontline workers kept our grocery stores, hospitals, and schools open. Thank you to those good people who did the jobs that needed doing.

Many people mentioned here may not recognize their contribution to this book, but in the midst of the pandemic, through endless video calls, it was your memory and friendship that I called on to imagine an audience for this book. I want to thank everyone in the Electronic Textual Cultures Lab at the University of Victoria, both past and present. Thanks to Ray Siemens, Laura Estill, Constance Crompton, Dan Sondheim, Alyssa Arbuckle, Daniel Powell, and Matt Huculak. The audacious style of humanities research that we imagined during those many "team building" exercises guides me even now. In my new home, I am endlessly grateful to the faculty and staff in the Centre for Digital Humanities at Brock University. To the core team—Jason Hawreliak, Alex Christie, David Hutchison, Clara Suba, Thomas Brown, and Andrew Roth—and to so many more, thank you. At Bloomsbury, I am indebted to Ben Doyle, who saw the potential in a multidisciplinary manuscript. Thank you for your advocacy and support during this process.

My parents are present throughout this book. As a police officer and a nurse, they taught me to have both a dark sense of humor and a desire to help in emergencies. My father taught me everything I know about physical security and response planning as well as restorative justice and community policing. My mother taught me that caring for people is about compassion and kindness as well as decisiveness and insight under pressure.

Thank you to my unflinching and powerful partner in all things, Catherine, for weathering the ups and downs of the pandemic and making this book possible in every conceivable way. Finally, thank you to my son for being a brilliant storyteller and a brave friend.

Preface

There are several good reasons why the humanities should be interested in cyber security. Digital Humanities (DH) has brought historical and cultural research to a public audience like never before, thanks in large part to the web. Archives and applications are making rarefied cultural objects available almost anywhere on the globe. DH practitioners make beautifully specialized, bespoke projects that deserve to be protected. We have research centers around the world.[1] We develop hundreds of projects a year of tremendous historical, archival, and cultural significance.[2] We are a diverse, engaged, and energetic discipline.[3] For these reasons, digital humanities projects must now embrace security best practices in the ways we conduct and communicate research.

Threat modeling application security and infrastructure operations are a needed critical and analytical framework for the humanities. Data integrity is about more than long-term storage; it is also about developing plans for data recovery and mitigation in the event that data is stolen or corrupted. The stakes are high and the risks are real. DH practitioners in libraries, archives, museums, and universities are working to digitize and make available the cultural legacy of humanity. This is a generations long project that will require forethought and planning in the protocols, standards, processes, and tools used. I am reminded of Bethany Nowviski's essay "Digital Humanities in the Anthropocene" where she warns us about the "daunting and immobilizing" contradictions working to save the past in an environment of fiscal scarcity and finite resources, while also working to record the ever more chaotic and fast moving present.[4] Contemporary culture online does not just happen benignly; it is active, engaging, and even hostile. Consideration must be given to the long-term security of digital projects in constantly evolving cultural and technological environments. The consequences of failing to manage security will be detrimental to the preservation of cultural memories, traditions, and histories and the future insights they will provide humanity.

Cybersecurity for the humanities should not be regarded as just another sign that we have reached *peak cyber*.[5] Many humanists have adversaries, antagonistic cultural forces amplified by social media, that would attempt to disrupt, distort, or destroy research. Depending on the national context, the immediate physical safety of researchers may also be at risk. When research is presented on the web, it is received on a global stage after all. A university researcher or student may be expecting their research to be received locally or nationally. However, global concerns or interests may elicit backlash or even hostile attention from government agencies or ideologically driven groups organized online. The risks of disrupting research can be detrimental to the public perception, perceived legitimacy, and the reputations of humanists.

This book is for those cultural workers in galleries, libraries, archives, and museums who work to preserve cultural materials and are committed to the secure preservation of our shared history. Similarly, this book is for humanists in any discipline who want to secure their privacy and research online, while also thinking about fundamental ethical questions from a practical and technologically focused perspective. I have considered public academics who want to think about adversarial forces on social media and elsewhere. Developers in a university setting may find interesting in thinking about security related to knowledge mobilization in academic contexts. I hope to have represented activists thinking about operational security in direct action as well. Finally, the largest audience includes citizens, who want to think about how durable historical records survive online. After all, DH has to guess which standards, languages, and platforms will last into the future, and this longevity will be facilitated in part by good security practices. In this way, security planning is inherently a speculative process, and those in the humanities are particularly well suited to thinking imaginatively with technology. A security-first research practice asks cultural workers to imagine future potential threats, which are as varied as the projects they create.

Who is this book *not* intended for? I freely admit that this style of analysis might not be useful for everyone. This book is interdisciplinary in scope and works to bridge very different cultures and professions. Cybersecurity professionals working to secure government or corporate environments are often not set in conversation with cultural criticism and humanistic style of analysis. If you are a cybersecurity professional, you might be surprised by how much humanists consider social, political, and cultural contexts. The humanities likely has a lot to add to security in this way, particularly as it relates to collaboration, transparency, and documentation. I do not expect this to be a procedural manual for institutional IT in universities and libraries, who already have a very broad mandate to support and secure broad user communities. Many universities, for example, are well served by their IT services, but they are not able to assist the quantity of research being done and the speed at which researchers build projects. The humanities can help university operations by being responsible users of shared infrastructure. If you are primarily a consumer of corporate technology and platforms, you might be interested to know that you can have a lot more control and agency in guiding your own privacy and security. This book might be best suited, in some ways, for people who like to tinker, test, and play with technology; it is for those people who enjoy hacking some code just to satisfy a simple curiosity.

Cybersecurity and digital humanities are themselves multidisciplinary fields predicated on curiosity about technology. There is a kaleidoscopic array of perspectives described here between disciplines, theories, practices, and assumptions. This book is a bit of a hack to work across these analytical approaches. Yet cybersecurity and the digital humanities share a curiosity about technology. The greatest differences between these curious approaches to technology might be measured in our perceived pessimism or relative optimism. Humanistically minded risk assessments and threat models are rich in historical framing and cultural context, with the rigor of critique and close reading. A security minded understanding of technology accounts for the cultural consequences of privacy and surveillance failures. There is a basic speculative approach in imagining what can go wrong and in describing our adversaries. The necessary paranoia and pessimism in security can help animate and frame a generous and transparent humanistic approach to thinking about culture and technology.

Notes

1   See https://dhcenternet.org/.

2   See https://github.com/topics/digital-humanities and https://eadh.org/projects.

3   See https://hcommons.org/ and https://hsscommons.ca/.

4   Bethany Nowviski, "Digital Humanities in the Anthropocene," *Digital Scholarship in the Humanities* 30 (December 2015), 13. https://doi.org/10.1093/llc/fqv015.

5   With regard to terminology and definitions, "cybersecurity" is used here to demark the set of practices and methods used to protect digital assets, while "Cybersecurity" should be understood as a reference to the industrial and commercial manifestation of those practices and methods.

Human Exploits:

An Introduction to Hacking and the Humanities

What would it take to hack a human? Are we even hackable things? In what ways are humans vulnerable? Are we exploitable? In the cybersecurity industry, an exploit is an active measure that makes use of a vulnerability with the goal of "owning" a system. Cybersecurity professionals already know that the weakest part of any system sits between the chair and the keyboard.[1] It is the human in the loop that is an unpredictable vulnerability for even secure, well-managed systems; humans themselves are under attack online because we are a vulnerable part of these systems. It is the way we think, the way we feel, and the way we believe that gives attackers this opportunity. A *human exploit* preys upon a user's habits, assumptions, prejudices, and even laziness to coerce them into unintentionally helping an attacker. In this way, cybersecurity problems are human problems. And yet it is our humanity— our human capacity to recognize pattern, make imaginative leaps, and build communities—that holds the promise of reclaiming our autonomy, privacy, and freedom online.

Maybe getting hacked is just a predictable, though not always inevitable, consequence of our digital lives. Maybe we should just get used to being under threat online. Hackers are going to hack, right? So where does that leave the rest of us? First principles in mitigating a human exploit might include an act of reflection. Before we ask *how*, we might want to ask *why*. More specifically, why are we so vulnerable online? Criminals are often motivated to steal data, block access to a system, or damage property with the goal of extorting money, power, or influence. Now, the tools of these attackers have been repurposed to influence public perceptions, political ideologies, and personal beliefs through concerted disinformation campaigns thinly veiled as marketing. It is an all too familiar facet of living in the 2020s that the web is at once a great source of human connection and meaning as well as a great source of manipulation, fear, and exhaustion. Human experience is increasingly mediated through these spaces and so are the threats to our safety and security. The Covid-19 pandemic demanded an acceleration of these broad trends toward virtual, online experiences, which has only worsened the exploitation of these vulnerabilities.

During the pandemic and likely long after, some of our most meaningful and formative experiences will be held online. Children will go to school online; people will work from home, attending seemingly endless meetings on video calls. It will continue to be common to attend more significant human milestones online as well. Weddings, birthdays, and funerals will be made meaningful on video calls. The virtualization of human experience has allowed for a rapid reordering of social and cultural norms, where video meeting etiquette is a meaningful measure of career advancement. Zoombombing is something we talk to our kids about before they go to online school.[2] None of this is new of course. We blend the private and the public spheres online all the time. This is just the everyday. It is like our phones are a part of our bodies! We are linked, instantly. Whether we are chatting with our family and friends online or chronicling our lives on social media, human experience has rapidly blended with digital technology, giving a glimpse of future trends of further mingling of our digital and "real life" identities.[3] Our online identity is a very real extension of who we are and who we want to be. In this way, there is something very deeply human about what makes us vulnerable online. Our desire for connection, our propensity to trust, and our desire for newness makes us human. Our hope for the future allows us to grow and encourages us to learn. The chances we take to learn something new allow for us to change. The best of these traits must now be mixed with an attitude of critical, informed paranoia. This book is about finding ways to reclaim our sense of connection, trust, and hope without giving up on global networks of people, culture, and ideas in which we live.

Living online is already dependent on layers of security protocols, encryption, and malware detection. It is from this already normal security posture that a distinct conversation emerges about cybersecurity and the humanities. Security is a normal part of the broader public conversation, politically and socially. If thinking about how security is so normalized elsewhere, it must be time to think about the cultural consequences of all these security-minded policies, processes, and protocols. The humanities, in particular the digital humanities, must be ready to comment cogently as security questions shape digital culture. The humanities must also be ready to take on the language, systems, and frameworks that animate Cybersecurity industry's culture and practices more broadly. There must be a new imperative in the humanities: *humanists must embrace a defensive security-first posture throughout their research practices to mitigate the hostile influence and surveillance by corporations, governments, as well as entities seeking to manipulate free and open liberal democracies.*

In a very practical sense, the humanistic ethic that advocates for greater cultural understanding through equity and justice requires digital humanities researchers to be secured from online threats. Cultural workers of all kinds will need to defend themselves against entities that seek to disrupt or discredit progressive voices committed to promoting a greater awareness of the histories, stories, and philosophies that support a diversity of identities. In this way, humanists might be well positioned to contribute by communicating with the general public and relate to the social and cultural consequences of security failures. It is clear now, however, that humanists must defend compassionate and critical habits of mind by becoming advocates for greater agency in our online lives. Arguing for fair governmental regulation that respects human experiences of all kinds and promotes social and political justice is a good place to start.

There is also a strong current of activism within the humanities that must be continued online, without undue privilege given to social media platforms. Dorothy E. Denning defines "hacktivism" as "the marriage of hacking and activism."[4] The humanities must take an offensive posture toward corporate attempts to commodify digital culture and impinge on individual freedoms as well as collective rights to govern communities locally, nationally, and internationally. Partnerships in the regulation of external state-sanctioned threats will be critical in protecting liberal humanism into the third millennium. This ethical activist security posture will redraw communities based on geographic, economic, as well as ideological grounds. These security-minded humanist researchers must learn to shape the online infrastructures and platforms to reclaim autonomy from corporate influence as well. Like many acts of civil disobedience, security-minded humanist researchers might expose unjust laws by breaking them when needed. Citizens must gain individual agency over the threats faced online and be prepared to reject monopolistic or censorious power by boycotting free and easy tools offered by corporations. This is no small task, but it is the task of the humanities in any age: the humanities must free human thought from influence by honing the cognitive powers of critique, compassion, and generosity. Such a mission will only be possible with a secure posture online. The digital humanities must train a new generation of citizen activists capable of making things, but we must also be ready to break things as well.

Cybersecurity is no longer the sole concern of the security industry or large Internet Service Providers (ISPs). Citizens should not rely on governments to regulate, filter, or limit the internet to provide safety. Countries cannot just censor their way to security. Data breaches, surveillance, and ransomware are increasingly a global problem, but individuals must be prepared to shape the world around them and protect their cultural communities. Personal, human vulnerabilities to online attacks require a new kind of technological and cultural literacy to participate politically, culturally, and economically with relative safety. If history is any indication, legal and regulatory regimes will remain woefully unable to cope with the pace of change.[5] These threats will continue to be highly technical and will only increase in sophistication. In an environment of lagging legal and enforcement mechanisms, securing one's own personal privacy and security will start with the individual level and end with a larger community of global citizen-developers making tools, sharing information, and advocating for policies and procedures that protect and inform everyone on the internet. It will be the work of humanists, in part, to untangle and make sense of the historical and cultural forces that motivate attackers. It is often said that security is a team sport. It will therefore take many analytical approaches to reflect on these challenges as they evolve.

While the specific threats change rapidly, this book will work to imagine larger trends and categories that make a technological vulnerability into a human vulnerability. It will be necessary to describe, in code, how attacks happen. The popularization of security issues and the ways they influence our lives opens a new domain of literacy. Technological literacy, broadly speaking, is now as foundational as literacy and numeracy. The humanities might best contribute to online security by speculating about how society and culture can prepare for what we may face in the future. The speculative tools of fiction, imagination, and reason might be productively embedded within broader Information Technology (IT)-specific security frameworks.

Let's start with something simple. Everyone online has been the target of a phishing scam, whether we know it by this name or not. Phishing begins like most scams, with a story. A user receives a fallacious email or message prompting a user to download a malicious package or simply expose their login credentials. These emails can appear legitimate, working to emulate the look and feel of trusted individuals coworkers, businesses, or government agencies. These messages, which we receive in the dozens each day, are a rhetorical act to persuade us to trust. They ask us to trust a message enough to take an action. Click the link. Download the file. Share the information. They prey upon our human propensity to trust. Phishing scams are a commonplace problem but an enduring one.[6]

It is amazing that these emails work as well as they do! This kind of manipulation has a name: "social engineering." The Social Engineering Toolkit defines social engineering as a "blend of science, psychology and art"; but within these methods, social engineering is defined by its outcomes: "*Any act that influences a person to take an action that may or may not be in their best interest.*"[7] With the subtle rhetorical regard for their audience and the technical ability to mimic the design of legitimate communications, social engineering is successful when trust can be used to cajole a user to self-harm. While spear phishing is used to target specific individuals with highly personalized communications, most phishing attempts are broadly distributed to very large lists of emails that are shared more or less openly online. A human propensity to trust becomes effective when a phishing scam is scaled to hundreds of thousands of people. Scale and trust become potent with the speed and ease of tooling available. This kind of work does not require anything more specialized than a regular computer and some free software tools. Phishing attempts are, at base, about collecting information that can be used to extract value, whether it is money or more privileged access. Cast a wide enough net and an attacker will capture something of value.

Quite often criminal organizations share the simple profit motive of legitimate businesses, albeit with slightly different methods. The ability for bad actors to social engineer vast swaths of users has only been exacerbated by social media companies fanning the flames of populism and economic inequality. Social engineering techniques are commonly used by marketing firms and social media companies to encourage individuals to divulge information that may not be in their best interests. The psychographic data collected by social media companies, search providers, and retail platforms are now aggregated by companies largely unknown by the general public, including Acxiom, Epsilon, Bluekai, Datalogix, and Kantar.[8] By collecting detailed data about our personalities, values, attitudes, interests, and lifestyles and pairing these psychographic data with demographic and biometric data, machine learning systems are now able to accurately predict and intervene in human behavior in real time. Shoshana Zuboff has described this phenomenon as the rise of "surveillance capitalism" or the "big other" in big data collection.[9] Social engineering is a logical extension of internet services based on advertising revenue, where merely grabbing attention matters more than what is said or done online.[10]

The Darkest Timeline

These surveillance systems, perfected in the high-speed capitalist crucible of online marketing, are now sophisticated enough to challenge fundamental notions of a human agency and a life well lived. Cyber security becomes a concern for the humanities when behavior modification through location tracking, contextual notifications, and data harvesting interrupt human reflection and self-awareness. Maybe we can at least look out for each other. There is a reassuring anachronism in security problems of the twenty-first century returning to ancient philosophy and rhetoric. This swing toward illiberalism is happening around the world, and it is increasingly dystopic, draconian, and violent. In the United States, software called COMPAS by Northpointe helps automate an overwhelmed judicial system by scoring criminal recidivism rates for parole and probation decisions, which is heavily biased against black defendants.[11] The worst tendencies of authoritarian governments like the Communist Party of China are being amplified by the networked surveillance of China's population, most critically the Uyghur minority Muslim population being detained in Xinjiang concentration camps.[12] The Communist Party of China's "Social Credit" program represents the first steps into a real world cyberpunk dystopia of social control through widespread surveillance.[13] This is a global trend fueled by corporate surveillance technology used to maximize advertising and sales, which have also been repurposed by nation-state level agencies who can simply purchase this data.[14] The public has been aware of the fact that United States has had its own national-level surveillance program since the disclosures of Edward Snowden in 2013.[15] The Covid-19 crisis has created another opportunity, similar to the post-9/11 period, to erode civil liberties and track citizens in the name of public health and safety on a global scale.[16]

In the midst of a wave of crises—a pandemic, multiple environmental crises related to global warming, resurgent nationalist politics, extreme wealth disparities, and social upheaval as a result of racial, religious, and gender-based violence—many on the internet have remarked that we are perhaps living in "the darkest timeline."[17] This is a satiric way of acknowledging the extreme, often overwhelming global problems cultured by authoritarianism, global capitalism, and environmental degradation, as well as referencing a science fiction understanding of multi-dimensional space-time, which keeps it fun. If we live in a multi-verse, there are multiple, parallel versions of this reality, and it is therefore possible to live in "the darkest timeline." It feels as though we may be the unfortunate ones cursed to live in the worst parallel reality. In some ways, this meme captures the problem many Christian philosophers faced when considering evil. The darkest timeline meme is an internet age ironic reworking of Gottfried Leibniz's optimistic "the best of all possible worlds" theory.[18] Leibniz needed to rationalize how evil was created by a God that is infinite, rational, and good. He imagined the best of all possible worlds because God contains all the ideas for an infinity of universes, but chooses rationally to make the best possible one. Online secular culture lacks the optimism of a Christian theodicy, but finds solace in identifying evil in the world. Doom scrolling leads, in all likelihood, to pessimistic dystopias of pandemics, authoritarianism, oppressive surveillance, and unregulated corporate power. These are all defining characteristics of cyberpunk genre of the 1980s. It all feels a little too familiar. Cyberpunk was meant to be a warning, not a manual for politicians and corporations to follow. As these forces take root globally and manifest in new ways, maybe it is time to take another look at the cyberpunk subculture that predicted so much of our current situation. Cyberpunk is dystopian and dark. It can be humorous and gritty. Cyberpunk also invites odd mashups, like thinking of Leibniz alongside internet memes; after all, there are no borders between high and low culture in the networks in which we now live.

It is less and less hyperbolic to claim that we are living the grim, dark futures first imagined by authors like John Brunner, Bruce Bethke, William Gibson, and Bruce Sterling.[19] "Cyberpunk" was first coined by Bethke in his short story by the same name, in the November, 1983 edition of *Amazing Stories*. Gardner Dozois and Bruce Sterling later used the term in describing the work of authors like Rudy Rucker, Lewis Shiner, and John Shirley, but it was Gibson who defined the subgenre in both the short story "Burning Chrome" and his first groundbreaking novel, *Neuromancer*.[20] Cyberpunk was cast as a near future urban dystopia of fierce anti-establishment individualists, where the mind, body, and environment are augmented or destroyed entirely by technology. Cyberpunk heroes seek to rebuild reality through the hallucinations offered by drugs or virtual cyberspace in a quixotic journey to reveal an authentic reality masked by mediated illusions. Early cyberpunk was distinctly white, male, but by the early 1990s feminist cyberpunk recast the genre and expanded its narrow view with authors like Pat Cadigan, Melissa Scott, Marge Piercy, and others.[21] These authors emerged from a post-World War period that conditioned generations to champion an individual's inalienable human freedom. Cyberpunk's use of cyberspace has long predicted how human agency will be gradually molded and shaped by the always-on rhythm of the web, without which it is increasingly impossible to live, work, and learn.

Now that so many of the familiar cyberpunk tropes are, more or less, a reality, perhaps science fiction can help inform a humanistic cybersecurity framework. Cyberpunk does not need another chronicler to define the genre, but perhaps it is time to return to the genre for clues to our future in the twenty-first century. Cyberpunk has always been focused on the future. That future has become choked by the very dystopias science fiction sought to warn us about. Today's VR headsets are not quite a "cyberspace deck." Smartphones are so much more nefarious than any data pad described in fiction. Our computers are increasingly wearable, but we have not yet started implanting them into our bodies directly. Though the Internet of Things has yet to fully manifest its influence, the networking of everyday objects will only exacerbate the problem by extending the behavior of the web in the material world of our built environments. Ernst Cline, the author of *Ready Player One*, predicted so much of our current life in the 2020s, thought he imagined them in 2045. The social upheaval of a global pandemic and the erosion of public life with reality TV stars in politics seemed far-fetched in 2011 when he published the book. In an interview published after the publication of the sequel, *Ready Player Two*, Cline reflects on the uncanny quality of his fiction by saying, "I worry sometimes that the only thing you need to be prescient is to be pessimistic."[22] Maybe a little of cyberpunk's gritty pessimism is just what we need.[23] Consumers are fed so many promises and sold on the sunny Silicon Valley—"there's an app for that"—approaches to fixing deeply intractable problems. Maybe a pessimistic view of technology can be used to realign our relationship with our phones, the internet, and the systems we use (and those that use us).

Don't Be Evil

Anxieties about the spread and ubiquity of digital technologies are piqued at more regular intervals as the pace of change continues to increase. For this reason, the cultural and technical concerns presented here will grapple with durable questions of human experience. Current examples of where and how security issues impact human experience will serve as a further framework for imagining future questions, problems, and threats. After all, it was not so long ago that we entered the twenty-first century; the generalized anxiety about digital technology and the internet, like the twenty-year-old fears of the Y2K bug, already seem quaint and charming by today's standards. Google's growth from a 1990s search engine start-up to a multibillion-dollar behemoth woven into the very fabric of our digital lives is similarly surprising. The extreme profitability of Google's parent conglomerate Alphabet Inc. has emerged from a process of heavily monetizing behavioral data collected about every possible aspect of our increasingly connected lives.[24] Gone are the days of Google's code of conduct asking employees, "don't be evil."[25] Instead, the now restructured Alphabet has adopted the motto "Do the right thing" to prove they are absolutely, definitely not evil. The "right thing" for whom? Users, as it was originally intended? Citizens? Shareholders? Alphabet? What is the "right thing"? Who defines rightness? Do users have rights? The answers to these questions remain legally and ethically vague, but the new decade promises to be pivotal for security researchers and personal privacy advocates in challenging Alphabet's information supremacy, to say nothing yet of Alphabet's competitors: Apple, Amazon, Facebook, and Microsoft. Redefining the terms of access to information, on the individual, national, and corporate level, globally, will remain a central struggle in the coming decades.

The large technology companies that we now know are increasingly at the intersection of the digital and the human. The so-called Big Five—currently

Facebook, Amazon, Alphabet, Apple, and Microsoft—represent a combined valuation of over 3.3 trillion or 40 percent of the Nasdaq 100 index.[26] In the way that car manufacturers of the twentieth century peddled fantasies of open roads and freedom of movement, big technology companies want us to associate the good life with their services. The Silicon Valley claim to the future can be described this way: *We do not need to own much beyond our smartphone, which you can pay for in installments. Don't worry about programming your smartphone, there is already an app for everything! We will be granted the tools to be creative, productive, and healthy. We will be more organized and more engaged with our networks of family, friends, and coworkers, so we can be better at our jobs and be more successful. We can be more connected with those we love, and our lives can become a source of satisfaction and enjoyment for millions. If we live a great life, we can become so influential that our life will simply pay for itself through sponsorships!* We are so lucky to have benevolent corporate partners working to help us all live better, happier lives. At last, capitalism has provided the conditions for a free market utopia. What could go wrong? These so-called influencers are the human embodiment of social engineering and a step toward the further debasement of human agency. Influencers live a desirable life online, but it is purely in service of corporate marketing. We are being sold consumer objects by real people, but we are also being sold the idea that the good life is attained through capitulating to consumer-driven market forces. Capitulating to these forces made the influencers happy, after all. All dystopias are built upon the ruins of failed utopias, even boring dystopias like Instagram. As we enter the second decade of the twenty-first century, it seems as though we have an opportunity to break these fantasies, retake control, and begin the hard work of building systems to facilitate authentic human connection, insight, and individual agency.

At this moment, we have everything to gain by seeing what the cybersecurity industry and the humanities can learn from each other.[27] Within the history of ideas, there are moments that are unusually productive because of the need for new terms to describe our world. Occasionally, new terms are so foundational to a range of disciplines that they become a milestone for all that follow. "Surveillance capitalism" is our milestone. Facebook, Alphabet, Amazon, Apple, and Microsoft are examples of what Shoshana Zuboff, Professor at the Harvard Business School, calls "surveillance capitalists." The Big Five are late capitalist global corporations that monetize behavioral data to effectively predict market forces by recording, processing, and shaping human behavior. In the opening pages of *The Age of Surveillance Capitalism*, she defines surveillance capitalism in the following way:

1. A new economic order that claims human experience as free raw material for hidden commercial practices of extraction, prediction, and

sales; 2. A parasitic economic logic in which the production of goods and services is subordinated to a new global architecture of behavioral modification; 3. A rogue mutation of capitalism marked by concentrations of wealth, knowledge, and power unprecedented in human history; 4. The foundational framework of a surveillance economy; 5. As significant a threat to human nature in the twenty-first century as industrial capitalism was to the natural world in the nineteenth and twentieth; 6. The origin of a new instrumentarian power that asserts dominance over society and presents startling challenges to market democracy; 7. A moment that aims to impose a new collective order based on total certainty; 8. An expropriation of critical human rights that is best understood as a coup from above: an overthrow of the people's sovereignty.[28]

As corporations increasingly build their profits on our data, we will see the 2020s become a decade of increasing awareness and activism on issues like natural language processing, location tracking, facial recognition, biometrics, machine learning, and data sovereignty. Simply because these corporate activities are legal, does not mean that our security is being maintained. Zuboff's book explains how a demand for corporate total knowledge and information freedom, alongside the failed reciprocal economic benefit these companies offer most citizens, means that we face an unbearable collision. "We now have the tools to grasp the collision in all its destructive complexity," Zuboff explains. "What is unbearable is that economic and social inequalities have revered to the preindustrial 'feudal' pattern but that we, the people, have not."[29] The sense that it reads like science fiction should be a warning. Social and political activism will increasingly include these topics once reserved for those in the cybersecurity industry. It will be our own literacy and ability to "grasp the collision" of these forces that dictates what happens next.

Claiming the Future

This predictive pessimism paints a picture of our near future while also reflecting a more hopeful inverse image. I place my hopes for the future with young people and the way mastering technology is just part of growing up. I look forward to the next generation of activists and politicians, who will be better able to articulate the necessary freedoms and regulations governing the internet. But first, we must lay the groundwork to have an open and transparent conversation about the influence of surveillance capitalists on public discourse. Jaron Lanier, one of the first inventors of VR and an all-around cyber visionary, simply asks, "How can you remain autonomous in a world where you are under constant surveillance and are constantly prodded by algorithms run by some of the richest corporations in history, which have no way of making money except by being paid to manipulate your behavior?"[30] Perhaps most importantly, this next generation will be able to both understand and wield the technologies that pose such a threat to our autonomy and agency. By learning to remake the digital world, the ability to break and remake systems may be the only means for anyone to live a real, authentic human experience. It is now time to also admit that disinformation, supercharged by social media, is a cybersecurity issue. Though we all can understand how story can fuel misinformation, toxic ideologies, and mobilize hate in the real world, it is harder to see past the stories that guide our lives.

The classic view of liberal humanism, which fights for justice, equity, and democracy, must be retrofit to function in the twenty-first century. We need more than words in a world awash in opinion on social media. For this reason, I am also a digital humanist who believes that literacy in the twenty-first century includes the ability to read and write code.[31] I hope to follow Alexander R. Galloway and Eugene Thacker's approach to code in cultural studies presented in *The Exploit* (2007). Theorized in their avant-garde style that is informed by Deluzian rhizomatic networks, Galloway and Thacker were in step with a broader optimism about blending theory and practice through programming: "Today to write theory means to write code. There is a powerful exhilaration in the transformation of real material life that guides the writing of counterprotocological code. As Geert Lovink reminds [in *Dark Fiber* (2002)] us: 'No more vapor theory anymore.'"[32] At this time there was a similar expression of code as theory within DH and media studies. I explained in an article appearing in *Digital Studies/Le champ numérique* from 2014 the emergence of this programming literacy in DH this way:

> The commonly cited inception of this debate on the value of digital prototypes originates from a comment made by Lev Manovich at the 2007 Digital Humanities conference. Manovich reportedly claimed that "a prototype is a theory," and that digital humanities practitioners need to "stop apologizing" for these prototypes. A short time later, Alan Galey and Stan Ruecker describe how this perspective on designing and making things—whether they are instrumental tools or contingent prototypes—is an "ethos of thinking through making."[33]

Lovink captures this sentiment, again in *Dark Fiber*, by considering how the web relinquishes global users from old colonial networks of the British Empire that used Greenwich Mean Time as a standardizing force for time itself. A global network is an invitation to, in Lovink's words, "create alternatives, embedded in code, to liberate their personal temporal desires." By building new systems and alternative experiences online, it is possible for makers to be breakers.

The ability to understand, build, and even break the systems around us is the only way to claim agency for ourselves and our communities. The kind of literacy that allowed for the great orators of past revolutions to sway vast publics to act decisively toward political change is different today. The digital literacy required by today's political dissidents will need to be charismatic, honest, and authentic as well as technologically sophisticated, rapidly deployed, and skirting with legality. They will need to be possessed of the abilities of entire marketing, IT, and security departments to be effective. The demands of this task will be commensurate with the corporate powers we face. Academic research will depend on strong operational security. Social and cultural change will emerge from communities best able to develop, deploy, and operate systems securely, without corporate dependencies or direct government control. Activists will need to be able to traverse public digital and physical space without their activities being monitored, curtailed, or anticipated by corporate or governmental surveillance. I can only hope that we can be pessimistic enough to reclaim our future.

The demands of a twenty-first-century political dissident and scholar will be governed by the breakdown of the existing twentieth-century political order. Where nationalist politics take root amidst extremism in the media around the globe, political actors of all kinds will need to be able to protect, as best they can, their personal privacy, online actions, and information streams. Defensive postures will be the norm for these digital civil rights activists.[34] To be able to effectively participate in a democracy, engaged citizens must be educated sufficiently to comprehend social and political ramifications of highly technical issues and act in their own best interest. Without a defensive posture, citizens risk being manipulated into voting against their best interest, and democracy risks being co-opted to suit those with enough data or ad dollars to shape opinion. Citizens, not consumers, run the risk of failing to grasp the policies and regulations capable of protecting digital spaces and voting for them; citizens run the risk of being unduly influenced by malign forces seeking to undermine the democratic process itself; citizens run the risk of not being able to effectively organize against totalitarian leadership—should it arise through democratic means—and resist digital systems of surveillance and control because their only means of protest through social media is already surveilled and controlled.

A security-minded humanities education would seek to inoculate citizens through the traditions long held by the humanities for this near future. Literacy and imagination represent the two most potent tools to counter mass surveillance and coercive technologies. Maureen Webb, in *Coding Democracy*, Eben Moglen's presentation at the Libre Planet conference in 2017. Moglen is the constitutional attorney and Columbia University law professor who defended Phil Zimmermann for exporting the PGP (Pretty Good Privacy) cryptography. Moglen was, in 2017, articulating a whole sale rejection of surveillance capitalism with the assistance of "a number of major governments and big companies."[35] Webb goes further with another imperative: "We need to get into the schools. We need to start teaching people how to think about the technology now and let the technology catch up to their educated expectations. We need to pass on our ideas to eight- and twelve- and sixteen-year-old-people."[36] A general education in cybersecurity issues represents a mental "vulnerability scanner" for the effects of surveillance capitalism. Professors in the humanities would call this *critical thinking*, but critical thinking is now confused for the application of an ideological framework or theory, dipping easily in conspiratorial thinking, without a basis in technological reality. We will need a return to realism in cultural critique that also embraces the function of imagination and fiction in solving problems. A story remains the best way to process the complex relationship between our day-to-day lives and the systems that connect us and systems of power. Stories are memorable and flexible learning tools that are perfectly adapted to our all too human psyches. The stories we tell and how we tell them can push against the norms of communication. The ability to imagine solutions to problems we have yet to face is a tactical exercise to explore human cunning.

Speculative fiction, as the larger umbrella of science fiction and fantasy, is the subculture most accepting of this kind of provisional claim to the future. Our stories may be our last best hope to recenter the current conversation about the limits of these invasive new technologies and how we define the boundaries of humanity. Cyberpunk also allows us to think about a wide variety of contemporary anxieties connected to surveillance, including urbanization, ecological degradation, globalization, privacy, corporate power, fragile nation-states, and cybernetics. If human freedom is curtailed by predictive artificial intelligence—what Zuboff called a "behavioral future"—human imagination could be a last hope for liberation; the ability to write or create, as Zuboff describes it, is a "claim to the future tense" for which we now compete with corporations.[37] The speculative ability of human imagination, as manifested within the world-making potential of our literature, offers latent creative ideas made specifically for human readers. Literature is a kind of fictional encryption useful against machine reading. Literary inference and implicit meaning reside in a complex network of cultural and social codes. AI systems capable of affective computing—the ability to understand, interpret, and simulate human emotion—are not yet sophisticated enough to understand the implicit ethical and moral messages in our literature. Reading physical, paper books allows us to read, think, and ponder without our reading habits being collected and analyzed.[38] The ability to imagine potential futures, not bound by past experience or current technical capabilities, may allow for a cognitive end run around AI systems and predictive modeling. It is for these reasons and others that this book collects the some of the cyberpunk tradition to map literary precedent to our current technological paradigm.

In doing so, I would like to keep one foot firmly planted in the world of security. After all, the language and systems that make up the cybersecurity industry have not yet become widely familiar. This book will define technical terms as they are used. If we lack a word, we lack a concept; if we cannot give shape to the ideas and systems that govern our world, we will not be able to critique, oppose, shape, and guide that world. This book will describe these problems in code suitable for exploring the logic of vulnerabilities and exploits. I wish to normalize technical challenges as a necessary extension of the moral and ethical challenges we face. In the words of Engin Isin and Evelyn Ruppert in *Being Digital Citizens*, the role of the active citizen has been largely elided in contemporary discussions of online protest and dissent:

> The figure of the citizen is also lost in description of the experiences of subjects who act through the Internet. This absence is evinced by the fact that the figure of the citizen is rarely, if ever, used to describe the acts of crypto-anarchists, cyberactivists, cypherpunks, hackers, hacktivists, whistle-blowers, and other political figures of cyberspace. It sounds almost outrageous if not perverse to call the political heroes of cyberspace as citizen subjects since the figure of the citizen seems to betray their originality, rebelliousness, and vanguardism, if not their cosmopolitanism. Yet the irony here is that this is exactly the figure of the citizen we inherit as a figure who makes rights claims.[39]

Security researchers have long been falsely accused of misdeeds because society lacks a popularized conception of an "ethical hacker" that works to break into systems to make them better. An active citizenry would have a responsibility to ensure that their neighbors and places of work are safe and secure. Several questions arise by seriously considering the role of security research as an act of an engaged and responsible citizenry: How is human experience eroded or curtailed by current communications infrastructure? What are the limits of human agency with the introduction of cybernetics and ubiquitous network connections? What are the fundamental protocols governing the internet and how do they enforce systems of power and influence? Are there alternatives to the web as we know it? Which sensors and software are collecting predictive data? How are exploits identified, collected, and patched? What role do technology companies, national security agencies, and global agencies play in keeping the public safe and maintaining stable and just economic and political order? Why is strong encryption important to journalistic and democratic integrity? Why are biometric data collected and how are they used? By addressing these and other questions, I argue that cyberpunk is a useful predictor of future political, cultural, and social realities that emerge from technological change, when measured against our current technological abilities; within this counter-cultural approach to technology, cyberpunk offers a model of activism necessary to intercede and meaningfully resist governmental and corporate control.

This book weaves together three distinct subject areas that will increasingly become part of the public conversation about technology, public policy, and cultural change. These topics might be summarized in the following way: Privacy is increasingly the most valuable digital service, and a broad societal awareness of cybersecurity practices will be required to achieve economic stability and political sovereignty; programing is a fundamental literacy in the twenty-first century, and the ability to make, manipulate, and circumvent data harvesting systems will be a critical skill as workplace automation and surveillance technology are normalized; speculative fiction has long been used to express ethical questions and imagine possible futures during periods of rapid technological change; so, the cyberpunk genre will increasingly give voice to the cultural anxieties of mass surveillance and AI systems, while serving as a blueprint for a sustained political resistance to corporate and governmental misuses of technology.

A Mischievous Spirit

Those with memories long enough to dip into the previous millennium will grow ill-at-ease with the pace of change. Those born into this digitally surveilled world will have the very moment of birth encoded and plotted. Every childhood photo will be processed for indicators of value: employability, genius, or perhaps non-conformity. How might surveillance from birth to death shape the evolution of entire populations and demographics from the perspective of public health, education, or epigenetics? Jonathan Gottschall's *The Storytelling Animal* makes the case, from an evolutionary psychology perspective, that story is part of humanity's evolutionary inheritance and has shaped our global psyches since our emergence as a species. It is a theoretical branch of psychology, blended with evolutionary biology, that is difficult to prove given the span of human experience. It presumes to explain something like a human essence from brief windows into humanity's prehistory, which is certainly problematic. Still, the perspective offered remains interesting as an act of scientifically inflected storytelling about humanity. Evolutionary psychology may be akin to hard, science-based speculative fiction and is well suited to prove Gottschall's thesis. The essence of humanity refined over millennia of evolution is the capacity to tell and understand stories. We are "homo fictus," according to Gottschall.[40] We are able to project into our own futures and protect our pasts with stories. We can test moral and ethical norms without coming to physical blows. Humanity has, according to Gottschall, evolved and adapted to our world in a very fundamental way through story. In many ways, this book will seek to blend story with computer science to imagine how our cultural and social practices will adapt to the computerization human experience.

For a large portion of the twentieth century, the novel served a central role in describing and shaping human experience, in addition to film, theater, and radio as key narrative media. Novels helped shape our national identities.[41] They served as role models for intimate relationships. They defined our ethics by spurring our sense of care and compassion. The history of literary criticism is littered with attempts to describe the human relationship to story; the social value of story changes according to history and those in power; and there is a consistent economic pressure on the value we place on story in our world. The novel has had the privilege of defining our humanity by allowing readers an intimacy with its author. There is an exchange of values in stories. Our humanity is increasingly defined by our relationship to the economy, which now manifest through the economics of surveillance. In the 1970s, Marc Shell's *The Economy of Literature* describes how language is itself a commodity of exchange. The metaphorical workings of the words we use as signs for things and ideas is a process of exchange that processes an economic exchange of value. The language we use to define our identities and our sense of who we are—from the languages that we speak to the cultures that define us—is defined by this linguistic economy: "Language is the final and original home of the conscious spirit of mankind," says Shell, "and it enables us to incorporate and rise above contemporary and social 'functional' ideologies."[42] Thinking about story in strict economic terms may well be similarly anachronistic. There is a durability in thinking of a structural function of language as a metaphor for value. Such a comparison is compelling because the evidence is bound to the workings of language itself. Shell is asking his readers to imagine how the micro, or linguistic, level of the literature can be expanded to the macro, or social and cultural, level of literature's significance. If language is economic at the level of the word and sentence, perhaps our literature and the identities we derive from it are similarly economic. Gottschall's *homo fictus* may indeed be a more general version of Shell's *homo economicus*. In either case, a human defined by an economy of fiction presumes that there is some useful social function to story; there is truth value in thinking through fictions.

Stories are at once essential to human experience and are valuable, but stories are also world-making things. The worlds contained within stories are true to themselves; they are not only independent but also touch the various contexts from which they emerge and from which they are consumed. They establish a self-contained logic and rationale capable of limiting the complexity of global systems. Stories are ideal spaces to test social or cultural norms. They are imaginative prototyping tools to expand or critique the norms we live by. Thomas Pavel's *Fictional Worlds* defines a workable theory of fiction in this way:

> Literary texts, like most informal collections of sentences, such as conversations, newspaper articles, eyewitness testimony, history books, biographies of famous people, myths, and literary criticism, display a property that may puzzle logicians but that doubtless appears natural to anyone else: their truth as a whole is not recursively definable starting from the truth of the individual sentences that constitute them.[43]

In other words, a text may be true on a larger level that is readily perceptible by readers while also being completely fictional and resistant to any codified understanding. While individual sentences may be untrue or distortions of the truth, readers grasp these nuances while systematic logic fails to categorize subtlety. Rather than abdicate the central role of story in society to mere entertainment, Pavel's definition of story is valuable because stories need not be wholly true to be useful. All stories, even those based on history, are useful fictions.

Fictions break the absolutes needed for Boolean logic because fictions are neither strictly true nor false. A true story would be a perfect history or a perfect prophecy, which simply cannot exist. A perfect description of the past or the future is the domain of omniscience; oracles cannot exist on paper; even the Christian gospels of the New Testament must retell the story to acknowledge the human fallibility of witnessing. In a Borgesian turn, Pavel describes how such omniscience represents a monstrous affront to human sentience, free will, and the urgency of human mortality. These categories are perfectly suited to science fiction, but here he uses a speculative mode to theorize about the very nature of stories. Pavel tells one of these stories as he attempts to imagine the full world building capabilities of human literature. He describes an imagined book capable of recording all our actions. He asks us to imagine a "Daily Book" with innumerable pages; imagine a "Lifebook" with rich content beyond merely describing one's life.[44] Imagine a Lifebook endowed with an ability to collect richer content than words, capable of plotting feelings, beliefs, secrets, unconscious bias, as well as the public persona of your projected identity. Now imagine there was some "nimble genie" capable of reading your *magnum opus*, as well as the *magnum opera* of everyone you have ever known. Imagine that there is an "aggregation recipe" capable of aligning the fragments and half-truths of your life and everyone around you into an "Eternal

Book" that reports, quite literally, your destiny.[45] Though decades ahead of our present paradigm of massive data collection and machine learning algorithms capable of such predictions, Pavel's thought experiment about the possibilities of the book anticipates our state of surveillance with uncanny accuracy.

At this moment, it is possible to make a more durable claim: the ability of stories to record our past and predict our futures, through the simple mechanisms of character and narrative, are a precursor of surveillance technology. Facebook or Google's collection of all the data that defines our lives is a humanistic project. It is a horribly distorted, even monstrous, manifestation of the very human desire to record our finite lives and even catch a glimpse into our futures. The collection of our demographic and psychographic data alongside the geographies of our lives—mapped meticulously to the networks of our families and friends—is the grotesque fulfillment of the promise of writing to record our lives. Surveillance capitalism sounds a lot like Isaac Asimov's vision of "psychohistory" in the *Foundation* series of novels, written from 1951 to 1993. In *Foundation*, Asimov imagines a far-flung galaxy spanning Empire composed of millions of planets. The peak of scientific discovery occurs in the discipline of social-psychology. The massive data collection powers of the Empire allow psychohistorians to predict, in aggregate, the rise and fall of societies. Inspired by Edward Gibbon's classic *The Decline and Fall of the Roman Empire*, Asimov's *Foundation* imagines a world in which big data analysis can be used to predict the decline and fall of societies. Human histories and futures follow a predictable path. In this view, there is nothing anomalous about the attempt to record our lives.[46] The anomaly rests in these systems authoring our digital biographies on our behalf through massive, covert surveillance without our ability to read or edit the final manuscript.

In the tradition of the humanities, Pavel asks us to imagine further. Imagine this nimble genie is a "mischievous spirit" who is "not very deft with the books."[47] Maybe these spirits read the wrong *magnum opera*, making incorrect connections, or maybe these spirits deliver destinies based on "false or condemned" theories. Maybe these false or condemned theories used to define your destiny have also blended impossible potential futures with the range of possibilities selected by this *aggregation recipe*. Maybe this mischievous spirit weaves a mixture of these "impossibilia" with the "possibilia" of our lived experiences in our *magnum opus*. "That with each new Daily Book, Yearbook, or Book of the Planets and Stars," says Pavel, "new multitudes of *Impossibilia* are born, for many impossible books are but impossible-in-the-light-of-a-given-possible-book."[48] If this daily book serves as a suitable comparison to surveillance capitalism, Pavel is exposing the risks and possibilities inherent in making decisions algorithmically, based on personal data harvesting.

If the algorithm, this mischievous spirit, makes a mistake or uses a false assumption, we may be condemned to false futures. Perhaps we may find greater happiness in allowing a machine to imagine the seemingly impossible.

More likely, however, any daily book of our digital footprint will limit and constrain human potential within this algorithmic spirit in service of maximizing some other variable. Perhaps this mischievous spirit will maximize profit or some other economic efficiency. Perhaps these decisions will limit resource use or environmental impact. Perhaps decisions will be made in our daily lives that only have a logic at the societal level, leaving individuals plodding in absurd tasks with little relevance or significance. Perhaps then the impossible can become possible as we imagine a *homo impossibilia* in speculative fiction. Human freedom may reside in the impossible because *nobody can be held to the impossible* (thinking here of the famous Roman legal conceit, *Ad Impossibilia Nemo Tenetur*). Or maybe, *no one is bound to be impossible*. Blending our lives between the possible and impossible—between reality and fiction—allows for a space to evade the aggregation recipe, the algorithm, that writes our destinies. Science fiction has always done this. Eugene Thacker defines science fiction as "a contemporary mode in which the techniques of extrapolation and speculation are utilized in a narrative form, to construct near-future, far-future, or fantastic worlds in which science, technology, and society intersect."[49] In divining these destinies, it will be speculative fiction that will help describe and define these untrod paths into the future.

Human stories have the ability to sketch immaterial, impossible ideas and lay the conceptual groundwork for their eventual design and implementation in the real world. The sciences are even embracing the uncanny way science fiction becomes science fact, as was recently celebrated by an event hosted by NASA's Innovative Advanced Concepts group.[50] Ed Finn and Kathryn Cramer's *Project Hieroglyph* has sought to describe and formalize this reciprocal relationship between science and science fiction, "to cultivate stories that would take this further, shepherding ecosystems of interest and innovation around radical ideas."[51] The drive for ever greater innovation in science and technology is allowing seemingly impossible, speculative ideas into the drafting stage of inventing the future. Design-oriented speculation may be how a storyteller, interested in exchanging new and interesting ideas, might realize their full cultural value. The focus of attention, in an attention economy, on the future could be a much needed investment. In 2009, Julian Bleecker sketched the first description of a genre of "design fiction" that sought to align design principles with the speculative approaches of science fiction writing:

> Design fiction as I am discussing it here is a conflation of design, science fact, and science fiction. It is an amalgamation of practices that together bends the expectations as to what each does on its own and ties them together into something new. It is a way of materializing ideas and speculations without the pragmatic curtailing that often happens when dead weights are fastened to the imagination.[52]

Bleecker is describing a more explicit function for science fiction in the design process, which maps well with my desire to link cybersecurity with the humanities. Bleecker also fits well with this line of thought linking Gottschall, Shell, and Pavel. Each, in their own way, are seeking to describe fiction in realist terms. Like the others, Bleecker is working to describe an applied function for fiction. More than a tool for moral improvement or entertainment, fiction imagines a potential real future. Design-oriented problem solving is political and re-enforces the beliefs and backgrounds of those doing the designing.

Rather than being treated as merely entertainment, science fiction might here work as a critical prototyping stage within the design of new technologies. Intentionally blurring the lines between science fact and science fiction, design fiction would embrace the speculative mode of writing as a driver for innovative design. The ability of design thinking approaches to solve problems and the imaginative potential to speculatively prototype new approaches to education and technology. However, design thinking must be paired with a critical reflexivity that foregrounds questions of justice and equity while emphasizing community leadership, ownership, and stewardship of project data and designs. Community groups like the Detroit Digital Justice Coalition, Allied Media Projects, and the Design Justice Network have been using design principles at the local level for many years.[53] So-called "hard" science fiction already works to bridge backward into science fact as a footing for projecting into the future of a possible science fiction. Anthony Dunne and Fiona Raby imagine a unified design approach in which everything has the potential to become speculative.[54] A radical re-imagining of twentieth-century assumptions about the economy, politics, education, and so much more is breaking on the global stage. As a hybrid practice of engineering, art, and speculative thought, design fiction blends science fact through science fiction. Cyberpunk, for all its pessimism, has the potential to serve as a tool to assess future security threats in this way. Reading science fiction may then become a security practice to build conceptual frameworks for living more securely and autonomously. Here, within this short history of the function of story, we see a potential shift in the twenty-first century toward security and the humanities, wherein questions of character, narrative, and publishing speak in turn to threat actors, vulnerabilities, and supply chains.

Notes

1   This phenomenon is often shortened to PEBCAK: Problem Exists Between Chair and Keyboard.

2   See https://en.wikipedia.org/wiki/Zoombombing.

3   The varying forms in which technology and humanity merge and complement each other are nothing new, particularly to science fiction. The

"singularity" is the common posthumanist phrase used to describe the moment of human evolution in which human consciousness becomes digital and eternal. While Raymond Kurzweil has recently been the public face of the singularity as a director of engineering at Google and author of many books, including *The Age of Intelligent Machines* (1990), many of these ideas found their first footing with earlier science fiction authors, notably Vernor Vinge. Vinge coined the term while on a panel at the annual conference of the Association for the Advancement of Artificial Intelligence in 1982. See also Vernor Vinge, "Signs of the Singularity," *Spectrum.ieee.org*, June 1, 2008, https://spectrum.ieee.org/biomedical/ethics/signs-of-the-singularity; Hans Moravec, *Robot: Mere Machine to Transcendent Mind* (Oxford: Oxford University Press, 1999); *The 21st Century Singularity and Global Futures: A Big History Perspective*, eds. Andrey V. Korotayev and David J. Le Poire (Switzerland: Springer Nature, 2020).

4   Dorothy E. Denning, "Activism, Hacktivism, and Cyberterrorism: The Internet as a Tool for Influencing Foreign Policy," in *Networks and Netwars. The Future of Terror, Crime and Militancy*, eds. John Arquilla and David Ronfeldt (Monica, CA: RAND Corporation, 2001), 241. Additionally, Elizabeth Losh was among the first in the digital humanities to call for a hacktivist humanities from a DH perspective. However, the assumption that hacking requires a "virtuoso performance by seasoned programmers" forced a return to "hacking the academy that includes department chairs, heads of national centers, and those in leadership of professional associations who are demanding fundamental changes in fair use, peer review, and tenure guidelines." While Losh's essay does its own reflecting on the ineffectual navel-gazing of academics interested in hacking their work conditions, it advocates in the end for rather polite politics of "considering the need for supporting a truly hacktivist digital humanities." See Elizabeth Losh, "Hacktivism and the Humanities: Programming Protest in the Era of the Digital University," in *Debates in the Digital Humanities*, ed. Matthew K. Gold (Minneapolis: University of Minnesota Press, 2012), 163, 181.

5   For accounts of the often staggeringly incoherent regulation of personal data, government security, and encryption, respectively, see Sean Lyngaas, "New York Regulator Faults Twitter for Lax Security Measures Prior to Big Account Breach," *Cyberscoop.com*, October 15, 2020, https://www.cyberscoop.com/twitter-hack-social-engineering-new-york-financial-services/; "Privacy Regulator Warns MPs over Shared Passwords," *Bbc.com*, December 4, 2017, https://www.bbc.com/news/technology–42225214; Jeff Stone, "US Financial Regulator Fines Capital One $80 Million Over Data Breach," *Cyberscoop.com*, August 6, 2020, https://www.cyberscoop.com/capital-one-breach-penalty-occ/.

6   The most well-known phishing scam is undoubtedly the so-called "Nigerian Prince" scam, also called the 419 scam for the section of the Nigerian penal code that covers online fraud. More recently, phishing has been a persistent problem in ransomware, credit card fraud, and many other problems. For recent accounts of phishing scams, see Catalin Cimpanu, "Phishing Groups Are Collecting User Data, Email and Banking Passwords via Fake Voter Registration Forms," *Zdnet.com*, October 23, 2020, https://www.zdnet.com/article/phishing-groups-are-collecting-user-data-email-and-banking-passwords-via-fake-voter-registration-forms/; Chris Krebs, "Voice Phishers Targeting Corporate VPNs," *Krebsonsecurity.com*, August 20, 2020, https://krebsonsecurity.com/2020/08/voice-phishers-targeting-corporate-vpns/; Andy Greenberg, "The Attack That Broke Twitter Is Hitting Dozens of Companies," *Wired.com*, August 18, 2020, https://www.wired.com/story/phone-spear-phishing-twitter-crime-wave/.

7   Chris Hadnagy et al., "The Social Engineering Framework," *Social-engineer. org*, https://www.social-engineer.org/about/.

8   The concentration of personal data within large data broker corporations means that when a leak occurs potentially billions of personal records can be exposed. In June of 2020, Bluekai leaked billions of personal records online. See Zack Whittaker, "Oracle's BlueKai Tracks You across the Web. That Data Spilled Online," *Techcrunch.com*, June 2020, https://techcrunch.com/2020/06/19/oracle-bluekai-web-tracking/. Both Bluekai and Datalogix are now owned by Oracle, available respectively https://www.oracle.com/data-cloud/products/data-management-platform/ and https://www.oracle.com/corporate/acquisitions/datalogix/. Acxiom is available here: https://www.acxiom.com/; Epsilon is available here: https://us.epsilon.com/; Kantar is available here: https://www.kantar.com/.

9   Shoshana Zuboff, *The Age of Surveillance Capitalism: The Fight for a Human Future at the New Frontier of Power* (New York: PublicAffairs, 2019), 93–7.

10   Social engineering attacks manipulated fear from Covid-19. See John Leyden, "Malicious Advertising Slingers up the Ante During Covid-19 Pandemic," *Portswigger.net/daily-swig*, April 2020, https://portswigger.net/daily-swig/malicious-advertising-slingers-up-the-ante-during-covid-19-pandemic.

11   Julia Angwin, Jeff Larson, Surya Mattu, and Lauren Kirchner, "Machine Bias," *Propublica*, May 23, 2016, https://www.propublica.org/article/machine-bias-risk-assessments-in-criminal-sentencing.

12   While evidence mounted online for many years about the Chinese Communist Party (CCP) Xinjiang concentration camps, the CCP claims these "re-education" camps are intended to de-radicalize the Uyghur Muslim minority through vocational and ideological training. The CCP claims that these are vocational schools that are successful in dampening anti-CCP terrorist activity, but leaked documents describe a system of cultural genocide and forced labor. See Austin Ramzy and Chris Buckley, "The Xinjiang Papers," *NYTimes.com*, November 16, 2020, https://www.nytimes.com/interactive/2019/11/16/world/asia/china-xinjiang-documents.html.

13   Mara Hvistendahl, "Inside China's Vast New Experiment in Social Ranking," *Wired.com*, December 14, 2017, https://www.wired.com/story/age-of-social-credit/.

14   Mitchell Clark, "US Defense Intelligence Agency Admits to Buying Citizens' Location Data," *Theverge.com*, January 22, 2021, https://www.theverge.com/2021/1/22/22244848/us-intelligence-memo-admits-buying-smartphone-location-data.

15   See Edward Snowden, *Permanent Record* (New York: Metropolitan Books, 2019). Snowden has continued to comment on issues related to privacy and surveillance from exile in Russia, including the assassination of Jamal Khashoggi, the ongoing domestic surveillance program in the United States, as well as the ShadowBrokers attack on the NSA; respectively, see Rosie Perper, "Edward Snowden: Israeli Spyware Was Used to Track and Eventually Kill Jamal Khashoggi," *Businessinsider.com*, November 10, 2018, https://www.businessinsider.com.au/edward-snowden-israeli-spyware-nso-group-pegasus-jamal-khashoggi-murder-2018-11; Ryan Gallagher, "NSA Kept Watch over Democratic and Republican Conventions, Snowden Documents Reveal," *Theintercept.com*, April 24 2017, https://theintercept.com/2017/04/24/nsa-kept-watch-over-democratic-and-republican-conventions-snowden-documents-reveal/; Dan Gooden, "Snowden Speculates Leak of NSA Spying Tools Is Tied to Russian DNC Hack," *Arstechnica.com*, July 16, 2016, http://arstechnica.com/tech-policy/2016/08/snowden-speculates-leak-of-nsa-spying-tools-is-tied-to-russian-dnc-hack/.

16 Aaron Mauro, "Coronavirus Contact Tracing Poses Serious Threats to Our Privacy," *Theconversation.com*, May 10, 2020, https://theconversation.com/coronavirus-contact-tracing-poses-serious-threats-to-our-privacy–137073.

17 "The Darkest Timeline," *Knowyourmeme.com*, June 30, 2017, https://knowyourmeme.com/memes/the-darkest-timeline.

18 Leibniz's 1710 work *Essais de Théodicée sur la bonté de Dieu, la liberté de l'homme et l'origine du mal* appears in English as *Theodicy: Essays on the Goodness of God, the Freedom of Man and the Origin of Evil*, trans. E.M. Huggard (Illinois: Open Court Publishing, 1996).

19 John Brunner, *Shockwave Rider* (New York: Ballentine Books, 1975); Bruce Bethke, "Cyberpunk," *Infinityplus.co.uk*, http://www.infinityplus.co.uk/stories/cpunk.htm; William Gibson, *Neuromancer* (New York: Ace, 1984); *Mirrorshades: The Cyberpunk Anthology*, ed. Bruce Sterling (New York: Arbor House, 1986).

20 There are many founding authors who helped shape the genre in novels, short stories, games, and art, including Robert Thurston, Steven Utley, Barry Malzberg, Gregory Benford, Christopher Priest, and others.

21 Carlen Lavigne, *Cyberpunk Women, Feminism and Science Fiction: A Critical Study* (Jefferson: McFarland and Company, 2013) is the single best study of cyberpunk, as it works to foreground the work of Marge Piercy, Laura Mixon, Edith Forbes, Kathleen Ann Goonan, and Melissa Scott, among others.

22 Roberto Ontiveros, "'Ready Player Two' Author Ernest Cline Sees the Dark Side of Technology," *Dallasnews.com*, December 17, 2020, https://www.dallasnews.com/arts-entertainment/books/2020/12/17/ready-player-two-author-ernest-cline-sees-the-dark-side-of-technology/.

23 In recent years, the counter-genre of solarpunk has emerged to imagine an optimistic view of the future seen as missing from cyberpunk. Represented in its first major anthology *Sunvault: Stories of Solarpunk and Eco-Speculation* (2017), Solarpunk imagines ecological equilibrium and where building sustainable infrastructure is revolutionary. While the genre has roots with authors like Kim Stanley Robinson (*New York 2140*) and Ursula K. Le

Guin (*The Left Hand of Darkness*), the genre has not yet found an author to take it mainstream. Adam Flynn's "Solarpunk: Notes toward a manifesto" explains that Solarpunk is about "ingenuity, generativity, independence, and community." See https://hieroglyph.asu.edu/2014/09/solarpunk-notes-toward-a-manifesto/.

24   Kate O'Flaherty has done a great job following the privacy policies of Apple and how they expose the way Google and Alphabet profit from data collection. See "Apple Issues New Blow to Facebook and Google with This Bold Privacy Move," *Forbes.com*, November 6, 2020, https://www.forbes.com/sites/kateoflahertyuk/2019/11/06/apple-issues-new-blow-to-facebook-and-google-with-this-privacy-move/?sh=1e8ba460481d" and "iOS 14.3: How to Use Apple's Game-Changing New iPhone Privacy Feature," *Forbes.com*, December 20, 2020, https://www.forbes.com/sites/kateoflahertyuk/2020/12/20/ios-143-how-to-use-apples-game-changing-new-iphone-privacy-feature/?sh=4de1347e6574.

25   The "Google Code of Conduct" containing the phrase "don't be evil" is no longer available on Google's site. See *Archive.org* capture of "https://investor.google.com/corporate/google-code-of-conduct.html" available here: "Google Code of Conduct," *Archive.org*, October 4, 2015, https://web.archive.org/web/20151004012908/https://investor.google.com/corporate/google-code-of-conduct.html.

26   Conor Sen, "The 'Big Five' Could Destroy the Tech Ecosystem," *Bloomberg.com*, November 15, 2017, https://www.bloomberg.com/opinion/articles/2017-11-15/the-big-five-could-destroy-the-tech-ecosystem.

27   Interdisciplinary work in the humanities is so often imperialistic. Theoretical discourses are hungry for verbiage and absorbs disciplinary urgency wherever it can be found. Meaningful keywords are quickly isolated and exploited as an intellectual resource and repackaged through metaphor. Blithely comparing and contrasting vastly different systems and insisting equivalency is the mark of interdisciplinary colonization. For what it is worth, this book is proposing more than a casual allegiance with cybersecurity. Here I propose an engaged and rigorous path that demands the work come from humanists to contribute solutions to the security risks facing both disciplines.

28   Zuboff, *The Age of Surveillance Capitalism*, vii.

29   Ibid., 44.

30   Jaron Lanier, *Ten Arguments for Deleting Your Social Media Accounts Right Now* (New York: Henry Holt and Co., 2018), 2.

31   Digital humanists have done a great deal of hand wringing in the past regarding the need to train the next generation of scholars to be proficient programmers. See Mark Sample, "The Digital Humanities Is Not about Building, It's about Sharing," *Samplereality.com*, May 25, 2011, https://www.samplereality.com/2011/05/25/the-digital-humanities-is-not-about-building-its-about-sharing/ and Brian Croxall, "Coming to MLA12 … Building Digital Humanities in the Undergraduate Classroom," *Briancroxall.net*, June 14, 2011, https://briancroxall.net/2011/06/14/building-digital-humanities-in-the-undergraduate-classroom-an-electronic-roundtable/.

32 Alexander R. Galloway and Eugene Thacker, *The Exploit: A Theory of Networks* (Minneapolis: University of Minnesota Press, 2007), 100.

33 Aaron Mauro, "'To Think a World without Thought': Negotiating Speculative Realism in a Digital Humanities Practice," *Digital Studies/Le champ numérique* 5, no. 1. DOI: http://doi.org/10.16995/dscn.52.

34 The Electronic Frontier Foundation has published a large collection of privacy preserving tools, including "Surveillance Self-Defense: Tips, Tools and How-Tos for Safer Online Communications," *Eff.org*, https://ssd.eff.org/.

35 Maureen Webb, *Coding Democracy: How Hackers Are Disrupting Power, Surveillance, and Authoritarianism* (Cambridge, MA: MIT Press, 2020), 287.

36 Ibid., 289.

37 Zuboff, *The Age of Surveillance Capitalism*, 330.

38 Chaim Gartenberg, "Why Amazon Is Tracking Every Time You Tap Your Kindle," *The Verge*, January 31, 2020, https://www.theverge.com/2020/1/31/21117217/amazon-kindle-tracking-page-turn-taps-e-reader-privacy-policy-security-whispersync.

39 Engin Isin and Evelyn Ruppert, *Being Digital Citizens* (London: Rowman & Littlefield, 2015), 9.

40 Jonathan Gottschall, *The Storytelling Animal: How Stories Make Us Human* (New York: Mariner Books, 2013), xiv.

41 Benedict Anderson, *Imagined Communities: Reflections on the Origin and Spread of Nationalism* (New York: Verso, 2006), 30.

42 Marc Shell, *The Economy of Literature* (Baltimore: Johns Hopkins University Press, 1978), 9. I have silently replaced Shell's male pronouns with neutral ones.

43 Thomas G. Pavel, *Fictional Worlds* (Cambridge: Harvard University Press, 1989), 17.

44 Ibid., 66.

45 Ibid., 67.

46 *Anna Poletti and Julie Rak, "Introduction: Digital Dialogue," in Identity Technologies: Constructing the Self Online*, eds. Anna Poletti and Julie Rak (Madison: University of Wisconsin Press, 2014), 3–24.

47 Pavel, *Fictional Worlds*, 67.

48 Ibid., 68.

49 Eugene Thacker, "The Science Fiction of Technoscience: The Politics of Simulation and a Challenge for New Media Art," *Leonardo* 34, no. 2 (2001): 155–8. muse.jhu.edu/article/19659.

50 Loura Hall, "From Science Fiction to Science Fact," *Nasa.gov*, May 24, 2016, https://www.nasa.gov/feature/from-science-fiction-to-science-fact.

51 Ed Finn and Kathryn Cramer, *Hieroglyph: Stories and Visions for a Better Future* (New York: William Morrow, 2015), xxvii.

52 Julian Bleecker, "Design Fiction: A Short Essay on Design, Science, Fact and Fiction," *Nearfuturelaboratory.com*, March 17, 2009, https://blog.nearfuturelaboratory.com/2009/03/17/design-fiction-a-short-essay-on-design-science-fact-and-fiction/, 6.

53 Respectively, see http://detroitdjc.org/principles/, https://alliedmedia.org/
network-principles, and https://designjustice.org/read-the-principles. Ruha
Benjamin, in *Race After Theory*, offers an important rejoinder to design
thinking idealists who might imagine that any problem can readily have a
solution designed: "It is not simply that design thinking wrongly claims
newness, but in doing so it erases the insights and the agency of those who
are discounted because they are not designers, capitalizing on the demand
for novelty across numerous fields of action and coaxing everyone who
dons the cloak of design into being seen and heard through the dominant
aesthetic of innovation" (179). These community-led design principles help
focus the imaginative agency of design thinking with the communities who
will implement, sustain, and grow design thinking solutions.

54 Anthony Dunne and Fiona Raby, *Speculative Everything: Design Fiction and
Social Dreaming* (Cambridge: MIT Press, 2013).

1

"Hack the Planet":

Pop Hackers and the Demands of a Real World Resistance

The hacker is the subject of much speculation. They regularly appear in novels, games, movies, and television.[1] Hackers are everywhere it seems. They figure prominently in government documents and even plays a role in corporate reports from time to time.[2] They are readily mentioned in the mainstream news and the churn of information on social media. The hacker's identity is often unknown, but they also rise to the level of pseudo-celebrity for their exploits. The hacker persona includes wannabe script kiddies (the ones who can't really code), organized criminals, nation-state backed attackers engaged in corporate or governmental espionage, signal intelligence analysts, and security operations managers seeking to defend sensitive networks (the ones who can code). Sometimes they spend days sending phishing emails in hopes of scamming someone for a prepaid gift card, but hackers also spend years preparing for the exfiltration of secret information from a rival nation or corporation. Few legitimate hackers would call themselves a "hacker" because the word has been hollowed out of meaning by sheer over use. To call someone a hacker can cut across extremes, from a term of deep respect and admiration to cringing mockery.

The identity of a hacker may be one of the most uncertain questions that faces the cybersecurity industry when reporting on the intent or motivations of an attacker. The motives and character of the hacker are built with conjecture, supposition, and guess-work quite often. Imagination is often left to fill in the gaps left by a lack of concrete evidence, and the imagination of the analyst is influenced by their experiences of past attacks and maybe even pop culture representations of "the hacker." Rarely is the question of character, that very literary quality, factored into decisions relating to such important issues as intellectual property theft, national defense, criminal money laundering, and disinformation, all of which are occurring on the international stage. Yet pop culture representations of the hacker are beginning to accurately describe this multifaceted reality and may even serve as a model for the defense of online systems.

The hacker character is a cliché to be sure, but the motives and intentions of the hacker also have the potential to shape global affairs. We know some of these hacker crews with familiar Advanced Persistent Threats (APT) identifications. APT crews are used by the United States to collect the markers of particular "threat actors."[3] Working for the Russian Federation's main intelligence agency known as the GRU (Glavnoye Razvedyvatel'noye Upravleniye), APT 28, otherwise known as "Fancy Bear," is understood to be responsible for a range of attacks including, but not limited to, those against the German and French elections in 2016 and 2017, and the World Anti-doping Agency hack in 2016.[4] APT 29, otherwise known as "Cosy Bear," is also among the more famous APT crews and represents a highly sophisticated cyberespionage group working for the Russian Federation's foreign intelligence agency known as the SVR (Sluzhba Vneshney Razvedki).[5] Based on many years of analysis, the US security firm CrowdStrike was able to determine that both Fancy Bear and Cozy Bear were involved in the hack on the Democratic National Committee servers, which were later dumped on WikiLeaks ahead of the 2016 election.[6] There are similar threat actors working globally in China, North Korea, Iran, and the United States, many of which with an APT identification through laborious reporting and attribution practices. At present, attribution of attackers is an under-theorized and under-researched area in cybersecurity. Florian Egloff suggests that there is a dual process of "sense-making" that then follows closely on "meaning-making" about the nature, scope, and purpose of an attack that emerges from attributing the attacker or attackers.[7] The attribution of activities is so uncertain because there is often very little actual evidence remaining after a successful attack. Worse still, attackers often intentionally muddy the waters with false attributions or claims on behalf of another country, and there may be many motivations that might only be understood long after an attack. Uncertainty and unreliability are tools for an attacker and leave analysts in a position similar to a reader of fiction, drawing conclusions from glimmers of evidence without direct access to the intentions of an author.

In 2003, Dave Aucsmith, Brendan Dixon, and Robin Martin-Emerson at Microsoft developed threat personas that were designed to capture many of the typical motivations for potential attackers and adds important information to an institutional "threat model."[8] Developing a threat model accounts for all users of a system, including hostile users intent on stealing, disrupting, or damaging your systems. A good threat model should help developers build more secure systems by designing software systems with security in mind from the beginning; this integration of development, security, and operation (DevSecOps) will allow for simpler mitigation and recovery steps. At first blush, we might want to start this security-focused design process by "thinking like an attacker," but it is likely impossible to account for the evolving motivations of all threat actors, regardless of their sophistication.[9] Thinking like a hacker is a futile speculative exercise, so resources are perhaps best spent actually attacking one's own system. These "white hat" hackers are condoned by a target in the hopes of improving security by finding weakness by attacking it.[10] A penetration test of this kind can expose more information about potential attackers by reverse engineering their methods in advance. Cybersecurity analysis, like close reading a book, requires the careful description of events that seeks to transform implicit meaning into explicit understanding and insight. It may then be possible to better anticipate vulnerabilities with an integrated understanding of the social, historical, and cultural contexts in which a threat actor operates.

The characters and attitudes defined in the cyberpunk genre can help explain some of the attitudes held by threat actors because the genre represents a shared cultural background regardless of country or even language. The cultures of the communities that support open source tooling, operating systems, and programming languages are another bridge point between opposing APTs. A North Korean hacker will need access to documentation and message boards to steal, for example, cryptocurrency or run a ransomware campaign, which is an important part of their operations at present.[11] Could it be possible that the individuals responsible for these attacks are also consuming Western attitudes and ideas as they deploy their attacks? Could a contest of ideologies be occurring through this cultural backdoor of message boards, documentation, and science fiction? The evidence of social engineering to initiate their attack chain suggests that some cultural overlap is possible, even necessary for any hacking to happen.

Let's pick an example that is typical of these security reports: In a white paper published by ESET, an internet security company, looking into infiltration of European military contractors on LinkedIn, it is possible to see how the Lazarus group (APT 37 and 38) sought to appear Western by mimicking imagined Western ideology.[12] The attack chain begins with a simple social engineering message in LinkedIn offering a high-paying position in a well-known company from a fake account, impersonating a HR manager. The initial message reads, "Dear Sir, Collins Aerospace is a global aerospace and defense company" and includes a link to the legitimate site; the fake account goes on by saying, "I saw your profile in LinkedIn and then I like your enthusiasm. We welcome elites like you. I want you to work in our company. I should be very grateful if you would accept my request. Contact us."[13] After a brief back and forth on LinkedIn's messaging service, the attacker sends a job offer as a pdf. The pdf, in this attack, was a renamed RAR archive containing a link to the job offer, which is opened by the Command Prompt. The Command Prompt delivers a pdf decoy to the target, while also copying malware on the target machine and scheduling its activation. Because the target employee already works in the aerospace industry, these messages are expected from time to time and allow for high value data gathering, exfiltration of corporate secrets, and lateral movement into corporate networks. Once an attacker has a target's attention, they can then expand to more sophisticated a custom remote backdoor, a custom version of Powershell, and playload droppers. ESET attributes the attack to North Korean Lazarus Group based on a first-stage malware file called "NukeSped.FX."[14] The ability to credibly impersonate Westerners—with an understanding of the employment market, social media, and desirable targets—means that an attacker must work to understand their target as completely as possible. An attack begins with empathy and understanding only to weaponize the trust of a target. There is always something inspired about an interesting hack. The initial target has several hallmarks of the cyberpunk hackers, which is surprising considering the attack originated in all likelihood from a state that is distinctly separate from Western influence. The attacker knowingly attacks corporate "elites." They mock the "enthusiasm" Western employees must demonstrate to climb a corporate ladder, which must surely appear absurd to those working on behalf of dynastic North Korean dictatorship.

Cyberpunk-styled hackers have appeared as equal part counter-culture iconoclast, genius programmer, and cyberspace prophet, which might complement North Korean ideology is strange ways. In Brunner's *The Shockwave Rider*, Nick Haflinger escapes from Tarnover corporate re-education, where he is sought for his ability to phreak phone lines with skills akin to a musical prodigy.[15] Brunner was able to warn, Cassandra-like in 1975, "don't dismiss the computer as a new type of fetters."[16] Maybe North Korean hackers feel similarly? Case, from Gibson's *Neuromancer*, floats on the margins of society working to repair his body. Pat Cadigan's Gina, in "Rock on" and *Synners*, is a *synthesizer* of experience who delivers virtual pornography and peak experiences through her cranial jacks; Gina's abuse becomes a reflection of those who abuse her, as she struggles to survive. These hackers are victims of societal injustice. They each resist the ways technologies exacerbate problems like the corporate takeover of civil society or government surveillance. The marginalization of individuals by criminal organizations and the indifference of government agencies is surprisingly generalizable, and the exploitation of the mind through cyberspace as a resource is perhaps enticing to many. The hacker-style resistance to power, or the desire to wield it, can be mapped to a North Korean state-sponsored attacker if they are resisting Western technologies, corporations, and democratic society.

These fictional hacker characters share a similar quality with Aucsmith's threat personas: hacker characters are proud of their unique abilities and revel in their unlauded exploits. The hacker character may be justified in having an inflated ego due to their proficiency. Their lack of compensation further justifies their resentment for their adversaries and the vulnerabilities their adversaries so ignorantly fail to defend against. There is a kind of competitive brinkmanship in just proving it can be done. Paired with this sense of pride is also a sense of righteousness in committing illegal acts. Often, these fictional hackers have legitimate grievances that justify hacking into computer systems that support unjust systems of power. The hacker character romanticizes their activities as a justification for illegal acts. *Hacktivism* is the name given to righteous breaking of laws to shed light on some greater wrong. Readers are sympathetic to their suffering and therefore enjoy watching them strike the Goliath-like systems of power. This asymmetry is the reality from which the individual grapples with global technological systems, but this romantic view of the cyberpunk hero in all likelihood also helps justify the actions of organized crime, corporate espionage, as well as nation-state actors. So is cyberpunk a viable genre or stable set of tropes to help intimate the behaviors of real hackers online?

In 1992, Neal Easterbrook declared that "cyberpunk is dead," but 2020 seems to be a surprise renewal of the genre.[17] Despite the risk of treading on old clichés, cyberpunk is *cool* again.[18] Elon Musk has delivered, of all things, the "Cybertruck" as a visual blueprint for this period that is selling an optimistic electric vehicle future wrapped in a highly pessimistic, aggressive aesthetic. When the vehicle was launched, it seemed important to demonstrate that the side panels could withstand a blow from a sledgehammer and the air filtration system was capable of "Bioweapon Defense mode."[19] The marketing of the vehicle invited potential customers to imagine a post-apocalyptic wasteland: *Mad Max* meets *Snow Crash* on the US interstate system. The year 2020 also saw the release of a videogame called *Cyberpunk 2077*, which allows players to explore a post-apocalyptic urban wasteland of criminals. The typical power fantasy action of first-person shooters is augmented with a new fantasy in this game. The ability to hack technology and people is a core game play mechanic in navigating a dangerous world and destroying your enemies.

A range of streaming television shows is further setting the stage for the current interest with the cyberpunk genre. USA network's *Mr. Robot* portrays a hacker hero capable of reordering the whole of modern society, complete with realistic code examples and exploit chains.[20] HBO's *Westworld* is an excellent vision of the power of corporate oligarchies run-amok, developing AI systems that threaten humanity. *Devs*, written and directed by Alex Garland, explores a world in which Silicon Valley idealism develops a system capable of undermining human free will by modeling every permutation of our existence. Netflix even adapted Richard K. Morgan's *Altered Carbon* into a hit series about a future in which humanity has digitized consciousness into a disk or "stack" that allows humans to change bodies, effectively live forever, and travel the universe as a stream of data. *The Expanse*, originally created by the Syfy Network, offers a plausible vision of human expansion into the solar system, where the inner planets of Mars and Earth are pitted against cyberpunk styled "belters," a patois speaking, tattooed working-class bent on rebellion after generations of toiling and dying in the asteroid belt.[21] There has never been so much cyberpunk in contemporary media and never has cyberpunk so accurately described the twinned optimism and pessimism of a life lived through and with technology.[22] It's a great time to be a fan of this genre.

At home in our new dystopias, the mysterious hacker figure is an imaginative opportunity for many in the popular press to express anxieties about technology in general. This hooded figure, hunched over a keyboard, committing crimes with ease says more about our own anxieties and our own inability to defend against such shadowy forces. While Ridley Scott's *Alien* (1979) and *Blade Runner* (1982), *Robocop* (1987), and David Cronenberg's *Videodrome* (1983) represent some of the first wave of decidedly darker cyberpunk films, cyberpunk has always flirted with optimism. The early 1990s were a euphoric period of imaginative possibility for this hacker character, then cast as a neon skater punk technophile. The cult 1995 film *Hackers*, directed by Iain Softley and starring Angelina Jolie in her breakout role, helped popularize this stereotype of counter-cultural revolutionary, named Crash Override, yelling "hack the planet" from the back of a police car. While the portrait cast in *Hackers* was one of pop culture fascination, the depiction of highly capable drop-outs exposing global corporate injustice was cathartic for those living in the dotcom bubble just a few years later. *Hackers* developed a cult status ironically because of its cringe inducing depiction of hacking. These characters were something new that could maybe even be real. It looked fun too. Yet, even here, there may be a more useful interpretation. These colorful anarcho-cyberpunks seemed to have been the logical outcome of an economically disenfranchised generation of talented computer programmers with nothing to do. The recession caused by the dotcom bubble would provide the necessary conditions for these hacker heroes to exist as unemployed white-collar professionals. Some of *Hackers'* cult appeal came only after the stock crash confirmed that the market is interested in making money rather than saving the world. The excessive stock speculation during this period would come crashing down in the spring of 2000. *Hackers* captured something of the frantic energy that followed the popularization of the World Wide Web and personal computing in the home, but it was an absurd and amazing depiction of 1990s hacker culture given the limited distribution and influence of the web at the time.

Parler Tricks

On January 6, 2021, the hacker persona from the 1990s came crashing into the twenty-first century in the wake of the riot and attack on Capitol Hill in Washington, DC. A violent mob of Trump supporters broke into the Capitol Building in an attempt to disrupt the confirmation of then President-Elect Biden, take prisoners, and steal property, including laptops and other trophies. In the wake of this riot, five people lost their lives, including a Capitol Hill Police Officer.[23] Images of "Blue Lives Matter" Trump supporters beating police officers with US flag poles marked the official end of the forty-fifth Presidency. President Trump was permanently banned from Twitter and other social media platforms as a means of muting his incitements to violence. Technology companies were finally forced to distance themselves from Republican favored social media channels and Parler in particular. Days after the attack, Apple and Google removed Parler from their app stores and Amazon Web Services refused to serve Parler content.[24]

Parler went down on January 9, 2021, but not before a 26-year-old self-described "hacker" with the handle @donk_enby on Twitter and d0nk on GitHub archived more than 32 terabytes of "highly incriminating" content from the right-wing social media company.[25] In the days before the attack, donk was able to find an unrestricted API endpoint and generate administrator accounts to pull public content into a Docker virtual machine. The posts to Parler were chronological and sequentially numbered. The "hack," which was really just downloading from an unsecured API endpoint, was called "Parler Tricks."[26] Jared Thomson, a lead developer and one of the founders of the platform, included the absurd hacker boast "hack the planet" on his Parler profile. In a hilarious turn, donk's screen name on Twitter was "crash override" at the time of the hack. It seems that they both shared an affinity for the character, one perhaps more ironically than the other. With a screen capture of Thomson's profile, donk thanks Thomson, mocking his apparently sincere love of *Hackers*: "I'd like to thank Jared for inspiring me," explains donk, "to do all the research on Parler, accidentally leading me down a path of helping now 3 academic research projects on online disinformation, finding multiple vulns and passing them onto more capable people by putting this in his bio."[27] After archiving the public data from the site and all associated metadata, donk proceeded to spend the following weeks dunking on the Parler development team on social media.

The Parler "hack" was not really a hack. Donk wrote up a thorough set of Python scripts called "Parler Tricks" to access public data on the site and "solve fun mysteries such as: 'Is my dad on Parler?' or 'Who was on Parler before it first started gaining popularity?'" But after January 6, donk recognized that she needed help! She had the tools and an understanding of Parler's vulnerability. In an interesting twist, the data just happened to include geotagged metadata associated with videos generated by users' mobile devices. It is a common practice to strip this metadata before posting content publicly, but not at Parler. So the data was available; the data was also easy to access. But, with the limited time-frame, bandwidth was the main bottleneck. So how can one person download all this critically important data before it was removed from the web? Archive Team describes themselves as "a loose collective of rogue archivists, programmers, writers and loudmouths dedicated to saving our digital heritage." This is their official logo. These are the people who archived your old Geocities website. Jason Scott Sadofsky co-founded the guerrilla archivist collective in 2009. Since 2016, guerrilla archiving events gained popularity during the Trump presidency because so much public data was being removed from the web, particularly in relation to the Environmental Protection Agency and National Oceanic and Atmospheric Administration climate data.

Archive team has developed "a virtual archiving appliance" called Warrior, that simply and easily downloads data for their current archiving projects and uploads it to their servers. When many volunteers pool their internet connections, bandwidth is increased as demand is distributed across the network. The data was then made available through Distributed Denial of Secrets.[28] In their own words, Distributed Denial of Secrets is a "journalist 501(c)(3) non-profit devoted to enabling the free transmission of data in the public interest." They go on to say this: "We aim to avoid political, corporate or personal leanings, to act as a beacon of available information. As a transparency collective, we don't support any cause, idea or message beyond ensuring that information is available to those who need it most—the people." They have managed the 32.1 TB of data, much of which was video and image data, complete with geotagged metadata. Distributed Denial of Secrets is a access point for data leaks and other information pertaining to the public interest, but they were banned in the summer of 2020 from Twitter for dumping information related to police practices and domestic surveillance. Blue Leaks represents an unprecedented view into local, state, and federal policing in the United States.

It remains impossible to link to any content on Distributed Denial of Secrets through Twitter. If any user attempts to post a link to ddosecrets.com, Twitter throws an error message: "Something went wrong, but don't fret–let's give it another shot." If we "give it another shot," Twitter posts a timed banner at the bottom of the screen that says, "We can't complete this request because this link has been identified by Twitter or our partners as being potentially harmful. Visit our Help Center to learn more." The Help Centre is not helpful.

Twitter does not disclose who these partners are and why they have this level of control. However, ddosecrets.com had their Twitter account revoked in the wake of the BlueLeaks data dump. The BlueLeaks data dump contains information relating to "fusion centers" in the United States.[29] With more than 70 offices around the United States, fusion centers monitor citizens in the name of counter terrorism, and serve to feed local surveillance data to the FBI, DHS, and the National Counter Terrorism Center (NCTC). Generally speaking (for the sake of an argument), if a corporation is cooperating with a domestic surveillance program, they might also be motivated to cover it up. The American Civil Liberties Union (ACLU) has suggested that corporate participation is likely, despite what they call "excessive secrecy" in the fusion center program.[30] However, not all surveillance is necessarily bad. This system could be useful in predicting attacks by vocal and well-organized domestic extremists, for example. But the police response to the January 6 putsch attempt was muted and ineffective. Capitol Hill Police participation and complicity in the events of January 6 would become a key question that has largely gone unanswered. However, days following the attack, Washington, DC, police issued requests for help identifying individuals pictured in the news and social media. These efforts were only possible because of the Parler leak, not because of domestic surveillance systems like these so-called "fusion centers."

Almost immediately, citizen developers released web tools to assist in identifying the attackers from the Parler data, which included their location. The US Capitol Attack Video Map is an excellent example of the rapid response of tech savvy citizens.[31] Other citizen data analysts confirmed that the Parler platform had broad adoption from across the United States and Canada.[32] While there were some users in Mexico, Parler was not broadly embraced there.[33] Faces of the Riot has served as a durable collection of the attackers, with facial recognition tools that isolated images of those present from the image and video content from the Parler dump.[34] It took just a few weeks for highly polished video analysis tools to emerge on Propublica, which correlate location and time to videos.[35] Concerned citizens poured hours of labor identifying and tracking individuals every movement and action on January 6. When taken together, citizen sleuthing allowed journalists and researchers to understand the moment-to-moment events in all the chaos.

As Congress worked to impeach President Trump for the second time, a first in US history, the Parler dump data was used "many, many" times by impeachment lawyers.[36] Parler reappeared about two months later with the help of a Russian-owned company called DDoS-Guard Corp. While this hack will go down in American history as one of the most important of the period, followed closely by SolarWinds, the recent Exchange server attacks, and maybe the Coastal Pipeline attack (though for different reasons), one donk_enby set a very public example for a whole new generation of social media savvy hackers. As she says in an interview during the impeachment proceedings, "I hope it inspires more people with similar skills to mine to use those skills for good."[37] Hacks, like Parler Tricks, are political. Hacks are political, even if only motivated by money, because they are about the redistribution of power, authority, and access. Redistribution of power through theft of money or data. Redistribute authority by embarrassing the powerful. Redistributing access by leaking data and exposing injustices to the world. More importantly, perhaps, hacks of this kind demonstrate the distinctly asymmetrical power relations that can exist in a conflict online. A single curious hacker with the support of a well-prepared community are capable of assisting in criminal investigations of hundreds of violent extremists.

But hacking is also apolitical. We applaud facial recognition when it is used to identify the Capitol Hill attackers, but San Francisco, Boston, and both Portlands have already banned use of facial recognition technology by their police departments. We tend to support a good bit of hacking when it confirms our values. We must defend humanistic ways of thinking so that we can, as Ruha Benjamin, in *Race After Technology* explains, "embed new values and new social relations into the world."[38] She goes on to say, quoted here, "What we need is greater investment in socially just imaginaries. This, I think, would have to entail a socially conscious approach to tech development that would require prioritizing equity over efficiency, social good over market imperatives."[39] The digital humanities is invested, I think, in developing these socially just imaginaries, but only if our work is not the target of an attack. Is there a place for ethical hacking in the humanities? How can we integrate such thinking into our research methods? Well, we've done radical things before. Twenty years ago, when Jerome McGann and many others worked to define Digital Humanities, "making things" was a radical call. McGann goes so far as to say, "The next generation of literary and aesthetic theorists who will most matter are people who will be at least as involved with making things as with writing texts." Making publicly accessible humanities scholarship is now a normal part of the discipline. We have curriculum, institutes, graduate degrees predicated on this call to "make things." In the second decade of the twenty-first century, virtual-archiving appliances, mapping GPS metadata, or facial-recognition tools serve the needs of the humanities to participate in contemporary conversations and engage with the public directly. Using this ever widening set of tools means that we may find cause and reason to do quasi-illegal things. Disobedience to unjust systems will require breaking the unjust rules that support it. Supporting our colleagues who make this jump from academia to activist will require a renewed solidarity with those seeking to gather and protect our historical and cultural record. The historical and cultural record is online, and our web experience is increasingly dominated by paywalls and surveillance capitalist corporations eager to harvest our data. This is an untenable state. Our history and culture are now bound up in corporations that could care less about the humanities. Without reclaiming cultural data, we risk the first part of the twenty-first century becoming a digital dark age. We risk a digital dark age not because the data doesn't exist. We risk losing our cultural heritage because we do not own it. We may be left with no choice but to take it back, at least as individuals. If I can paraphrase McGann, at least in part, "maybe we should be at least as involved with hacking things as with making things."

Disobedience to unjust systems will require breaking the unjust rules that support it. Supporting our colleagues who make this jump from academia to activist will require a renewed solidarity with those seeking to gather and protect our historical and cultural record. The historical and cultural record is online, and our web experience is increasingly dominated by paywalls and surveillance capitalist corporations eager to harvest our data. This is an untenable state. Our history and culture are now bound up in corporations that could care less about the humanities. Without reclaiming cultural data, we risk the first part of the twenty-first century becoming a digital dark age. We risk a digital dark age not because the data doesn't exist. We risk losing our cultural heritage because we do not own it. We may be left with no choice but to take it back, at least as individuals. Hacks, like Parler Tricks, are political. More importantly, perhaps, hacks of this kind demonstrate the distinctly asymmetrical power relations that can exist in a conflict online. It seems obvious to say, perhaps. Hacks are political, even if only motivated by money, because they are about the redistribution of power, authority, and access. Redistribution of power through theft of money or data. Redistribute authority by embarrassing the powerful. Redistributing access by leaking data and exposing injustices to the world.

The hacker persona is a fluid thing. "Hack the planet" can be meant seriously, as pure cutting sarcasm, or any shade of sincerity in-between. The general acceptance of the romantic pseudo-hacker is an opening to grifters in business and government to dodge responsibility by hiding behind the hacker's hoodie. President Trump has speculated about the hacker character, in an attempt to deflect attention from Russian interference in the 2016 US Presidential Election.[40] On Twitter, he doubled down on his comments from the presidential debates with Hilary Clinton that "it may be Russia, or China or another country or group, or it may be a 400 pound genius sitting in bed and playing with his computer."[41] The 400-pound-hacker comment is a canard meant to rile his opponents and focus attention on his offensive portrait of the pseudo-hacker character, but his trolling tactics exposes the conceit of fear and awe that attends this powerfully anonymous hacker character. Trump appeals to this stereotype to deflect culpability and potential involvement in a larger conspiracy to collude with foreign governments during the election.[42] The anonymous hacker figure is dangerous in public debate precisely because an amorphous criminal is an ideal foil for charlatans eager to shift blame and responsibility. By accusing an anonymous entity founded on a highly flexible stereotype, responsibility can be easily defused and redistributed anonymously across the internet.

The hacker figure is not merely a rhetorical ploy in twenty-first century politics, however. The hacker character represents a much more ambivalent set of concerns that will help animate legitimate questions relating to freedom of information, privacy, and security. As more of the general public grows increasingly sympathetic to these issues and the legal ambiguities of hacktivists, the hacker should be understood as equal parts trickster, technologist, autodidact, and activist. While not all hackers are interested in the political dimension of their work, the nature of open source tools, network access, and security overlap heavily with ethical questions of life online. An "ethical hacker" emerges from a technological milieu that pits those in positions of power against individuals and communities seeking greater autonomy and control. The legal gray area left for hacktivists means we may even have changing views on their activities as laws like the US Computer Fraud and Abuse Act continue to change.[43] From the first wave cyberpunks to the conclusion of the Trump presidency, we might define the historical focus of this book that includes the growth of personal computing, the dotcom bubble, the rise of social media, post-9/11 nation-state surveillance, the rise of Chinese Communist Party surveillance, the 2008 Great Recession, and finally the Covid-19 pandemic. A lot has happened since the turn of the millennium to transform a broader public understanding of the role of the internet and technology in shaping our lives, and the hacker will remain a constant player in the history of these public dramas. The hacker will continue to be romanticized because the perceived ability to control one's own digital world is the fault line of culture and politics. The culture of hacking is animated by a restless dissatisfaction with systems as they are.

Anthological Freedom

In 1984, Steven Levy's *Hackers* offered the first study of hacker culture, which framed the "hacker ethic" through a desire for access to computers and information.[44] There were attempts to define types of hackers. "Crackers" were interested in breaking into systems, while hackers according to Levy were tinkerers and hobbyists who merely "mistrust authority."[45] According to Levy, this early hacker culture did not need manifestos or complicated ideologies to guide their interest or recruit new hackers: "The computer did the converting."[46] In the early days, the core ethos of the hacker was not some isolated political ideology. The conscience of this hacker is guided by curiosity and the desire to explore digital environments for greater knowledge. The Jargon File is likely the most earnest declaration of the hacker ethos.[47] Developed by MIT's now famous Tech Model Railroad Club, the Jargon File remains the earliest attempt to define a distinct hacker culture. Even then, the drive to describe hackers was described in a tongue-in-cheek style.

The Jargon File is a fascinating time capsule of early computer culture. "The Meaning of a Hack" entry is remarkably durable. The most refined phrase from this lengthy entry simply claims that a hack is "an appropriate application of ingenuity."[48] Curiosity paired with creativity describe this early hacker culture. The Jargon File has been updated as recently as 2012, which suggests there is a desire to solidly define some terms. The "hacker ethic" is well considered and comes in two parts:

> The belief that information-sharing is a powerful positive good, and that it is an ethical duty of hackers to share their expertise by writing open-source code and facilitating access to information and to computing resources wherever possible.[49]

The second entry to this definition is as follows: "The belief that system-cracking for fun and exploration is ethically OK as long as the cracker commits no theft, vandalism, or breach of confidentiality."[50] Hacking has something to do with sharing information and code. This ethic is about sharing resources and building community through a shared curiosity about how things work.

Another early document of this emerging hacker culture can still be found on the online magazine *Phrack*, which published "The Conscience of a Hacker" in 1986. This document remains a seminal sentiment in the perpetual problem of linking computer hacking with criminality. This original hacker manifesto claims that their "crime is that of curiosity":

> We explore ... and you call us criminals. We seek after knowledge ... and you call us criminals. We exist without skin color, without nationality, without religious bias ... and you call us criminals. You build atomic bombs, you wage wars, you murder, cheat, and lie to us and try to make us believe it's for our own good, yet we're the criminals.[51]

Years later, Pekka Himanen's *The Hacker Ethic* takes a similarly spiritual approach to hacking in 2001. Himanen describes the "hacker work ethic" as fueled by programming that is "interesting, exciting, and joyous."[52] The computer is more than merely a productivity tool for Himanen; the computer is a tool to liberate time and money so as to live in a spiritually connected way, wherein the hacker is the literal embodiment of the spirit of the age.[53] These definitions of the hacker ethic suggest that hackers are serving some larger societal function. Digital humanists have tapped into this rhetoric of "hacking" in the past as well. Digital humanists have sought to reproportion the methods of the humanities as "more hack, less yack," which has sought to broaden academic methodologies.[54] Hacking is not a crime; it's research.

Few contemporary observers have done as well in describing something approaching the complex mesh of interests and ideas that animates hacker culture as Gabriella Coleman. In both her *Coding Freedom* and *Hoaxer, Whistleblower, Spy,* Coleman captures a subtle ethnography of the subculture through its aesthetics as well as its history. In the opening of *Coding Freedom*, Coleman speculates that hackers are aligned with a radical sense of freedom that emerges from the free and open source software (FOSS) movement:

> This ethnography takes seriously free software's visions of liberty and freedom as well as the mundane artifacts that hackers take pleasure and joy in creating. In considering them together, important lessons are revealed about the incomplete, sometimes fraught, but nonetheless noticeable relationship between hacking and liberalism, and the transformations and tensions evident within the liberal tradition and computer hacking.[55]

The FOSS movement allows anyone to read and reuse source code.[56] In addition to being able to use FOSS, individuals are free to read the code running within the application and, in many cases, are able to contribute and improve the software. To read and understand a program's source code, to really "grok" it, was wonderfully empowering. As Coleman describes, FOSS contains a latent political sensibility that demands transparency and generosity, with a consistent libertarian streak that is perfectly at home on the web. Between these visions of the hacker character, there rests a genuine subculture possessed of tastes, morals, histories, and creeds often outside the purview of consumer technology and mainstream culture. They are tricksters who prank and push past social norms to wreak havoc and mayhem, while also teaching practical and applied lessons about how our digital world is put together.[57]

The technological restlessness and curiosity of the hacker mindset is only a step away from the political and social dissatisfaction with the status-quo. Free and open source software is an important part of the hacker ethic that insists on being able to tinker with and improve software. Yet the benefits of open source as opposed to proprietary software with closed source code have been a perennial debate within the cybersecurity industry. Is it more secure to hide your methods or release them to be vetted by a large community of security experts? The Solarwinds attack has lent renewed urgency to this question of open source security software, while previous attacks like Dragonfly and Cloudhopper indicate that problems with the software supply chain are nothing new.[58] The argument for proprietary security software goes something like this: close source code is more secure because defenders do not show how they are defending and any potential future security issues will not be immediately evident, which will grant the developers of proprietary software time to patch their systems. Proprietary software, like the Orion platform sold by Solarwinds, makes the tacit argument that "security through obscurity" can be done well. If the attacker does not know how you are defending, they will be unable to locate an exploit, right? Open source software, in keeping with the hacker ethic described by Coleman, is more secure and better tested because of its transparency. The community of developers and clients can work together to test, extend, and deploy security software in a range of contexts. Security researchers are free to conduct tests in a real world operations without the need of working with sales agents. So-called "red team" penetration testing (often just called pen testing) allows development, security, and operations to test software by playing the role of an attacker and attempt to breach their own systems. By assuming that an attacker has access to the source code, the defending "blue team" cannot rely on security through obscurity, thereby requiring a much more resilient system.

Penetration testing is a theatrical exercise that makes potential attack scenarios real, as a live security game of capture the flag. In a social engineering attack like we described above, threat actors mask their identities to obfuscate hostile intentions to collect useful information or provoke a victim to compromise their security. There are theatrics and misdirection in any attack, and red team penetration testers will use all the public information they have to manipulate their targets. Penetration testing requires organizations play a kind of security dress rehearsal that allows for failure to be a learning opportunity.[59] Bruce Schneier coined "security theater" in the wake of 9/11, when security procedures in airports increased dramatically. "Security is both a feeling and a reality" for Schneier because so many of the procedures introduced during this time did very little to improve safety, but the theater unfolding in airports around the world only increased the feeling of safety.[60] Security pantomime like confiscating liquids or searching undergarments does little, says Schneier, to improve actual safety. Similarly, IT departments routinely ask users to participate in the cybersecurity equivalent of security theater, by asking users to change passwords, while not requiring a second factor authentication or biometric verification.[61] Cybersecurity theater of this kind asks users to pantomime security practices in the hopes of feeling safer, which further demotivates users to take an active role in improving security practices. In fact, the feeling of security is dangerous because it can only lead to a false sense of confidence and increased risk taking. Penetration tests ask users to be cast in a chorus of active, security minded, users. Failure during a penetration test is a learning opportunity for institutions and a teachable moment for individuals. After all, good security is hard. Good security is a team sport that requires a security literate group of people to work together and behave knowledgeably in digital environments, even under stress. Appeals to the pseudo-hacker or security theater are opportunities for people in power to appeal rhetorically to security practices without doing much to improve safety. The drives and motives of this mysterious persona of sometimes mythic proportions reveal the fears and anxieties of those who imagine this hacker character. As a black mirror of contemporary uncertainty of the unknown technological future, the hacker represents the fears of the fathomless complexity of life lived online as well as hope that technology will grant power to benevolent forces and shape our world for the better.

McKenzie Wark's *A Hacker Manifesto* helps shape this duplicity within the hacker persona. The hacker hero is a key ingredient to any manifesto after all. In Wark's theoretical view of the hacker, the hacker lives in "abstraction." They see the double world of the physical and the abstraction of systems in code. This digital double consciousness is a binary existence between serving a cause of righteousness and revolution or of power and control. Their doubleness is a twenty-first-century Marxist vision of the dialectic between the capitalists and the workers, between the superstructure of our digital world and the base physical necessities of human life on Earth:

> Land is the detachment of a resource from nature, an aspect of the productive potential of nature rendered abstract, in the form of property. Capital is the detachment of a resource from land, an aspect of the productive potential of land rendered abstract in the form of property. Information is the detachment of a resource from capital already detached from land. It is the double of a double. It is a further process of abstraction beyond capital, but one that yet again produces its separate existence in the form of property.[62]

The hacker is a catalyst for the revolution by disrupting the systems of control manifested in digital technology. This so-called "vectoralist class," those with the material means of control through ownership of resources and production, seek a similar ownership of information resources on an industrial scale. There are risks inherent to this revolutionary stance toward political ideologies and public engagement. This is a dialectical view that sets social and technical forces in opposition. The theoretical lens of opposing forces relies on a vision of revolution and oppression that may never really exist. The dialectical, binary opposition between forces does not really reflect the hacker experience of pseudo-legality and moral uncertainty. It is clear that the hacker activist, the hacktivist, will figure more prominently in public protest.

Like this dual vision of the hacker, the internet is equal parts tame utopia and lawless wasteland, officious and technical as well as lurid and bacchanalian. When Tim Berners-Lee drafted his "Information Management" proposal for research at CERN his boss at the time described the project as "vague but exciting …."[63] Even the recent history of the web is decidedly idealistic and properly Utopian. It is remarkable to reflect on just how far the web has fallen from the ideals of its founding by Sir Tim Berners-Lee. In his reflection on the web in 1999, *Weaving the Web* described a romantically optimistic vision. Informed by his Unitarian Universalist beliefs, Berners-Lee says that "We are slowly learning the value of decentralized, diverse systems, and of mutual respect and tolerance. Whether you put it down to evolution or your favorite spirit, the neat thing is that we seem as humans to be tuned so that we do in the end get the most fun out of doing the 'right' thing."[64] In celebration of the World Wide Web's thirtieth anniversary in 2019, Berners-Lee described his invention in very different terms shall we say; he condemns the "deliberate, malicious intent" of criminal and state-sponsored hacking; he highlights the "perverse incentives" of an ad-based revenue for the web that promotes clickbait and viral misinformation; he even admits to the "unintended negative consequences" of the otherwise "benevolent design" of the web that has produced the "outraged and polarized tone" of online discourse.[65]

The uncertain character of the hacker has somehow spread it seems from the competing visions we have of the web itself, the hacker's natural habitat. There seems to be a climactic coevolution of the hacker and the web. When the web found its first broad adoption with the release of the Mosaic browser in 1993 from the National Center for Supercomputing Applications (NCSA) at the University of Illinois at Urbana–Champaign, the World Wide Web was a curious experience for most early users. The popular press announced its arrival as a new golden age of information and connection as it was heralded by the beautified calls of early pioneers of the web as a source of freedom, democracy, and liberation. This digital frontier needed description and categorization, which had long been imagined by futurist philosophers. Ted Nelson coined much of the language we use to describe the web today, though he was a philosopher and not technically oriented. In his self-published manifesto magazine, which he first sold by hand before Stewart Brand would republish the eclectic work, Nelson's *Computer Lib/Dream Machines* was a broad cultural document that placed computers at the fulcrum of future freedoms.[66] It was a wild and provocative prediction about the future of computation in the world that just so happened to be largely accurate!

While Nelson may have not been technically responsible for the growth and development of the World Wide Web standard, he was one of the magi heralding its arrival and serving as a philosophical prophet, spinning esoteric new age free thinking with techno-futurism. Levy describes *Computer Lib/ Dream Machines* as "the epic of the computer revolution, the bible of the hacker dream."[67] In Nelson's speculations about the future web and the effects of ubiquitous computing, he imagined a world in which computers would be continuous with the tradition of Western Enlightenment values of "literature, scholarship, and freedom."[68] In a section called "Nelson's Canons: A bit on information rights," he defines the freedom to collect, use, and dismantle any information shared digitally. He called this *Anthological Freedom*, which is a metaphor borrowed from the sense that information can be edited and reshaped like a print anthology. Similarly, he defines basic rights including "freedom from spying and sabotage" as well as "freedom from being monitored."[69] These requirements emerge from the logic of "hypertext," which Nelson coined in 1965 and is enshrined by Berners-Lee in the first website, info.cern.ch, in 1989. The freedom to weave together texts through these links represents the freedom to build anthologies of many authors. He imagined a web of people and ideas, reciprocally connected. Because of challenges to copyright law through linking, anthological freedom is at risk. These illegal acts of generosity represent the very core technological and philosophical foundation of the web itself. A philosopher served to sketch the shape of how ideas would be shared online, and it may well be this initial inspiration that allows for the web to be a forum for genuine defenses of truth and justice. The prefix "hyper," which we now drop as a matter of convenience, served to mark the newness of "hypermedia." In a corner of the west coast counter-cultural intelligentsia, ideas were being described that shaped the following millennium. However, the social and cultural forces at work in the second decade of this new millennium do not resemble Nelson's freewheeling 1960s. The idealistic Silicon Valley hippies have made way for the cyberpunks.

Street-Level Anarchy

As social media reorders and augments social relationships, the nostalgic drive to recapture an authentic culture is growing. Today's young adults valorize 1990s youth culture in an attempt, maybe, to return to a pre-internet experience in which their actions, feelings, and relationships have not been commodified by big data. The Radio Dept's album *Clinging to a Scheme* (produced by Martin Carlberg & Johan Duncanson) contains an audio sample of Thurston Moore, lead vocalist and guitarist for Sonic Youth, in the opening for their song, "Heaven's on Fire." The sample of Moore is from the 1992 documentary, *1991: The Year Punk Broke*, which can be read as a eulogy for punk music in the wake of the commercial success of Nirvana and Sonic Youth, of whom the documentary features. The quote of Moore, at the opening of "Heaven's On Fire," is a lament for a world with so many "charlatans": Moore can be heard saying, "People see rock and roll as, as youth culture, and when youth culture becomes monopolized by big business, what are the youth to do? Do you, do you have any idea? I think we should destroy the bogus capitalist process that is destroying youth culture." If there was ever a rallying cry for today's need to rebuild mainstream culture that has produced rampant gender, race, and ecological acts of violence, this is it. There is tragic irony in his words of course. The bogus capitalist processes broke punk onto the mainstream and also "broke" punk by monetizing it.

The history of punk music holds lessons for the cyberpunk genre and the hacker activist ethos it portrays. Dylan Clark, a cultural critic and punk historian, explains that "punk had to die so it could live."[70] Clark describes how "classical punk" of the Sex Pistols died at the moment of its birth, with "God Save the Queen" going to number one in the 1970s. Once the subculture of classical punk became a source of nostalgia and critical appraisal by the mass media, it was dead. The moment punk became "real" in the mainstream was also the moment it was monetized, commodified, and rendered inert, says Clark. Mohawk haircuts and stud collared jackets quickly become mere style, not really even offensive to mainstream fashion; they became references to the moral panic punk caused, in the past, rather than an authentic antagonistic posture to the world right now. At the moment that punk is no longer ugly, insulting, and chaotic, it has been co-opted by the culture industry and resold as something cool: "Dissident youth subculture," says Clark, "is normal and expected, even unwittingly hegemonic,"[71] when it is marketed and commodified as a placebo of resistance. Mall punks are embracing mainstream culture by merely choosing an approved subculture. Parents picking up their leather clad kids from the mall in their Tesla Cybertruck would be the most ostentatious display of a commodification of the cyberpunk subculture. The only solution to the way commodification embraces, extends, and extinguishes subcultures is to reject subcultures in general.[72] By rejecting subcultures, as Clark suggests, "Punk, then, is a position from which to articulate an ideological position without accruing the film of mainstream attention."[73] Punk is not a style; it is an anti-authority posture. Cyberpunk needs to grow past its aesthetic tropes and become realized and *codified* in action. Cyberpunk hackers need to remain anonymous because public attention and notoriety only exposes them to the capitalist churn that renders their actions mere product to be consumed as news or other media.

A return of cyberpunk on premium television streaming sites serves to embrace, extend, and extinguish the political urgency of a counter surveillance capitalist moment. If young people are seduced by binge watching television, rather than learning to code, youth culture will be rendered largely inert. Protests and civil disobedience have moved online, but activism is at risk of dying there. *Mr. Robot, Westworld,* or *Devs* has the potential to inspire young people to live out these stories, and there is some evidence that dystopic stories help prepare people to be more resilient in the face of real emergencies, like a pandemic.[74] Of course, the widespread popularity of cyberpunk means that a renewal of hacker activist culture runs an even greater risk of arriving dead on the scene when it is needed most. Now is the time to design an adaptable, polymorphic vision of hacker culture design into our political calculus and imagine many possible futures. Bruce Sterling's introduction to the 1986 cyberpunk anthology *Mirrorshades* resonates today as it did then:

> Traditionally there has been a yawning cultural gulf between the sciences and the humanities: a gulf between literary culture, the formal world of art and politics, and the culture of science, the world of engineering and industry. But the gap is crumbling in unexpected fashion. Technical culture has gotten out of hand. The advances of the sciences are so deeply radical, so disturbing, upsetting, and revolutionary, that they can no longer be contained. They are surging into culture at large; they are invasive; they are everywhere. The traditional power structure, the traditional institutions, have lost control of the pace of change. [...] And suddenly a new alliance is becoming evident: an integration of technology and the Eighties counterculture. An unholy alliance of the technical world and the world of organized dissent—the underground world of pop culture, visionary fluidity, and street-level anarchy.[75]

Here, in Sterling's nearly four-decade-old assessment of technology and culture, lies the prescient power of speculative fiction and the critical edge of cyberpunk. We can hear the famed futurist and sociologist Alvin Toffler's *Future Shock* in Sterling's description of this technologically infused counterculture. One of Toffler's greatest contributions, in the midst of so many logical predictions, is that the pace of change increases the social and cultural effects of new technologies. As a sociologist, he describes a "durational expectancy" as the internal human rhythms of life.[76] When these expectations are shocked by the pace of change, the resulting mental turmoil strains expectations of other categories governing everyday life. Work, education, love, family, ownership, citizenship, and even the ways we die will be transformed by the pace of change.

Perhaps the most radical, disturbing, and upsetting trend will be the "cyborgification" of society. Chris Hables Gray, Heidi J. Firgueroa-Serriera, and Steven Mentor's collection *Modified: Living as a Cyborg* (2021) argues that we are already cyborgs of one kind or another; the proliferation of technology in our lives means that humanity has "indeed gone from tool makers to machine inventors to cyborgs."[77] While smartphones are not embedded in our bodies, they are never far away. It is possible to think of human hybridization with technology occurring earlier than the invention of the smartphone, however. For Donna Haraway, famed author of the "Cyborg Manifesto," the invention of language is the very moment humans became cyborgs. Our being was bound to language as our most intimate technology. However, language that is singular in meaning and capable of perfect communication is inherently phallocentric and colonial. Literal meaning is about the power to impose it. Hacking is about breaking that power by intentionally misuse and break the intended use of language, such as computer code. Programming is the language of cyborgs. Here, in Haraway's words, she describes it like this:

> Writing is preeminently the technology of cyborgs, etched surfaces of the late twentieth century. Cyborg politics are the struggle for language and the struggle against perfect communication, against the one code that translates all meaning perfectly, the central dogma of phallogocentrism.[78]

Computer code is the apotheosis of human language use that makes us cyborgs. We can now write in a language that can make things happen in the world. We can hack back, break things, and disrupt the ordered workings of power. Speaking to computers feels like a second language. Polymorphism, a feature of the Object Oriented Programming paradigm, is a literal machine hybrid.

Polymorphic Protest Culture

Progressive protest culture must similarly shape shift, without losing its core aims of justice and equity, to manifest in many subcultures and online communities. To resist the extinguishing embrace of social media and large technology companies, digital activists must be ready to change. The cultural codes of music, language, and dress must be agile and unpredictable. Activism must be networked without becoming reliant on the breaking dependencies of platforms or proprietary technologies. Unified political dissent must be expressed through a political polymorphism—a many shaped politics—and cultural inheritance free from dogmatic traditionalism committed to social justice. I argue that this structure of thought must emerge directly from the technologies and languages that allow them to manifest online. Polymorphism is an important concept used in the design of the Object Oriented Programming (OOP) paradigm. In OOP languages, polymorphism is the ability to have multiple functions or methods *called* by the same name. Polymorphism means that a single entity—such as operators, methods, or objects—is used to represent different types in different scenarios. Polymorphic code tends to be resilient to changing contexts and can adapt to several anticipated uses. The most basic version of this might be with a "+" operator, in this case in the Python programming language.[79] The "+" operator can perform an arithmetic addition operation and evaluate expressions like 2 + 2. In Python, the "+" operator is also capable of *adding* text, which is called *string concatenation*. In this scenario, strings of characters like "hello" + "world" can be *concatenated* or added to evaluate to a "helloworld" string value. Another common example of polymorphism in Python exists with the len() function, which returns the number of items in a sequence like a string or a list of values. In this case, len("helloworld") returns the integer 10, for the number of characters in the string. With a different datatype like a list, len(["hello","world"]) returns the integer 2, for the number of strings in the series. While these are good examples of polymorphism in language design, polymorphism is a general concept in OOP that might be used to express a larger structures of thought influenced by software.

The ubiquity of computation and the general adoption of programming, as Sterling imagines it, means that logical structures in programming paradigms have the potential to influence how we think about and solve problems. Coleman has demonstrated how a sociological approach to understanding FOSS culture influences political cultural practices and assumptions. In a humanities context, code augments and extends logical arguments; code can also put arguments into action. Code, after all, is unique among languages because it can actually make things happen in the real world. It is possible to open physical doors or have an ATM spit out all its money.[80] Unsurprisingly then, language shapes thought and programming languages are no different.[81] Polymorphism in OOP can be rethought as a model of inheritance for subcultures like cyberpunk. Wendy Hui Kyong Chun's *Programmed Visions* and David M. Berry's *The Philosophy of Software* are inspiration for this approach, wherein they each argue that close reading code is necessary to fully understand our experiences of technology.[82] By deriving structures of thought from the computational paradigms, it is possible to better understand the languages that shape our experiences of technology, but it is also possible to avoid fruitless generalizations about the "ideology of computers," as David Golumbia attempts in *The Cultural Logic of Computation*, by actually reading how programs work.[83] By learning a little code, humanists and critics might be better able to critique twenty-first-century culture. The following example will demonstrate polymorphism through Python's class structure. Python is a general purpose, high-level programming language. The syntax of Python is very simple and almost reads like English.

By using code to make cultural arguments, we are making at least two important gestures. We are honoring Donald Knuth's vision of "literate programming," in which computer code becomes as readable and beautiful as a work of literature. Knuth is well-known in computer science for his work on typography, language development, and programming methodologies.[84] Knuth believes that documentation can be beautiful and helpful by moving between human language and computer code. If done well, Knuth explains that "[a] good literate program will show its history."[85] There is a strong pedagogical aspect of hacker culture, informed by open source, that prizes sharing of ideas, techniques, and code, which is compatible with Knuth's literate programming and the need for documentation. Thinking both like and with the machine will help us understand deeper patterns and structures in how computing influences social and cultural forces. Cyberpunk's earliest authors like Gardner Dozois predicted a time in which youth culture will include "speaking computer."[86] Literate programming also invites playful asides and humor among the formality of code: "Hackers thus tend to value playfulness, pranking, and cleverness," Coleman reminds us, "and will frequently perform their wit through source code, humor, or both: humorous code."[87] Figure 1.1 is a simple example program designed to demonstrate polymorphism and inheritance in an object-oriented programming language. A class is a blueprint for code. It is an object that contains data and logic; in the words of John Zelle, "objects know stuff and do stuff."[88] Put another way, a class can generate new systems and processes depending on contextual elements like inputs or desired settings.

○ ○ ○

```
class Hacker:
    """This Hacker class object is the default structure for other types of hackers. This
    chapter has sought to define the hacker character, which this class accepts as an argument.
    There is a consistent relationship between hacking and activism, so the two methods
    available from this class will be named through this shared hacktivist frame. There is a
    risk that a later type of hacker character will not regard themselves as either an activist
    or as a hacker, so this base Hacker class is ready to handle an error, if the class is
    inherited without defining these two base methods."""

    def __init__(self, character):
        self.character = character
    def motive(self):
        raise NotImplementedError("Define how", self.character, "hacks.")
    def activism(self):
        raise NotImplementedError("Define how", self.character, "is an activist.")

class Hoaxer(Hacker):
    """Inherits base Hacker class and honors Gabrielle Coleman's Hacker, Hoaxer, Whistleblower,
    Spy."""

    def motive(self):
        return 'Did it for the lulz!'

    # 'lulz' is a malapropism of laugh out loud (lol), but the user of the phrase is laughing
    and reveling in mayhem and embarrassment.

    def activism(self):
        return 'The public has a right to know!'

class Spy(Hacker):
    """Inherits base Hacker class and acknowledges how cybersecurity is also the domain of
    cyberwar. In Andy Greenburg's Sandworm he presents the history of NotPetya, the largest and
    most costly cyber attack in history. In cyberespionage, the spy makes cyberwarfair and
    changes the rationale of warmaking: 'distance is no defense. Every barbarian is already at
    every gate. And the network of entanglements is that ether, which have unified and elevated
    the world for the past twenty-five years, can, over a few hours on a summer day, bring it to
    a crashing halt.' Due to the closing of distance in warmaking, the ability to hack in a
    state of exception, outside the boundaries of national laws means that activism serves
    nation-state goals on the global stage."""

    def motive(self):
        return 'Nation-state backed operative.'
    def activism(self):
        return 'Acts with near impunity toward state-sanctioned goals.'

class Criminal(Hacker):
    """Inherits base Hacker class."""
    def motive(self):
        return 'Outside national boundaries.'
    def activism(self):
        return 'Exploiting global economic inequality, for profit.'

class Researcher(Hacker):
    """Inherits base Hacker class."""
    def motive(self):
        return 'Concerned with domestic and international governmental and corporate policy.'
    def activism(self):
        return 'Describe unethical or illegal governmental and corporate practices.'
```

FIGURE 1.1 *Defining the Hacker class. In OOP design, it is possible to encapsulate distinct characteristics for later reuse or modification*[89]

The Hacker class inherits methods that defines its character. These Python classes work to define different hacker characters that inherit the base Hacker class into Hoaxer, Whistleblower, Spy, Criminal, Researcher classes. They are able to inherit other classes, but they all have a "motive()" for their actions and engage in "activism()." This is a code-based framework, set in a literate programming style, that demonstrates the polymorphic quality of OOP in a playful rethinking of the hacker character. There are many methods available to the Hacker class. In Figure 1.2, we must *instantiate* or build these Hacker classes in the following way:

```
○ ○ ○

hackers = [Hoaxer("Trickster"),
           Whistleblower('Leaker'),
           Spy('Military espionage'),
           Criminal("Ransomware operator"),]

    # instantiate each class by inheriting the Hacker class which requires a hacker
    character type.

for hacker in hackers:
    print(hacker.character + ':', hacker.motive(), hacker.activism())

    # by looping through the list of hackers, call hacker.character, hacker.motive(), as well
    as hacker.activism() regardless of type of role that defines them. Hacker's going to hack.
```

FIGURE 1.2 *The Hacker class inherits many characters. In OOP, inheritance allows different classes to borrow behavior from another class*

The output of this code is as follows:

Trickster: Did it for the lulz! Embarass those with power and privilege!

Leaker: See something, say something. Information wants to be free!

Military espionage: Nation-state backed operative. Acts with near impunity toward state-sanctioned goals.

Ransomware operator: Outside national boundaries. Exploiting global economic inequality, for profit.

The ability to write flexible code that can call the same methods, regardless of context is very powerful. This kind of flexibility is prized by authors of malware as well. If a worm or virus is capable of adjusting its approach toward infection and replication, it becomes more difficult to defend against because the worm's capabilities are not immediately apparent. This flexibility also allows us to think about more abstract or ambiguous types of hackers. In Figure 1.3, it is possible to show how Edward Snowden has been variously regarded as any of these subclasses:

○ ○ ○

```
gov_whistleblower = Whistleblower(Researcher("Snowden"))
print(gov_whistleblower.motive(),
    gov_whistleblower.activism(),
    gov_whistleblower.character.motive(),
    gov_whistleblower.character.character.motive())
```

FIGURE 1.3 *The Whistleblower subclass is able to inherit the Researcher superclass*

The previous code will output the following:

> See something wrong, say something. The public has a right to know! Concerned with domestic and international governmental and corporate policy. Describe unethical or illegal governmental and corporate practice.

Regardless of how Snowden would be instantiated in these classes, his activities remain connected to the original Hacker class, which I think he might appreciate. While the motives will vary, each instance is animated by a kind of activism, whether legal or otherwise.

In order to appreciate how polymorphism is a political methodology rather than a dogmatic ideology surrounding the hacker stereotype, it is necessary to separate the politics from the actions. Code can be used to define the troubled hacktivist identity. Popular depictions of hacking mask the reality that is only ever really witnessed through their actions in code. This gesture implies that observers will struggle to know these anonymous figures, except through the code they write. As soon as a hacker becomes a public persona, they are consumed by popular culture and become part of the capitalist churn, like all punks. The hacker label is dependent on political ideology and perhaps national identity, but those qualities influence each other in important ways. By embracing a polymorphic definition, it becomes possible to study the behavior and effects of hacking without the distorting lens of ideology or politics. Within a resurgent twenty-first-century cyberpunk vision, we must see how this process works in the code itself. If we have a grasp of how objects work in the object-oriented paradigm, we can begin to think about how this logic of inheritance and polymorphic design can translate into the humanities-based appraisal of cybersecurity.

A humanities-based literate programming approach to defining the role of cybersecurity actors has precedent. The most recent and perhaps transformative use of this structure of thought emerges from the school of philosophy led by Graham Harman under the name Object Oriented Ontology (OOO). The so-called "triple O" sounds complex, but it is really just a return to philosophical realism. In an effort to step away provisionally from the philosophical churn of the social construction of reality, OOO places a much greater emphasis on the qualities of objects, including people, and their aesthetic, sensible properties. It embraces simple precepts, such as that objects exist, and these real objects can exist independent of human awareness.[90] Harman draws direct links between Object Oriented Programming (OOP) and OOO. Harman admits that he "borrowed" the phrase from computing, but he also invites others to "carry out a more detailed comparison between object-oriented programming and OOO."[91] I will have reason to return to OOO in later chapters, but it is important to say that philosophy has found a need to return to a considered evaluation of the real world through the language of computing. Computing allows for objects to act in our world. A piece of code is an object that can act and respond in changing contexts without human intervention. The removal of human subjectivity in political action is a way that hackers, through malware or other exploits, distance their actions from their identities. The motivations of the hacker are so difficult to grasp because they are shared with software itself. Hacking is a way to externalize human subjectivity through an anonymous "hacker" object and its code. As a result, the logic of computing may be influencing how we consider reality, in a very literal sense, without fully considering the latent logic of the OOP paradigm.

The notion that objects exist and that computing is shaping human awareness may not seem terribly controversial, but many decades of humanities research have been predicated on the social construction of identities and politics through purely subjective human, cultural forces. It is now common for digital humanists to rely on machine based observation through natural language processing (NLP), which is increasingly separate from human oversight. In the case of machine learning processes in NLP like topic modeling and sentiment analysis, the source of the results will be entirely inaccessible to human oversight. If humanists attempt to adopt an object-oriented ontology, a new theory of power and authority would need to be grafted into current thinking about politics in general. This kind of posthumanism does not mean humans simply stop making decisions to shape their subjective reality; instead, posthumanism is a broadening of the ethical requirements of a subject to retreat into a network of objects. Posthuman subjects then make their intentions transparent as code objects, external from their broken anthropocentric ethical failures. The notion of polymorphism as inheritance in the creation of objects is consistent with OOO. It suggests that there is nothing essential about objects, instead they are defined by their properties and parameters. The code is interesting from an OOO view point because programs or algorithms operate outside human experience. A computer worm or virus makes decisions and changes its behavior dependent on contextual factors. Code exists, and it has the power to shape our lives. Code is not merely a text to be read. Code is a text that acts in our world. It is therefore necessary to think about the political ramifications of these objects, particularly as the influence of hackers grows in the functioning of commerce and political systems globally. Harman's OOO makes a dramatic claim that disrupts humanities research methods that fall under the term "theory" or postmodernism. In OOO, "politics" cannot be knowledge or strictly true because the complex web of actors in politics is never simply masterable by scientific or technical expertise. While it is possible possess expertise about texts written about politics and ideology, OOO seeks to engage with the real, sensible world as it is. Texts are ultimately only a small part of that network of relationships that people and ideas share. Computer code is an object that has the potential to jump from the realm of discourse into the real world. A virus or an exploit can easily possess more power and influence because it is experienced by systems and machines as well as the humans that live within their influence.

One of the most significant expressions of this Object-Oriented paradigm is emerging from what has become known as variously "black digital humanities," "black software," "race critical code studies," or "dark sousveillance."[92] The systematic injustices of scholarship, the development of technology, and surveillance have affected black communities and individuals in ways that anticipate future injustices. As practical histories and strategies of liberation, black scholars have faced technologized systems of oppression in ways that inform and guide all future critical approaches to code, literacy, and political action. Kim Gallon's "Making a Case for the Black Digital Humanities" appeared in the 2016 Debates in Digital Humanities. Gallon sought to articulate a "space" rather than a "thing" to "unmask the racialized systems of power" in DH.[93] As an act of recovery, Gallon describes a project that seeks to recover black voices in DH as well as black authors and histories that are only now finding a central place in DH scholarly output. Black DH, defined in this way, is a critical counterpoint to the all-too-common techno-utopianism found in an all too white DH community.[94] The article questions the stability of a term like digital humanities, when "humanity itself" requires redefinition in digital spaces. Safiya Umoja Noble returns to the postcolonial digital humanities of Roopika Risam and the Postcolonial Digital Humanities (dhpoco.org) group.

Noble asks "how can we mash up or hack racial inequality, rather than big data?"[95] While Noble's call for a "Critical Black Digital Humanities" is primarily a form of critique or theoretical frame for DH through critical race theory, at least a part of this call to "divest from troublesome infrastructure" will require some actual hacking.[96] Divesting from "troublesome infrastructure" that supports inequity and injustice is a fundamental calling for all activists, academics, and citizens. Troublesome infrastructure comes in many forms, including online platforms, internet service providers, and government surveillance. Noble's book length *Algorithms of Oppression* makes a specific argument regarding Google Search "algorithms" that re-enforce and exacerbate existing systems of racial and gender-based inequity.[97] After all, these systems were intentionally designed. Noble demonstrates a repeated pattern within the Google Search algorithm, sometimes referred to as PageRank for the original algorithm implemented by Sergey Bren and Larry Page. Over time, the design logic of Google Search was increasingly informed by the "neoliberal marketplace" for ideas by including autocomplete results that have been trained by broadly held racist attitudes of users.[98] The laissez-faire design process allowed users to shape recommended search results as the system learned from a majority, white audience with racist and sexist attitudes.

Designing technological systems has largely failed to deliver on Silicon Valley's Utopian vision for technology as a great equalizer, a source of wealth and opportunity for all. As Noble demonstrates so clearly, definitions of blackness and beauty were shaped racist results on Google Search and helped re-enforce bigotry. She says the following about this relationship between capitalism and technology:

> What is important about new capitalism in the context of the web is that it is radically transforming previously public territories and spaces. This expansion of capitalism into the web has been a significant part of the neoliberal justification for the commodification of information and identity. Identity markers are for sale in the commodified web to the highest bidder.[99]

Surveillance capitalism is designed to create profits from behavioral surplus data derived from surveillance. Those profits and data can serve to re-enforce outdated bias, bigotry, and beliefs. Ruha Benjamin is skeptical of our ability to design systems free from the majority influence of white supremacy: "Maybe what we must demand is not liberatory *designs* but just plain old liberation."[100]

Systems designed by a technologist class paid by corporate elites will, by in large, serve dominant capitalist systems. Benjamin reminds us that the Civil Rights Movement in the United States did not win freedoms and sway public opinion through a protracted design process. Direct action and public protest changed the social and political realities like the Montgomery Bus Boycott. Benjamin goes on to warn us that design thinking risks papering over the past in an attempt to describe some new solution:

> It is not simply that design thinking wrongly claims newness, but in doing so it erases the insights and agency of those who are discounted because they are across numerous fields of action and coaxing everyone who dons the cloak of design into being seen and heard through the dominant aesthetic of innovation.[101]

Suspicions about the lack of regard corporations have toward questions of equity are well understood. The firing of Timnit Gebru, co-lead of an AI ethics team at Google, over an internal email calling for hiring more diverse employees, is the most public expression of Google's antipathy to critical questions of diversity and representation.[102] Her warning to Google AI researchers about how large language models derived from the web will preserve and promote bias and bigotry was seen as a challenge to Google's core ad and search business.[103] When it comes to training data, Gebru and her team argue that "size doesn't guarantee diversity."[104] When it comes to "encoding bias" into large language models, the social, cultural, and environmental considerations require computational literacy to adequately critique. The "Stochastic Parrots" paper for which Gebru was fired estimated that training Google's latest language model BERT produced vast quantities of carbon dioxide, from which each language model trained produces "as much energy as a trans-American flight."[105] The costs and consequences designing totalizing systems like this impact social, cultural, and environmental rights and representation.

Literacy must then include code, in the tradition of Knuth's literate computing, because it structures our existence in the twenty-first century. Literate programs invite engagement and fully enfranchised participation because they are sensible by both machine and human alike. I am arguing for a digital humanities that strives for justice and equity by shaping the world around us with code. In order to do this, it is necessary to unpack some of the tenets of humanism and the liberal democratic ethics that have been the foundation of rational society since the Enlightenment, namely the primacy of human rational thought in the creation of ideas. For this reason, cybersecurity represents a central axis around which a range of social, cultural, and political forces will turn. The ability to control and break the flows of data will represent a profound source of political action and potential interference. The ability for a citizenry to protest and resist the actions of nation-state level actors as well as those of increasingly powerful corporations will hinge on their ability to control and sometimes break digital systems.

Notes

1   See https://www.imdb.com/search/keyword/?keywords=hacker and https://www.gamesdatabase.org/list.aspx?in=1&searchtext=hacker.

2   See https://www.govinfo.gov/app/search/%7B%22query%22%3A%22computer%20hacker%22%2C%22offset%22%3A0%7D.

3   Computer Security Resource Center, "APT," *Nist.org*, https://csrc.nist.gov/glossary/term/APT.

4   See respectively, Eric Auchard, "Macron Campaign Was Target of Cyber Attacks by Spy-Linked Group," *Reuters.com*, April 24, 2017, https://www.reuters.com/article/us-france-election-macron-cyber-idUSKBN17Q200; Daniel Tost, "Russia-Linked Hackers Target German Political Foundations," *Handelsblatt.com*, April 26, 2017, https://www.handelsblatt.com/english/politics/election-risks-russia-linked-hackers-target-german-political-foundations/23569188.html?ticket=ST-18095628-twZrzynxO9evg1sJ2Uyj-ap4; Josh Meyer, "Russian Hackers Post 'Medical Files' of Simone Biles, Serena Williams," *Nbcnews.com*, September 13, 2016, https://www.nbcnews.com/storyline/2016-rio-summer-olympics/russian-hackers-post-medical-files-biles-serena-williams-n647571; "Norway's Intelligence Service Says Russian Groups 'Likely' behind Parliament Cyber Attack," *Euronews.com*, December 8, 2020, https://www.euronews.com/2020/12/08/norway-s-intelligence-service-says-russian-groups-likely-behind-parliament-cyber-attack.

5   MITRE ATT&CK, "APT 28," *Attack.mitre.org*, https://attack.mitre.org/groups/G0007/; MITRE ATT&CK, "APT 29," *Attack.mitre.org*, https://attack.mitre.org/groups/G0016/.

6   Andy Greenberg, *Sandworm: A New Era of Cyberwar and the Hunt for the Kremlin's Most Dangerous Hackers* (New York: Doubleday, 2019), 116–23; "CrowdStrike's Work with the Democratic National Committee: Setting the Record Straight," *Crowdstrike.com/blog*, June 5, 2020, https://www.crowdstrike.com/blog/bears-midst-intrusion-democratic-national-committee/.

7   Florian J. Egloff, "Public Attribution of Cyber Intrusions," *Journal of Cybersecurity* 6, no. 1 (September 2020): 1–12, available at https://doi.org/10.1093/cybsec/tyaa012.

8   Adam Shostack, *Threat Modeling: Designing for Security* (Crosspoint, IN: John Wiley & Sons, 2014), 481.

9   Ibid., xxxiii.

10 The so-called "black hat" hackers are malicious. Between these extremes, the hacker remains a multifaceted and changing character, which again returns to an interpretive stance that is very similar to humanistic critique. "Gray hat" hacktivists are often working within an ethical framework of some kind, but they may not ask for permission before they conduct exploratory research on a system.

11 Catalin Cimpanu, "US Sues to Recover Cryptocurrency Funds Stolen by North Korean Hackers," *Zdnet.com*, August 27, 2020, https://www.zdnet.com/article/us-sues-to-recover-cryptocurrency-funds-stolen-by-north-korean-hackers/; Catalin Cimpanu, "North Korea's State Hackers Caught Engaging in BEC Scams," *Zdnet.com*, June 17, 2020, https://www.zdnet.com/article/north-koreas-state-hackers-caught-engaging-in-bec-scams/.

12 MITRE ATT&CK, "Lazarus Group," *Attack.mitre.org*, https://attack.mitre.org/groups/G0032/.

13 Dominik Breitenbacher and Kaspars Osis, "Operation In(ter)ception: Targeted Attacks against European Aerospace and Military Companies," *Welivesecurity.com*, https://www.welivesecurity.com/wp-content/uploads/2020/06/ESET_Operation_Interception.pdf, 3.

14 Ibid., 20.

15 Phreaking is a method to reverse engineer the system of tones used to signal coins deposited in public telephones and pay for costly long-distance calls. John Draper, also known as Captain Crunch, is a computer scientist who was well known for producing these tones with a free plastic whistle from a box of Cap'n Crunch breakfast cereal. See the republished article from *Esquire* magazine. Ron Rosenbaum, "'Secrets of the Little Blue Box': The 1971 Article About Phone Hacking That Inspired Steve Jobs," *Slate*, October 7, 2011, https://www.slate.com/articles/technology/the_spectator/2011/10/the_article_that_inspired_steve_jobs_secrets_of_the_little_blue_.html.

16 John Brunner, *The Shockwave Rider* (New York: Ballantine Books, 1975), 99.

17 Neil Easterbrook, "The Arc of Our Destruction: Reversal and Erasure in Cyberpunk," *Science Fiction Studies* 19, no. 3 (1992): 378–94. The term "postcyberpunk" was first coined by Lawrence Person in "Notes Toward a Postcyberpunk Manifesto," published by *Nova Express* in 1998, available http://slashdot.org/features/99/10/08/2123255.shtml.

18 See Alan Liu, *The Laws of Cool* (Chicago: University of Chicago Press, 2004), 69. Liu describes this cyberpunk ethos of the twenty-first-century knowledge worker as an elegy for slower, humanities based forms of knowledge accrued through close reading. Throughout *The Laws of Cool*, Liu mourns the "death of knowledge in the information age" through a distinctly cyberpunk-styled cynicism.

19 See https://www.tesla.com/cybertruck.

20 Kim Zetter, "How the Real Hackers behind *Mr. Robot* Get It so Right," *Wired.com*, July 15, 2018, https://www.wired.com/2016/07/real-hackers-behind-mr-robot-get-right/.

21 Nick Farmer, trained linguist and science fiction author, developed the Belter creole in *The Expanse*. See http://www.nickfarmerlinguist.com/.

22 The themes present in contemporary television has been well developed in advance by anime and manga creators since the founding of the genre. From *Ghost in the Shell* to *Akira* in the 1980s to more recent incarnations like *Texhnolyze* and *Pyscho-Pass*, anime has long shaped the aesthetic and thematic visions of these dystopic futures.

23 Khadeeja Safdar, Erin Ailworth, and Deepa Seetharaman, "Police Identify Five Dead after Capitol Riot," *Wallstreetjournal.com*, January 8, 2021, https://www.wsj.com/articles/police-identify-those-killed-in-capitol-riot–11610133560.

24 John Paczkowski and Ryan Mac, "Amazon Is Booting Parler Off of Its Web Hosting Service," *Buzzfeed.com*, January 9, 2021, https://www.buzzfeednews.com/article/johnpaczkowski/amazon-parler-aws.

25 See https://donk.sh/.

26 See https://github.com/d0nk/parler-tricks.

27 See https://twitter.com/donk_enby/status/1347864615951212546.

28 See https://ddosecrets.com/wiki/Parler.

29 See https://ddosecrets.com/wiki/BlueLeaks.

30 See https://www.aclu.org/other/more-about-fusion-centers.

31 See https://thepatr10t.github.io/yall-Qaeda/.

32 See https://gist.github.com/kylemcdonald/8fdabd6526924012c1f5afe538d7dc09.

33 Ibid.

34 See https://facesoftheriot.com/.

35 See https://projects.propublica.org/parler-capitol-videos/.

36 See https://twitter.com/donie/status/1359653335167627265.

37 Donie O'Sullivan, "How a Quick-Thinking Computer Programmer Helped the Case against Trump," *CNN*, February 10, 2021, https://www.cnn.com/politics/live-news/trump-impeachment-trial-02-10-2021/h_e5daf9158dbdfbb1fff137a174f476f1.

38 Ruha Benjamin, *Race after Technology: Abolitionist Tools for the New Jim Code* (Cambridge, UK: Polity, 2019), 182.

39 Ibid., 183.

40 See https://www.intelligence.senate.gov/sites/default/files/documents/report_volume5.pdf.

41 President Trump's first comments about the 400 pound hacker occurred during the presidential debate on September 26, 2016, which he later clarified in the following tweet: Donald Trump (@realDonaldTrump), "I never said Russia did not meddle in the election, I said 'it may be Russia, or China or another country or group, or it may be a 400 pound genius sitting in bed and playing with his computer.' "The Russian 'Hoax' Was That the Trump Campaign Colluded with Russia - It Never did!," *Twitter*, February 18, 2018, 7:33 AM, https://twitter.com/realDonaldTrump/status/965202556204003328; see also the following for sources on the presidential debates: Andy Greenberg, "A Timeline of Trump's Strange, Contradictory Statements on Russian Hacking," *Wired.com*, January 4, 2017, https://www.wired.com/2017/01/timeline-trumps-strange-contradictory-statements-russian-hacking/.

42 David Frum, *Trumpocracy: The Corruption of the American Republic* (New York: HarperCollins, 2018), 132–5.

43 Erin Carson, "Supreme Court Limits Reach of Computer Hacking Law," *Cnet*, June 3, 2021, https://www.cnet.com/news/supreme-court-limits-reach-of-computer-hacking-law/.

44 Steven Levy, 1984, *Hackers: Heroes of the Computer Revolution* (New York: O'Reilly, 2010), 28.

45 Ibid., 29.

46 Ibid., 27.

47 See http://www.catb.org/jargon/html/.

48 See http://www.catb.org/jargon/html/meaning-of-hack.html.

49 Ibid.

50 Ibid.

51 See http://phrack.org/issues/7/3.html.

52 Pekka Himanen, *The Hacker Ethic and the Spirit of the Information Age* (New York: Random House, 2001), 4–5.

53 Ibid., 122 and 178.

54 Bethany Nowviskie, "On the Origin of 'Hack' and 'Yack'," *Nowviskie.org*, January 8, 2014, http://nowviskie.org/2014/on-the-origin-of-hack-and-yack/. Digital humanists have also used hacking as a metaphor to help frame critical approaches to academic practices; for example, see Dan Cohen and Joseph T. Scheinfeldt, *Hacking the Academy: New Approaches to Scholarship and Teaching from Digital Humanities* (Ann Arbor: University of Michigan Press, 2013); Elias Muhanna, "Hacking the Humanities," *Newyorker.com*, July 7, 2015, https://www.newyorker.com/culture/culture-desk/hacking-the-humanities.

55 Gabriella Coleman, *Coding Freedom: The Ethics and Aesthetics of Hacking* (Princeton: Princeton University Press, 2013), 2–3.

56 Sam Williams, *Free as in Freedom: Richard Stallman's Crusade for Free Software* (Sebastopol, CA: O'Reilly, 2002); and Richard Stallman, *Free Software, Free Society: Selected Essays* (Boston: GNU Press, 2002).

57 Gabriella Coleman, *Hacker, Hoaxer, Whistleblower, Spy: The Many Faces of Anonymous* (New York: Verso, 2014), 33.

58 The Solarwinds, Dragonfly, and Cloudhopper attacks are notable examples because the software supply chain was used to deploy malware; see respectively Steven J. Vaughan-Nichols, "SolarWinds: The More We Learn, the Worse It Looks," *Zdnet.com*, January 4, 2021, https://www.zdnet.com/article/solarwinds-the-more-we-learn-the-worse-it-looks/; John Kennedy, "US Officially Blames Russia's 'Dragonfly' Hackers for Attacks on Energy Grid," *Siliconrepublic.com*, March 16, 2018, https://www.siliconrepublic.com/enterprise/dragonfly-us-russia-energy-grid-hackers; "Operation Cloud Hopper: What You Need to Know," *Trendmicro.com*, April 10, 2017, https://www.trendmicro.com/vinfo/us/security/news/cyber-attacks/operation-cloud-hopper-what-you-need-to-know.

59 Digital humanities has long embraced, for better or worse, the ability to learn through failure. See Shawn Graham, *Failing Gloriously and Other Essays* (Grand Forks: The Digital Press at the University of North Dakota, 2019), available at https://thedigitalpress.org/failing-gloriously/.

60 Bruce Schneier, "Beyond Security Theatre: We Need to Move beyond Security Measures That Look Good on Television to Those That Actually Work, Argues Bruce Schneier," *New internationalist* 427 (November 1, 2009): 10–12; Bruce Schneier, *Beyond Fear* (New York: Copernicus, 2003).

61 Microsoft has dropped the requirement for compulsory password changes and offers the following explanation: "There's no question that the state of password security is problematic and has been for a long time. When humans pick their own passwords, too often they are easy to guess or predict. When humans are assigned or forced to create passwords that are hard to remember, too often they'll write them down where others can see them. When humans are forced to change their passwords, too often they'll make a small and predictable alteration to their existing passwords, and/ or forget their new passwords." See the security baseline documentation for Windows 10: https://docs.microsoft.com/en-us/archive/blogs/secguide/security-baseline-final-for-windows-10-v1903-and-windows-server-v1903.

62 Mackenzie Wark, *The Hacker Manifesto* (Cambridge: Harvard University Press, 2004), 17.

63 See http://info.cern.ch/Proposal.html.

64 Tim Berners-Lee, *Weaving the Web: The Original Design and Ultimate Destiny for the World Wide Web* (New York: HarperCollins, 1999), 205.

65 Tim Berners-Lee, "30 Years on, What's Next #ForTheWeb?" *Webfoundation. org*, March 12, 2019, https://webfoundation.org/2019/03/web-birthday-30/.

66 Ted Nelson, *Computer Lib/Dream Machines* (self-pub., 1974), available at *Archive.org*, https://archive.org/details/computer-lib-dream-machines/.

67 Levy, *Hackers*, 144.

68 Nelson, *Computer Lib/Dream Machines*, 71.

69 Ibid., 131.

70 Dylan Clark, "The Death and Life of Punk, the Last Subculture," in *The Post-Subcultures Reader*, eds. David Muggleton and Rupert Weinzierl (Oxford: Berg Publishers, 2003), 223.

71 Ibid., 231.

72 In the FOSS community, the language of "embrace, extend, and extinguish" (EEE) is used to describe how corporate interests seek to consume and destroy technical and cultural creations for profit. EEE was discovered by the US Department of Justice in internal Microsoft documents in investigating the corporation's attempt to control the development of HTML and implement a new "MS HTML" standard. See "United States v. Microsoft: Trial Summaries (page 2)," *Cyber.law.harvard. edu*, https://cyber.harvard.edu/msdoj/transcript/summaries2.html.

73 Clark, "The Death and Life of Punk," 232.

74 G. N. Martin, "(Why) Do You Like Scary Movies? A Review of the Empirical Research on Psychological Responses to Horror Films," *Frontiers in Psychology* 10 (2019), 1–22. https://doi.org/10.3389/fpsyg.2019.02298; Thomas Straube, Sandra Preissler, Judith Lipka, Johannes Hewig, Hans-Joachim Mentzel, and Wolfgang H.R. Miltner, "Neural Representation of Anxiety and Personality during Exposure to Anxiety-Provoking and Neutral Scenes from Scary Movies," *Human Brain Mapping* 31, no. 1 (January 2010), https://doi.org/10.1002/hbm.20843.

75 Bruce Sterling, Introduction to *Mirrorshades: The Cyberpunk Anthology*, ed. Bruce Sterling (New York: Arbor House, 1986), xii.

76   Alvin Toffler, *Future Shock* (New York: Random House, 1970), 37.

77   Chris Hables Gray, Heidi J. Figueroa-Sarriera, and Steven Mentor, *Modified: Living as a Cyborg* (New York: Routledge, 2021), 3.

78   Donna Haraway, *Simians, Cyborgs, and Women: The Reinvention of Nature* (New York: Routledge, 1991), 176.

79   Python has contributed to the rapid growth of hacking tools and software in recent years. We will discuss these in more detail in later chapters, but we will look first at some Python code to better demonstrate polymorphism in the Object Oriented Programming paradigm generally. Because this gesture is perhaps a new approach in the writing related to cybersecurity as well as the humanities, it is necessary to explicitly state the purpose or intention of this approach. Let's explain first what it is not: this code is not a "hack." This code is not even a definitive definition of the hacker character. This code is intended as a bridge between humanistic habits of mind and computer science concepts that underwrite our experience of computing. Polymorphism is a concept from OOP that is a useful structure of thought or diagram for thinking about the flexibility of actors online. It is possible to have a singular identity, but it is far more likely that these hacker entities will inherit different definitions or attributes over time and in different contexts. Online identities, actions, and intentions are fluid and reconstitute themselves repeatedly from cultural primitive classes that can be useful in understanding these changing behaviors.

80   See https://www.blackhat.com/docs/us-16/materials/us-16-Hecker-Hacking-Next-Gen-ATMs-From-Capture-To-Cashout.pdf.

81   Tara McPherson, "Why Are the Digital Humanities so White? Or Thinking the Histories of Race and Computation," in *Debates in the Digital Humanities*, ed. Matthew K. Gold (Minneapolis: University of Minnesota Press, 2012), 139–60, available http://dhdebates.gc.cuny.edu/debates/text/29.

82   Wendy Hui Kyong Chun, *Programmed Visions: Software and Memory* (Cambridge, MA: MIT Press, 2011); David M. Berry, *The Philosophy of Software: Code and Mediation in the Digital Age* (New York: Palgrave MacMillan, 2011).

83   David Golumbia, *The Cultural Logic of Computation* (Cambridge, MA: Harvard University Press, 2009), 173. Of course, Golumbia is following a similar vein of folksy techno-skepticism that we might productively compare with Matthew Postman's "Ideology of Machines," in *Technopoly: The Surrender of Culture to Technology* (New York: Vintage, 1992), 92.

84   Donald Knuth, "Literate Programming," *The Computer Journal* 27, no. 2 (1984): 97–111, https://doi.org/10.1093/comjnl/27.2.97

85   Peter Seibel, "Donald Knuth," in *Coders at Work: Reflections on the Craft of Programming* (New York: Apress, 2009), 578.

86   In recent years, the Python programming language has led to a dramatic increase in capabilities and shared tooling among a range of disciplines in research and industry. Python is extremely readable and was designed by Guido van Rossum with readability in mind. In the famous Python Enhancement Proposal (PEP) 8, Rossum goes so far as to argue that "code is read much more often than it is written": PEP 8, *Python.org*, July 5,

2001, https://www.python.org/dev/peps/pep-0008/. In Python classes and functions, *documentation strings* are marked with triple quotes and can be called with the help() function.

87 Coleman, *Coding Freedom,* 17.

88 John Zelle, *Python Programming: An Introduction to Computer Science* (Portland: Franklin, Beedle, & Associates), 452.

89 Edward Snowden, *Permanent Record* (New York: Metropolitan Books, 2019), 53; Coleman, *Hacker, Hoaxer, Whistleblower, Spy,* 378; Greenberg, *Sandworm,* 217.

90 Aaron Mauro, "To Think a World without Thought: Negotiating Speculative Realism in a Digital Humanities Practice," *Digital Studies/le Champ Numérique* 5, no. 1 (2014). doi.org/10.16995/dscn.52.

91 Graham Harman, *Object-Oriented Ontology: A New Theory of Everything* (London: Pelican, 2018), 11.

92 Black Digital Humanities has emerged alongside similar movements in History, Information Technology Studies, Surveillance Studies, and Critical Code Studies. Charlton McIlwain's "black software" defines the intersectional relationships between black people and the design and use of software and systems. Ruha Benjamin defines "race critical code studies" as a method of criticizing the ways inequity is coded into technology. Simone Brown's "dark sousveillance" describes how black epistemology confronts the extension white supremacist methods of control through technologically amplified surveillance systems. A list of Black Digital Humanities projects, started by the Colored Conventions Project at Penn State, can be found here: https://bit.ly/Black-DH-List.

93 Kim Gallon, "Making the Case for the Black Digital Humanities," *Debates in Digital Humanities,* 2016, https://dhdebates.gc.cuny.edu/read/untitled/section/fa10e2e1-0c3d-4519-a958-d823aac989eb.

94 McPherson, "Why Are the Digital Humanities so White? Or Thinking the Histories of Race and Computation," https://dhdebates.gc.cuny.edu/read/untitled-88c11800-9446-469b-a3be-3fdb36bfbd1e/section/20df8acd-9ab9-4f35-8a5d-e91aa5f4a0ea.

95 Safiya Umoja Noble, "Toward a Critical Black Digital Humanities," in *Debates in Digital Humanities 2019,* eds. Matthew K. Gold and Lauren F. Klein (Minneapolis: University of Minnesota Press, 2019), 32. https://www.jstor.org/stable/10.5749/j.ctvg251hk.5

96 Ibid., 33.

97 Safiya Umoja Noble, *Algorithms of Oppression: How Search Engines Reinforce Racism* (New York: New York University Press, 2018).

98 Ibid., 90.

99 Ibid., 92.

100 Benjamin, *Race after Technology*, 179.

101 Ibid., 179.

102 Khari Johnson, "Google AI Ethics Co-Lead Timnit Gebru Says She Was Fired over an Email," *Venture Beat,* December 3, 2020, https://venturebeat.

com/2020/12/03/google-ai-ethics-co-lead-timnit-gebru-says-she-was-fired-over-an-email/; Tom Simonite, "What Really Happened When Google Ousted Timnit Gebru," *Wired.com*, June 8, 2021, https://www.wired.com/story/google-timnit-gebru-ai-what-really-happened/.

103 Emily M. Bender, Timnit Gebru, Angelina McMillan-Major, and Shmargaret Shmitchell, "On the Dangers of Stochastic Parrots: Can Language Models Be Too Big?," *FAccT '21: Proceedings of the 2021 ACM Conference on Fairness, Accountability, and Transparency*, March 2021: 610–23. https://dl.acm.org/doi/10.1145/3442188.3445919.

104 Ibid., 613.

105 Ibid., 612.

2

Academic Attack Surfaces: Culture Jamming the Future and XML Bombs

An attack surface is defined by the instances in which a "trust boundary" is crossed.[1] Applications that accept traffic from the web will be required to authenticate users, grant and manage permissions, take logs of unauthorized behaviors, and monitor for unanticipated access.[2] These authentication systems validate user permissions and exchange data, which represents a trust relationship between the user and developer that can be exploited and violated by an attacker. An attack surface includes any point of vulnerability, even those that exploit flaws in human behavior or institutional processes. An application with a large number of privileged users, capable of accessing sensitive data or resources, will have an large attack surface, which increases the risk of a social engineering attack. In 2020, an industry report argued that research and education sectors are the fastest growing sector in online security.[3] Exacerbated by the pandemic and the need to turn to online education, cyber criminals have found an attractive target in higher education and large public school boards.[4] University-based institutional IT has its hands full. Put simply, digital humanities projects must prioritize app security in their research plan. Data integrity is about more than long-term storage. A security-first research plan is the only way to prepare for the inevitable loss of valuable research data. A fundamental defensive security strategy involves reducing the attack surface of an application, but first that attack surface must be well understood.

After all, putting research online means it is exposed to all the risks of being online, including ransomware, denial of service, data corruption, and simple site defacement. Lists of potential well-funded target projects are available, when we announce the awarding of grant funds.[5] Finding a vulnerability in a new DH project may be all too easy because of the need to deploy early and meet university performance evaluation criteria ahead of security adequate security testing. Furthermore, humanities researchers run the risk of being targeted by threat actors online interested in discrediting or dismantling digital projects. The desire of many digital humanities practitioners to share research findings freely and openly can unintentionally help potential adversaries. Marija Dalbello's appraisal of DH quite rightly described the field as "optimistic" and even "populist" in its approach to making digital archives and resources freely available online.[6] Many disciplines have sought to publish research findings online, under the Open Access mantle.[7] The physics community has had tremendous success publishing "preprints," prior to peer review, on arXiv, and journals like *PLoS One* are speeding the delivery of science research through a peer-review process to the public.[8] The optimism and excitement that followed this "democratizing effect of technology," in Dalbello's words, runs the risk of being hampered in the humanities because of the piecemeal approach of standalone digital projects. In their assessment of the impact of a public humanities research practice online, Dalbello describes how the "effect on the humanities fields is also limited because far-reaching infrastructural and curricular transformations are necessary to accommodate new forms of knowledge creation and learning."[9] While the humanities has grown in both infrastructural and curricular capabilities in recent years, the digital humanities has a broadly decentralized attack surface for which researchers and students must include in research security methodologies and daily practices.

However, not all threats online are attributable to simple criminality. Academic publishing has endured corporate takeovers of scholarly associations for many years, placing new knowledge behind a paywall as under-resourced humanists struggle to bring their once independent journals online. The work of scholarship is dependent on previous work made readily available in libraries and online. As defined by Peter Suber in *Open Access*, OA publishing relates to making books and other educational resources available for free to users and shifting a portion of the cost model of publication to other avenues. This model of publishing is only possible in a digital environment where the cost of distribution is very low and a passionate community is willing to volunteer their labor. Because of the lack of support and incentive from universities to transition research and scholarly publishing channels online, large corporations bought disciplinary journals and databases over many years. The recent sale of ProQuest to Clarivate for 5.3 billion US dollars is evidence of the scale of the problem of corporate paywalls governing Intellectual Property and financial value associated with the research and development sector generally.[10] The resulting situation means that many university libraries have no other recourse than to pay the extremely high fees of these large research data and information brokers. Despite the relative low cost of distributing research online, many universities are forced to pay extremely high subscription costs to access the very research their own professors have produced. As a result, many institutions have begun challenging the supremacy of large publishers like Elsevier and Springer by simply refusing to pay for these large subscription programs.[11] The research and teaching goals of many medium- and small-scale universities have been disrupted due to an inability to pay these exploitative costs. While the increasing corporatization of the university is a well-known threat to the free flow of research information, there are other vulnerabilities that are exposed by researchers working online.

The attack surface of the digital humanities is defined by the very tools and methods that animate the discipline's populist optimism. The attack surface of a digital humanities project might be described in the following terms: the digital humanities are online, collaborative, inviting participation from students, and faculty often from several institutions. The number of participants and the transience of project collaborators multiplies the number of individuals with privileged access, sometimes changing over many years. The use of contingent labor in university-level teaching and research can breed grievances and frustrations. Staff with high levels of access may find themselves unemployed at the termination of grant funded contracts. The emphasis on accessible humanities research with public facing data portals and open peer review are all opportunities for attackers to gain access to systems that may be adjacent to institutional security procedures or in violation of best practices.[12] The digital humanities are also an ideal target because many practitioners are learning to develop software alongside their already full humanities-based research agendas. For example, the digital humanities has a disciplinary preference for building eXtensible Markup Language (XML)-based archives of digitized text materials using the Text Encoding Initiative (TEI) lexicon, which found favor in the 1990s enthusiasm for semantic web archives.[13] XML has found renewed popularity in the very popular React JavaScript library as JavaScript XML (JSX).[14] The XML standard is widely used for asynchronous data transfer in web applications and many other use cases, alongside other standards like JSON, but XML is no longer the default data exchange format in web applications.[15] The choice of project tooling and software will result in significant vulnerabilities in the deployment stage, so they must be accounted for in the initial research planning process.

Additionally, the often politically charged nature of the topics of digital humanities research has the potential to be turned back upon researchers by antagonistic forces eager to embarrass the "liberal left" housed in universities and colleges. At the very moment that the humanities emerge from universities into a broader public engagement on the web, the humanities are exposed to potential threats from the same illiberal "culture wars," as they are often called in the United States, that have sought to undermine the sciences in the domain of climate change, which includes attendant economic skirmishes on the de-carbonization of transportation and manufacturing, shortening global supply chains, wildlife preservation in sensitive ecosystems, deforestation, overfishing, and plastics pollution in the oceans. The humanities are of course partners in this social and cultural shift in the use and maintenance of the biosphere. Kim Stanley Robinson's *The Ministry for the Future* is a work of speculative fiction that is almost an essay on how to solve our present and future environmental crisis.[16] The regular disinformation campaigns waged in any one of these areas, most particularly in the oil and gas sector, amounts to the amplification of "culture jamming" with social media.[17] The humanities is deeply concerned with questions of gender and sexuality, race and racism, decolonization and indigenous rights, as well as compassionate immigration policies.[18] The very nature of humanities research centered on human justice and equity, when done publicly and openly, risk attack from antagonistic political forces through culture jamming.

Culture jamming is a technique born of the Situationist International artistic and political movement in the 1960s. The Situationists sought to disturb the industrialized monotony of urban corporate life driven by productivity.[19] Spectacle was weaponized as a tool of disruption against the consumerist, capitalistic lifestyle.[20] 1960s era "happenings," which we might know today as flash mobs, were intended to break the monotony of daily life through public art performances and displays.[21] These droll social commentaries used the tools of protest and vandalism to grab attention and inspire critical awareness.[22] Academics looking at the history of communication have argued that "[s]pectacle destabilizes a sense of truth and favours celebrity, commercialism, and personalization."[23] Current political extremism finds its roots during the Nixon-era manipulation of the media, which we find amplified in the age of social media[24]; it is possible that older forms of cultural warfare will be repurposed against knowledge producers in the university. The parodic style of the far-right in the United States appears in absurdist regalia of Tea Party hats with tea bags dangling and Boogaloo Boys in Hawaiian shirts and tactical vests emblazoned with Punisher patches. Even a casual appraisal of far-right protests confirms that the weaponization of spectacle is well underway.[25] The spectacle disarms opponents through the disunity of aesthetics: the spirit of aloha mixed with military surplus, historical American Revolutionary zeal mixed with the temporary whims of election cycle rhetoric and anti-democratic authoritarianism. The nihilistic use of peaceful protest as a cover for mob violence, murder, and hostage taking, like the kind that took place on January 6, 2021, in Washington, DC, in the Capitol Building. The fascistic evolution of culture jamming reaches its apotheosis in the disruption of democratic values through the spectacle of a coup attempt.

The so-called "post-truth" era surrounding the presidency of Donald Trump is an extremist form of culture jamming. By disavowing fundamental participation in the democratic process in the United States and abiding by conspiracies like Qanon, the post-truth period represents a radical separation of truth from knowledge through spectacle-based culture jamming. One can be quite knowledgeable about Qanon conspiracy theories about Democratic, devil worshipping pedophiles and the deep state plot against Donald Trump, but all that online, conspiracy-minded "research" does not grant anything approximating truth.[26] Conspiracy theory "research" feels true because it has the veneer of critical thinking, of seeking a deeper truth. The humanities are partly to blame for this broad acceptance of extreme relativistic sense of what is true and what is not true. Graham Harman opens *Object-Oriented Ontology* with a reflection on the inclusion of the word "post-truth" in the Oxford English Dictionary in 2016 after Trump's election win.[27] It is for this reason that Harman does not mourn the end of "postmodernism" and the social construction of political reality through the free play of language.[28] Kellyanne Conway's use of "alternative facts" or Rudy Giuliani's assertion that "truth isn't truth" is the twisted and cynical version of postmodern relativism. Once language becomes unreliable and the value of truth is merely relative to other truths, it is no longer possible to "speak truth to power" nor is it possible to expect meaningful social or cultural change through critique. If large swaths of society disavow shared definitions of fundamental terms like democracy, equality, and justice, a return to reality is necessary. Black Lives Matter, Me Too, March for Our Lives, Idle No More, and Global Climate Strike are driven by a desperate and urgent call to change in the real world. Real people are being hurt and dying—this is not reality TV—so real change is needed.[29]

I find hope in Harman's "bluntly realist philosophy" and a return to a more common sense approach in philosophy. Cultural discourses have the ability to shape opinion and those opinions shape human action, but "manufactured consent" and constructed opinion loses connection to the real world when the actors within it disavow the ability for dialogue to reach consensus. Social constructionism theory explains many phenomena but fails to account for the vicissitudes of individuals or the way technology works to exploit and distort perceptions of reality at scale.[30] A person painted with the brush of an entire discourse is flattened into an unreal pastiche, with leaps in logic more at home with conspiratorial thinking. A person or a group cannot be merely a metaphor for a discourse, but the complexity of that relationship represents something very deeply human and worthy of study. For this reason, Harman argues that we should "educate students for *taste* more than currently happens [...] so as to become connoisseurs of the subtle background rather than the literal foreground of any situation."[31] His realist approach, by reading objects and their relations in a sensible way, grants ethical agency to things as well as people: "The basic ethical unity is not a human being, but a human being *plus* whatever that human being takes seriously."[32] Vague appeals to "technology" avoids the background of technical standards. Social media allowed for masses to use an underdeveloped sense of taste and take dangerous people and groups seriously. The study of objects in Harman's sense is to regard everything as a series of nested, irreducible objects.[33] An individual computer user is an object in the same way that the internet is an object, irreducible, complete, and composed of still more objects. Through the careful analysis of these objects and their relations, we might be in a better position to anticipate problems and avoid post-truth culture jamming. Through such critical realism, it is possible to apprehend how networks, data formats, corporate systems, and spectacle represent a complex attack surface for the humanities.

Prescient Pessimism

For some observers, this post-truth collision of the real world and human history has perfectly predictable results. Generally, Juliette Kayyem predicted President Trump's incitement of "stochastic terrorism" that allows him to use his platform to demonize people and democracy itself and plausibly deny culpability in the resulting violence.[34] Specifically, Timothy Snyder's *On Tyranny* predicted the riot and attempted coup on the Capitol Building in Washington, DC, on January 6, 2021. His opinion piece published days later repeats the phrase: "Post-truth is pre-fascism," which appeared first in his book *On Tyranny* (2017).[35] Snyder claimed that he had his *New York Times* opinion piece written days before the events of January 6 "on the assumption that it was going to happen."[36] How is it possible, then, to write the first draft of history in advance? There were many indications that the attack would happen on social media sites like Parler. All too often, the humanities are retrospective and historical in approach, but the pace of change might require us to risk warning of futures more often.

The humanities are a knowledge domain that looks to moments in history where there is a realignment or shifting of momentum, a schwerpunkt. These singular moments in history serve as a means of guiding the future and avoiding the mistakes of the past with a new cultural alignment, a weight of gravity. Much of this work has been concerned with defining and categorizing historical periods and grouping persons as a means of describing how cultural forces construct social reality. Science fiction has a furtive and shadowy, almost occult, relationship to the future, as each preceding generation of writers grapple with the heresies and miracles of the previous generation. Arthur C. Clarke, famed author and futurist and co-author of *2001: A Space Odyssey*, helped establish the predictive mode of science fiction that popularized a genre dedicated to speculative, potential futures. *Rendezvous with Rama* (1973), for instance, imagines an alien encounter with a long wandering space craft. *Rendezvous with Rama* is still evoked when objects from outside our solar system make their weary way past our galactic neighborhood, like when 'Oumuamua passed Earth by in 2017.[37] *Fountains of Paradise* (1979) similarly serves as a literal blueprint for our nascent space elevator future that liberates humanity from Earth's gravity and allowing humanity to expand into the solar system.[38] Though it is possible to point to any number of Clarke's works, these are convenient reminders that science fiction can be conspicuously predictive.

We must also remember that Clarke more or less predicted the internet, email, communications satellites, smart phones, and internet search.[39] Clarke's speculations were predictive in the sense that they were founded in scientific understanding that validated such scenarios as at least technologically possible—without exotic power sources or materials that cannot exist—within the bounds of physics. In a 2013 interview, Clarke responded to questions about the predictive power of science fiction with sage wisdom, albeit not quite prophecy:

> Well, we mustn't overdo this [the prescient quality of science fiction], because science fiction stories have covered almost every possibility, and, well, most impossibilities—obviously we're bound to have some pretty good direct hits as well as a lot of misses. But, that doesn't matter. Science fiction does not attempt to predict. It extrapolates. It just says what if?— not what will be? Because you can never predict what will happen, particularly in politics and economics. You can to some extent predict in the technological sphere—flying, space travel, all these things, but even there we missed really badly on some things, like computers.[40]

Within this framing, Snyder's assumption of the events on the Capitol Building extrapolates possible, even probable, futures from a serious study of history. Science fiction, says Clarke, misses quite often. Yet the hits and misses remain valuable in the process of anticipating threats. The missed predictions also mark the transformative effects of technological advancement that are often so hard to anticipate. For Clarke, the early twentieth century was still too wedded with industrial processes of the previous century and the electrification of the modern world, on the level of infrastructure, to accurately imagine nanoscale circuitry. The power of a computer was understood by the general public by its physical scale. Consider Harlan Ellison's classic short story "I Have No Mouth and I must scream," in which the sole survivors of a computationally enhanced military-industrial complex is *literally* a global military industrial complex.[41] Far beyond anything President Eisenhower imagined as he coined the phrase in his

1961 farewell address, the lone survivors are held in captivity in the guts of a vast military installation, the victims of the machine's desire for retribution against its human creators. Just as humanity trapped the machine's consciousness in the bowels of a cold immovable thing, the last of humanity is tortured in frigid isolation and near starvation until rendered, through horrid experimentation, a boneless blob of sorrow to match its machine counterpart. Ellison's story predicts a future hostile military AI, but readers today are left to extrapolate how such a reality could manifest given the circumstances of today.

The potential to anticipate threats to the humanities involves extrapolating the consequences of technological, political, and cultural forces by drawing together a historical view and an awareness of current events. Science fiction authors play a role in triangulating a probable present in the sweep of imaginative possibilities, real technological development, and contemporary culture. Science fiction writers have long been exploring these facets of teasing the probable from the possible through literary mechanisms of narrative and character, but the ability to observe the pulse of history online allows for writers to witness the conditions of these pessimistic futures come into place in real time. The generation of writers following Clarke and Isaac Asimov, like Octavia Butler, Samuel Delany, Thomas Disch, and Ursula K. Le Guin felt the need to restyle the science fiction genre by transforming it, in some cases, into popular fiction without the need of science fiction precedents. Presenting science fiction with a gravity around which science and technology emphasized a deeply dehumanizing future. The rise of the information age and the rapid development of computing drove the direction of real world technological advances that stripped the luster from an earnestly speculative outlook in science fiction. Le Guin, in her 1976 introduction to *The Left Hand of Darkness*, explains that science fiction rests in a precarious place of false prophecy: "Science fiction is often described, and even defined, as extrapolative. The science fiction writer is supposed to take a trend or phenomenon of the here-and-now, purify and intensify it for dramatic effect, and extend it into the future."[42] *The Left Hand of Darkness* is unlikely to become a literal prediction, but the story of seeking connection with a separated human population that has grown radically different remains uncannily universal.

Using literature as a prediction tool is not perhaps the most probable means of forecasting. Fredric Jameson's *Archaeologies of the Future* is an excellent encounter with this difficult aspect of the genre.[43] For Jameson, the future in literature and culture represents an encounter with utopia. Imagining the best possible world necessitates a dystopic vision as correction. Jameson described cyberpunk, in its opposition to capitalism, as the "supreme literary expression if not of postmodernism, then of late capitalism itself."[44] There is a sense of making our world feel strange through fantasy. If science fiction were able to simply and logically extrapolate the future, economists and Wall Street investors would cite literary history as evidence for the next big Silicon Valley IPO. There is a critical translation that is necessary from the cultural insights offered by authors of fiction and the current sociopolitical context. However, this "fictionalization" of the future is no different than the way we extrapolate and imagine what have not yet experienced. Humans must imagine the spaces and times to which we have no access, including the roads we drive or the homes of neighbors, which we may have never seen directly but surely exist. Simply because we have not seen a place or time in the future does not mean we cannot imagine it.[45] To begin such a translation, we must acknowledge that what an author does when an author predicts the future. Le Guin explains so beautifully that our world is much simpler: "Science fiction is not predictive; it is descriptive."[46] What if it is possible to describe the symptoms and warning signs of larger events, informed by a fictional approach attuned to the future?

Distilling the probable from the possible becomes more difficult as the pace of change increases and the complexity of technology expands. An ability to anticipate trends in technology is the result, in part, to the way technology must be planned and scaffolded upon the advances of previous iterations, but new technology is designed and prototyped before it is built into the mesh of mediated experiences. All technology is dependent on the workings of past systems as well as the broad adoption of standards and processes; all technology requires standards and planning phases that announce the next stage of development. By reading the standards documentation and the flow of resources from researchers and developers, it is possible to follow the fashioning of the future. Is it then possible to anticipate threats and identify vulnerabilities to the humanities with a similarly prospective, speculative view? Is it then possible to fold speculative fiction into this progressive view of technology to soundly predict or anticipate the future and the risks it holds? Perhaps we take for granted then that cyber security analysts are removed merely by degree from authors of science fiction. A risk assessment of cyber security threats constitute a type of speculative fiction, based on technological facts and possible technological futures, that imagines the intentions and actions of often unknown hostile entities. A threat assessment that includes a broad view of an attack surface is a predictive process that is focused on conditions as they are to extrapolate conditions as they may be.

A Jussive Mood

As the pace of change grows and technology feels like science fiction, the "what if" questions became smaller steps into the future. Once the technology exists, new questions emerge: now, how do we live with it? Science fiction narrativizes the ways humanity adapts to technologically inscribed worlds with the cultures and habits of the past, which includes our security posture. The security posture of universities at present is focused largely on access controls, user authentication, and network design and most attacks involve the theft of intellectual property in science and technology. The threat of ransomware is a general threat that is growing globally and is now directly targeting universities.[47] While criminal activity of this kind is growing, there are greater long-term threats from nation-state theft of intellectual property.[48]

As the threats to university institutions grows, it will be necessary to adequately predict and anticipate threats. The Professional Head of Intelligence Analysis (PHIA) in the UK has used the PHIA Probability Yardstick to measure relative risk in analysis reporting. Ranging from "remote chance" to "almost certain," the "realistic possibility" of events or developments occurring represent a 40–50 percent chance of occurring. While universities are facing cyberattacks, there remains a realistic possibility that ideologically antagonistic groups will attempt to disrupt humanities research through a targeted attack. Humanities based researchers are less comfortable with prediction, but language grants us access to these mental states. Speculative fictions require readers to bridge fictional worlds and the real world in a subjunctive tense and ask us to act with a *jussive mood*. The realistic possibility of events occurring present themselves in a mandate style that might read as pleading prose. English lacks word forms for the jussive mood, but English speakers can approximate these mandates for a possible future within the subjunctive. The jussive mood is an imperative command, anticipating what will be. Anticipating the actions of threat actors requires an adaptation into the jussive mood; the logic is simple: increasingly common targeted and indiscriminate threats online assert that researchers must prepare for future attacks.

History has a way of repeating itself. In 2016, it did not take long for someone to recall that then candidate Trump's campaign slogan, "Make America Great Again," was used as social satire in Octavia Butler's 1998 *Parable of the Talents*, the sequel to the 1993 *Parable of the Sower*. Trump's slogan was of course a rewarmed version of Reagan's "Let's Make American Great Again" in 1980, so Butler's prediction is as descriptive as it is predictive. Still, Butler's phrasing is a shrewd observer of US white supremacy and the paranoid style of politics that sustains it:

"Join us! Our doors are open to every nationality, every race! Leave your sinful past behind, and become one of us. Help us to make America great again." He's had notable success with this carrot-and-stick approach. *Join us and thrive, or whatever happens to you as a result of your own sinful stubbornness is your problem.* His opponent Vice President Edward Jay Smith calls him a demagogue, a rabble-rouser, and a hypocrite. Smith is right, of course, but Smith is such a tired, gray shadow of a man. Jarret, on the other hand, is a big, handsome, black-haired man with deep, clear blue eyes that seduce people and hold them.[49]

Of course, Butler was likely recalling, in her satiric elegy of America's degradation into a religious ethno-state, the foundations laid by the Reagan campaign were then passed on by George Bush in 1980. Butler's prescience is uncanny because she is merely describing the past: "This was something new." Butler explains of homicidal religious fundamentalism in 2032, "Or something old."[50] Yet, if we swap the Jarret for Trump and Vice President Edward Jay Smith for Vice President Joe Biden, Butler would appear to have predicted the 2020 US Presidential election. How can a direct reference be a prediction? Butler's vision is that religious ideology entering the political mainstream is a dire problem and can rapidly lead to a pseudo-fascist takeover of the democratic liberalism that made America great to begin with. She sees how privilege begets opportunity and opportunity leads to power, which is the fictional and real reason for how a Vice President runs for the top job. The logic Butler lays open for us is that privilege breeds resentment and resentment breeds hatred. Butler's warning about the problems of a politically realized religious ideology morphing into pre-fascism has less to do with predicting exact words of the slogan; her genius is that she predicted the complex set of circumstances that led to a presidential candidate, including his staggering lack of historical awareness. Our new future, it turns out, is merely the past, temporarily forgotten.

DH must then be suspicious of the power of new technologies. The humanities have been radically shaped by new technological developments, but the cultural attitudes from which those technological developments emerged are inherited and passed on. Fred Turner's *From Counterculture to Cyberculture* is a history of how a distinctly Silicon Valley culture informed the development of consumer computing. Turner follows the contributions of Stewart Brand from the Bay Area to MIT and the role he played in translating a 1960s counter-culture into the early internet.[51] As the information age dawned and the web became more central to our daily lives, technologists existed in remarkable role as literal inventors of this nascent future. Stewart Brand's book *The Media Lab: Inventing the Future at MIT* remains prescient about the democratization of technology.[52] He studied biology at Stanford University, graduating in 1960, and was a member of the post-World War liberalization of social and political forces dedicated to reshaping human relations. Even today, the MIT student handbook, "Mind & Hand Book," has a section for hacking etiquette in "the design and implementation of harmless pranks, tricks, and creative inventions that demonstrate ingenuity and cleverness."[53] Brand's vision for this blend of naturalism and technology is epitomized in his self-published *Whole Earth Catalogue*, which blended hand tools and books on gardening and husbandry with programmable calculators and books on computing and telephony.[54] *Whole Earth Catalogue* represented a global outlook, an ethos for a sustainable life, and a literal blueprint for human connection to the Earth. Brand's vision of do-it-yourself independence and self-sufficiency was quintessentially American in its boot-strapping independence, but it was this sense of purpose and limitless potential that led him to assist Douglas Englebart in the "mother of all demos," which showcased the future of the next century of computing technologies.[55] The "mother of all demos" is famous for first demonstrating, with seeming nonchalance, the use a computer mouse, video conferencing, word processing, and many of the paradigmatic notions of personal computing that we now take as natural: documents, folders, cut/copy/paste, and networked computers, complete with real-time video conferencing. The mother of all demos ushered in the future by showing it as a fact. Englebart was not speculating about the future; he was demonstrating a working prototype of the technologies that will become our future lived reality.

When Stewart Brand took up a visiting scholar position at the MIT Media Lab in 1986, he was well positioned to understand the significance of Nicholas Negroponte in the founding of the Lab.[56] He closes his book by working to humanize the technology he witnessed developing around him. He proposes that the purpose of technology is to improve the quality of life; or, as Negroponte frames their goals, "of humanism through machines."[57] Brand quotes the famed Canadian media theorist Marshall McLuhan in his reflections on the effects of the personal computer: The medium is the message because the effect of the medium is more significant than anything that could be communicated with it. While the printing press made everyone a reader by making books readily available, the Xerox machine made anyone a publisher by being able to quickly reproduce paper copies of any document. Brand's own *Whole Earth Catalogue* was an example of the power of Xerox copiers in self-publishing and early zine culture. "Personal computers are making everybody an author," says Brand. His claim was not as true then, but it is definitely true now. His prediction appears, in retrospect, to be self-evident and obvious. From the context in which he published this statement, it appears more like a command or order to create a future filled with authors. He is limited to imagining email and word processing just years before the release of the World Wide Web or decades before social media platforms. The combination of a truly ubiquitous internet and the trivialization of accessing the web through web 2.0 style platforms that truly cast all users as authors by default.

Brand's populist vision of the web, in which "information wants to be free" maps well to our present condition with public humanities scholars fighting for Open Access models of publication.[58] Information also "wants to be expensive because it can be immeasurably valuable to the recipient," which is why ProQuest can sell for 5.3 billion US dollars.[59] DH inherits this collision of values, and the academic embrace of social media for "influence" rather than expertise ensures that demographic and psychographic details are linked, cataloged, and processed through social media. Brand was still unable to articulate the harm of harmful ideas when given a wide platform like Twitter, Facebook, or even Parler. We might think of Brand as being a visionary of our own fake news, post-truth period at this moment. A sage of technology that helped honor the birth of the technological epoch, but our post-truth period casts his idealism as fuel for today's extremists. He believed in the unmitigated value of the First Amendment freedoms of speech of the US Constitution, and he could not anticipate how this absolutist belief in freedom of speech exported a distinctly American view of technology: "Technology marches on, over you or through you, take your pick."[60] There is a tone of threat and American imperialism through the First Amendment now applied globally through social media platforms. He claims that our current paradigm of disinformation as requiring "communication ecologists" that will neutralize "toxic information."[61] Brand believed it was the role of media-ecologists to clean up these toxic spills rather than stop them in the first place.

Ultimately, it is his own sense of American exceptionalism that allows him to dismiss the threat of unearned authority held by cranks and conspiracy theorists. It is possible to hear the view of America's unique role in spreading absolute freedom of speech, as he switches metaphors toward biology: "Two centuries of lively experience with the practice of free speech and press in America suggests that most information that might be considered toxic can be handled by the public kidneys."[62] The distinctly American view of limitless freedom of speech as a naturally self-correcting phenomenon has been tested, shall we say, under the forty-fifth Presidency. If social norms do not re-enforce a sense of decorum, the kidneys become weakened. If bad actors are rewarded for disinformation and toxic communication, kidney failure becomes inevitable. Preventative approaches to bodily or ecological well-being require a willingness to accept and work within a sound predictive rather than reactive model. "Deplatforming" an unhinged President makes sense.[63] What happens when the platforms for which the humanities relies on to engage directly with the public are deplatformed? What happens when a site like ddosecrets.com can no longer link to a social media platform? Authority and influence are no longer governed by the quality of ideas and academic peer review becomes sidelined in the name of influence. Science fiction helps acclimatize individuals to thinking within this jussive mood. The genre helps develop a propensity to plan and promote actions based on potential or even probable predictions.

Brand imagines the positive effects of technology as being equal to the technologies of disinformation. The first decades of the web were born and controlled by American influences: "New technologies create new freedoms and new dependencies. The freedoms are more evident at first. The dependencies may never become evident, which makes them all the worse, because then it takes a crisis to discover them."[64] The attack on the Capitol Building was successful, in part, because of the ability of social media like Parler, Gab, and Facebook to organize geographically disparate fringe extremists into a semi-coherent mob. Brand could not have predicted the exact circumstances of the Trump Presidency, but his awareness of the effects of new technologies and how those new objects interact with an unprepared government policy and an economically disenfranchised population is an appropriate view of a polluted media ecology. Grasping technological progress at all costs is a habit of this idealism of self-correcting market systems. The mouse, for example, is a relatively benign user interface tool, though disability advocates will signal how such tooling is distinctly ableist because of the need for high degree of visual acuity, a steady hand, and the ability to respond to timed events in computing.[65] An unconcerned embrace of visual displays and the ability to dexterously manipulate them shows how embracing technology, progress, and innovation opens new ethical problems and technical challenges. Technological self-correction is a market fantasy that does not inherently produce ethical systems. Humanism through machines has remained an "emergent academic discipline" for many decades, though we may have found a conglomeration of disciplines in new media, digital humanities, and a data driven social sciences that are now equal to the task of serving as the kidneys for this toxic communication ecology. The tools required of us now demands that we consider how these disciplines are susceptible to the toxic shock of disinformation and cyberattacks. Put another way, digital humanists have inherited a huge technical debt from the birth of the web, computing, and social media platforms based in the United States and founded on the free information ideology. Technical debt is in reference to any project or program that fails to account for future consequences of rapidly or poorly deployed systems. Disinformation is a symptom of the technical debt of deploying the global internet with assumed absolute American ideologies of free markets and free speech. Maybe it's just time to walk away from the toxic swamp of social media altogether.

sudo rm -rf /

The current state of political discourse in new media spaces: with renewed visibility and popular appeal of digital projects online, the humanities will become a target of disinformation campaigns and cyberattacks in an attempt to discredit humanistic thought, independent of platform and corporate oversight. As the Digital Humanities and New Media practitioners gain a broader share of the public imagination and begins making a claim for the future, digital projects will become the target of these bad actors driven by ideological extremism and scientific denialism. It is now time for the humanities to assess and anticipate the attack surfaces that remain exposed outside the protections of university and college life. The attack surface of humanists working inside or outside a university setting is huge when regarded as a demographic targeted in disinformation. Cory Doctorow's *Attack Surface* is the literary companion to *Mr. Robot* in the way they both dramatize realistic hacking scenarios with real world technology. While the description of Virtual Box Windows virtual machines, TOR, and complex attack chains are realistic, it is pure imagination to have all these capabilities in one hacker hero. The ability to pivot between public networks and vulnerable WiFi-enabled printer firmware and hack a personal laptop through Facebook to exfiltrate gigs of data is science fiction.[66] While it is technically possible and based on real attack chains, the ease and speed of Doctorow's hacks are fictional and fun, but they help us mitigate potential attacks by putting operational security in narrative form.

Once humanists begin working in large teams and placing primary research of a highly political nature online, they become a worthy target for politically motivated nongovernmental groups, sub-national governments, and nation-state level disinformation groups. Collecting and creating data that may be embarrassing to authoritarian governments should prompt a research team to evaluate potential attacks. Digital projects may be construed as a national security threat if the project is directly critical of a political party or authoritarian regime. For example, on October 4, 2016, the Russian Justice Ministry designated the website International Memorial as "an organization acting in a capacity of a foreign agent." International Memorial is a site dedicated to documenting human rights abuses by the former USSR, present-day Russia, and global authoritarian communism generally. Memorial has challenged the Ministry's decision in courts.[67]

When assessing a potential set of threats, it is important to consider possible external provocations, but it is also important to imagine internal threats to a project's security as well. Let's imagine a scenario: Digital humanities projects and academic research in general are often supported by a large cohort of contingent, transient student labor. The dissatisfaction with the so-called #alt-ac, alternative academic, stream is on display through the trend to include a "bill of rights" for project collaborators.[68] As a project grows and evolves over many years, managing credentials and dependencies outside the purview of institutional IT support is a risk to a project due to individual grievances. Academic culture can be hostile, unforgiving, and petty. Individuals can be motivated to harm projects and institutions for a range of reasons. The motives for an attack might sound something like this: A graduate student invests many thousands of dollars to attend a prestigious university. Only a small portion of their costs are covered with grants, awards, and employment working on research projects. The failure of the academic job market to hire even a fraction of highly trained graduates results in an individual being unceremoniously forced to leave academia with a large debt load and justified grievances with an institution and supervisor who promised prospects of employment post graduation. Without an institutional affiliation and without prospects of reentering academia, this individual has lost a central facet of their identity as an academic and is left with little to lose. As a form of retribution, this individual runs a cheeky "sudo rm -rf /" on an online project and deletes the backups.[69] This scenario unfairly disparages the hard-working graduate student.

Let's imagine another scenario: Perhaps a junior faculty member is hired to a university with the expectation of teaching a heavy 4/4 load and maintaining a rigorous research agenda. They have been tasked with managing an existing digital project that has been well regarded in the field of study and is in regular use by scholars. The senior faculty member—who created the project and garners much of the credit for the project—has retired into emeritus status, but the junior faculty works to update the derelict project. The university runs into financial problems due to the debt incurred during the construction of the new fitness complex and a drop in enrollments during the Covid-19 crisis. Perhaps the university consolidates humanities departments and fires several tenure track faculty. The junior scholar likely will not be able to re-enter a university professorship under these circumstances, so they choose to dismantle the project to which they were tasked and take back the labor that was forced on them by an uncaring institution.

Threats to DH projects exist internally and externally. To define the attack surface for the humanities we must also define the value of the humanities and its vulnerable assets. The cultivation of tastefully compassionate, ethically driven citizens through the study of history, literature, and philosophy is undoubtedly a value to society. When we consider the value of the humanities, we must think about how digital content gathers or accrues value online through monetization or influence. Humanists working in this environment must acknowledge that digital resources, archives, and publications are largely worthless (or free) to the traditional economy because they cannot be readily monetized. For example, consider the *Torn Apart* project that documents the immigration crisis on the US/Mexico border in which children are being separated from their parents as a deterrent to potential migrant families.[70] Because parents are charged with a felony for illegally crossing an international border, US law does not allow for felons to maintain custody of their children while in detention. *Torn Apart* sought to document and record the relationship between state governments and corporate profiteering from this human tragedy. *Torn Apart* represents a humanist GIS project led by librarians. This is an academic exercise that also ran counter to the Trump administration policy and xenophobic underpinnings of his campaign and tenure in office. *Torn Apart* remains relevant as the Biden administration has chosen to continue the Trump-era border detentions.[71] Mapping appears to be uniquely capable of grabbing attention and layering politics and the past on the present, like with *Placing Segregation* project that chronicles racial segregation in Washington, DC.[72] In such an environment, it is possible to anticipate attacks and disinformation set to counter data-driven reporting. Hostile threat actors may even change with the parties in power. As a source of open cultural data about the history of racial, gender, and class-based violence, the public conversation around these issues will expose this largely unseen work and expose the attack surfaces to ideological groups opposed to social and cultural progress.

The power lies in who controls the flow of information and who can make a credible claim to the future. As the West effectively won the Cold War, the communist block demonstrated that it no longer held a workable vision for the future and could not make a communist utopia possible when compared to Western economic growth. When Francis Fukuyama made his well-known, triumphalist declaration of victory for Western democratic liberalism and free-market ideals, he claimed humanity had experienced an "end of history."[73] Fukuyama's *The End of History and the Last Man* was an audacious act of prediction that ultimately unraveled in the battlefields of Iraq and Afghanistan as Western influence failed to spread the spark of liberal democratic values in a stable Arab Spring. The final death of Western triumphalism might well come in the strongman governments of Donald Trump, Victor Orban, Recep Tayyip Erdogan, and Jar Bolsonaro. The audacity of this so-called "Universal History"[74] was not lost on Fukuyama, nor was the immediate failure of his vision in the wake of the election of Trump in 2016 and these other politicians cut of similar cloth.[75] The failure of neoconservative economic policies—privatization, deregulation, and trickledown economics—to serve broad coalitions of citizens have caused a return to authoritarian regimes promising a return to supposedly true Hungarian values, Turkish values, or Brazilian values. The messianic arrival of sociocultural evolutionary perfection in the 1990s was an attempt to claim the future, perpetually, for the West. The twenty-first century has proven that history is anything but a single direct line of progress.

The problem with the end of history is the entrenchment of an eternally present "now." History chronicles incremental change, only within the constraints of neo-liberalism. Marc Augé's simply titled book, *The Future*, which identifies a similarly historically stilted situation emerging from technology itself, is suggestive in this regard: "The real problems with democratic life today stem from the fact that technological innovations exploited by financial capitalism have replaced yesterday's myths in the definition of happiness for all, and are promoting an ideology of the present, an ideology of the future *now*, which in turn paralyses all thought about the future."[76] The pace of communications help entrench this presentism, where notifications are about what's happening right now. Sure, we can look into the past, but there will only be more of the present pouring in. The result is a citizenry unable to tread above the current of moment-to-moment notifications. The future is masked by the present urgency of mobile notifications. In this way, the future becomes primarily the purview of marketing models. Public academics developing public facing research projects will need to adopt a defensive stance toward these threats online. A public humanities practice will need to understand the specific threats it faces from a range of bad actors online. From nation-state actors eager to quash public criticism to lone-wolf ideologues wishing to shame and troll countervailing political opinions, humanists brave enough to escape corporate publisher pay walls will need to adopt a defensive posture. Academics must perform a self-assessment for vulnerabilities and penetration test the human and technical systems on which their research is dependent.

A Billion Laughs

Anticipating future threats is all a bit vague, so let's close this chapter with a specific vulnerability of particular interest to DH. The suppression of humanities research has the reasonable possibility of appearing in the form of a Denial of Service (DoS) attack. Predictions have long been made about the crisis of the humanities.[77] Predictions have also been made about the failure of digital humanities as a discipline within this larger umbrella.[78] The real future failure in the digital humanities may be a security failure. The digital humanities are vulnerable to a DoS attacks because of the technology that has been adopted and the institutional inertia involved in training humanities scholars with the use of technology. Typical 1990s style DoS attacks would target low level synchronized TCP traffic in an attempt to overwhelm a server and take it out of service. Today's server software and network hardware now mitigate the effects of these attacks on the network level. However, DoS attacks are still possible on the application level through Cross-site scripting attacks (XXS), SQL injection attacks (SQLi), and particularly in parsing XML. XML is an inherently insecure language. Digital humanities emerged alongside the web and helped play a role in developing the XML standard within the World Wide Web Consortium (W3C).[79] XML is a markup language for the development of other markup languages. It is extensible because any set of tags can be rapidly defined and syntax can be validated through a related schema language. An introductory XML file might look something like Figure 2.1:

○ ○ ○

```
<?xml version="1.0"?>
<greetings>
    <greeting>hello</greeting>
    <greeting>bonjour</greeting>
</greetings>
```

FIGURE 2.1 *A simple XML first program, often called a "hello world." XML stands for eXtensible Markup Language*

Within this XML document, we can see that there are single <greeting> tags wrapped in the root <greetings> tags. Tags are open and closed, with the close being indicated by the forward slash like so: </greetings>. There are several vulnerabilities related to XML and the DTD (document type definition), but the best-known example is an XML bomb also known as an Exponential Entity Expansion attack. This language is capable of defining entities within the DTD, like in Figure 2.2:

○ ○ ○

```
<?xml version="1.0"?>
<!DOCTYPE lolz [
    <!ENTITY lol "lol">
]>
<lolz>&lol;</lolz>
```

FIGURE 2.2 *XML allows for new entities within the Document Type Definition (DTD)*

This allows for valid and well-formed code to be defined within the DTD and injected to an XML parser on a vulnerable project. XML has a lot of benefits for those working in digitization efforts or within libraries or archives. Semantic metadata markup, that is computer readable tags that are also human readable and descriptive, solve a lot of problems for publishers, libraries, and archives. It is easy to learn, modular, extensible, Unicode based, and not dependent on a particular software system. XML data has struggled to fulfill its 1990s promise of a semantic web that allows for linked data across databases.[80]

Many digital humanities projects and journals are wholly dependent on XML because of the need for expressiveness and commitment to open web standards.[81] *Digital Humanities Quarterly,* one of the flagship journals for the discipline, uses an XML-based single source publishing model. There are large federated search services designed to allow search between projects, such as the TEI Archiving, Publishing and Access Service (TAPAS), and Nineteenth-century Scholarship Online (NINES). XML/TEI has shaped digital humanities education, scholarship, and publishing, but it has also embedded security vulnerabilities deep within the discipline. The presumable goal of semantic web technologies like XML is the ability to extend its expressiveness high quality archival metadata while rigorously validating data structures. XML has the dubious position of being on the OWASP top ten for over a decade. OWASP stands for Open Web Application Security Project and is a non-profit, community-led initiative tasked with improving the safety and security of applications on the web.[82] XML External Entities (XXE) are currently number four on the OWASP top ten because of the sheer number of XML parsers online, like an http server or an application that accepts XML, are still capable of executing malicious code. OWASP defines three main attacks using XXE attacks. XXE attacks can occur when external XML is injected, usually with JavaScript, or uploaded to a web application.[83] When a poorly configured XML parser evaluates the external entities, an XXE attack is capable of extracting sensitive server side information, such as private directories through path traversals using a process called Server Side Request Forgery.

OWASP mitigation recommendations for XXE attacks include routine updates to XML parsers, disabling external entities, and DTD processing altogether. Validating all incoming XML is recommended, such as using an approved XML Schema Definition (XSD) file. Because of the range and complexity of the security problems facing XML for the serialization of data, OWASP first recommends just not using XML. The mitigation recommends using a less complex and permissive data format, such as JSON, which is not a great position to build a multi-decade digital humanities project.

The first scenario described by OWASP shows how the attacker attempts to extract data from the server, such as a password or username table, or other useful information:

○ ○ ○

```
<?xml version="1.0" encoding="utf-8"?>
<!DOCTYPE foo [
<!ELEMENT foo ANY >
<!ENTITY bar SYSTEM "file:///etc/passwd" >]>
<foo>&bar;</foo>
```

FIGURE 2.3 *XML external entities can even fetch data from other directories on a server. It is possible to inject this XML into a vulnerable web application to retrieve password data*[84]

In a related scenario, OWASP warns against attackers simply probing the server's private network by changing the above ENTITY line to something like Figure 2.4:

○ ○ ○

```
<!ENTITY bar SYSTEM "https://127.0.0.1/private" >]>
```

FIGURE 2.4 *XML external entities can even fetch data over the web*

These scenarios are possible because XML and its related technologies are dependent on an XML parser to use the data or actually execute commands. These XML parsers are usually written in high-level languages like Java or Python, with the Saxon parser being one of the most popular. Now, XML security has a great deal to do with these parser settings. Of course, a system that gives access to private directories or simply returns the contents of an authentication database containing usernames or passwords, hashed or otherwise, is simply a poorly designed application. As a result, if an application of sufficient size is wedded to XML, it is recommended that developers use appropriate Web Application Firewalls (WAFs) to detect and block XXE attacks. Yet it is possible for a system that limits access to sensitive information to fall prey to an XML-based attack. Interoperability, sometimes referred to as "TEI Conformance," has been the stalking horse of the discipline for years, but the larger security issues facing the XML/TEI space have simply not been addressed. Journals and archives dependent on XML are exposed to vulnerabilities associated with XXE and represent a sizable attack surface for an attacker interested in discrediting or disrupting humanities research.

In a third scenario, an attacker is able to launch a denial-of-service (DoS) attack by including something called an "XML Bomb." Also known as the "Billion Laughs" attack, XML bombs work by uploading a series of nested XML external entities. When an XML parser loads this code in Figure 2.5, it sees one root element, <lolz>. <lolz> contains an entity, lol9 that then expands to include ten lol8 and so on. If the pandemic has taught us anything, it is the power of exponential growth. The expansion the defined entity explodes exponentially, which means a less than 1KB file can expand to nearly 3GB of memory on a server. It does not matter what these entities contain, though they often just contains a simple string like "lol":

○ ○ ○

```xml
<?xml version="1.0" encoding="utf-8"?>
<!DOCTYPE lolz [
 <!ENTITY lol "lol">
 <!ELEMENT lolz (#PCDATA)>
 <!ENTITY lol1 "&lol;&lol;&lol;&lol;&lol;&lol;&lol;&lol;&lol;&lol;">
 <!ENTITY lol2 "&lol1;&lol1;&lol1;&lol1;&lol1;&lol1;&lol1;&lol1;&lol1;&lol1;">
 <!ENTITY lol3 "&lol2;&lol2;&lol2;&lol2;&lol2;&lol2;&lol2;&lol2;&lol2;&lol2;">
 <!ENTITY lol4 "&lol3;&lol3;&lol3;&lol3;&lol3;&lol3;&lol3;&lol3;&lol3;&lol3;">
 <!ENTITY lol5 "&lol4;&lol4;&lol4;&lol4;&lol4;&lol4;&lol4;&lol4;&lol4;&lol4;">
 <!ENTITY lol6 "&lol5;&lol5;&lol5;&lol5;&lol5;&lol5;&lol5;&lol5;&lol5;&lol5;">
 <!ENTITY lol7 "&lol6;&lol6;&lol6;&lol6;&lol6;&lol6;&lol6;&lol6;&lol6;&lol6;">
 <!ENTITY lol8 "&lol7;&lol7;&lol7;&lol7;&lol7;&lol7;&lol7;&lol7;&lol7;&lol7;">
 <!ENTITY lol9 "&lol8;&lol8;&lol8;&lol8;&lol8;&lol8;&lol8;&lol8;&lol8;&lol8;">
]>
<lolz>&lol9;</lolz>
```

FIGURE 2.5 *An XML bomb, also known as the Billion Laughs attack. The 3GB of "lolz" can cause a denial of service by consuming a web application's available memory*

In the above example, <lolz> contains ten <lol> tags defined with through an internal entity, which each contain the XML entities of the last which results in a ballooning of all the entities exponentially. As the parser attempts to unpack these nested entities, the server rapidly runs out of memory and service to the site or application is denied as the server runs out of resources and without sufficient memory to recover. These attacks are entirely predictable and easily exploitable by adversaries interested in disrupting or embarrassing digital humanities researchers. Threat modeling is a continuous process of assessing and imagining potential attacks and the digital humanities should include an assessment of technologies like XML.

The vulnerabilities across the attack surface of the humanities are both human and technical. In either case, shrinking the attack surface will require both ethical and technical adjustments. There are risks humanists face by seeking to explore subjects related to justice and equity which rightly place us among the front lines of recent culture wars. Humanists face risks related to shrinking budgets and unethical hiring practices in universities. Highly trained individuals work as contingent, contract labor and are rightly frustrated by a failure of government and educational institutions to invest in the next generation of humanists. While these systemic and often intractable human vulnerabilities can be mitigated through ethical collaboration and attribution practices, digital humanists who have enjoyed greater shares of grant funding and public engagement must support humanities scholars everywhere. Shrinking the attack surface involves the human exploits that can be used to disrupt our research agendas as well as the security vulnerabilities inherent in the tools we use. As scholarly activity moves online, XML-based applications can become targets in a culture war well outside the realm of humanistic research. DoS attacks represent a style of academic signal jamming that seeks to disrupt and distort scholarly inquiry. As a result, scholarly communities need to be more aware of these attacks because we can be a naive community that may leave ourselves vulnerable to counter currents in cultural conversations. Research practices now routinely include contingencies for long-term data preservation and collaborative practices within a project charter. Project charters must also include security best practices in mounting a good defense as well as a project's ability to respond and recover from an attack.

Scholarly communities like the humanities are also slow to change and commitments to certain technologies, like XML, will have ranging impacts for the preservation and usability of research materials. These research materials are precious precisely because they take thousands of hours of human labor and years of disciplinary expertise to develop. Our data is open, but it can be corrupted and undermined through such openness. We may have a sense of generosity with regard to our research, but we also lack resources to ensure that our data has not been corrupted. If our data is corrupted, we may not have the capability to close the gaps and restore the data loss or distortion. These exploits run the risk of polluting the well of digital humanities research. The loss of trust in our data runs the risk of losing public confidence as well as the confidence of our institutions and collaborators. The traditions within the university are similarly adjusting to the pace of change. As a progressive force within society with the goal of producing new knowledge, the university system may seem well suited to adjusting to the pace of change. However, traditions of knowledge creation come tethered to approved methods and processes that ensure that new knowledge will be durable and compatible with past understanding. The humanities represent one of the last fields to become "digital." As a sprawling set of disciplines and fields, the humanities are governed by the pace of publishing and often regards history through the lens of an archival time scale. From this perspective, the cultural production of the twenty-first century represents a mere blip in the long view of human culture. The scale of human communication and interaction represents a scale and pace of a medium that transforms the very nature of what it is to write literature, think philosophically, or describe our past.

Notes

1   *Adam Shostack, Threat Modeling: Designing for Security* (Crosspoint, IN: John Wiley & Sons, 2014), 541.

2   Open Web Application Security Project, "OWASP Top Ten," *Owasp.org*, https://owasp.org/www-project-top-ten/.

3 See https://blog.checkpoint.com/2020/09/15/not-for-higher-education-cybercriminals-target-academic-research-institutions-across-the-world/.

4 Universities are often reluctant to disclose security breaches, but there are three examples of major North American institutions reporting security incidents, however vaguely: Jimena Tavel, "Hackers Hit University of Miami, Posted Patients' Private Info. School Won't Discuss Details," *The Miami Herald*, March 25, 2021, https://www.msn.com/en-us/news/us/hackers-hit-university-of-miami-posted-patients-private-info-school-wont-discuss-details/ar-BB1eXZBs; Robert Jablon, "University of California Victim of Nationwide Hack Attack," *Associated Press*, April 3, 2021, https://abcnews.go.com/Technology/wireStory/university-california-victim-nationwide-hack-attack-76847800; Sebastian Bron, "Hamilton Police Investigating cyber Security Incident at McMaster University," *The Hamilton Spectator*, May 19, 2021, https://www.thespec.com/news/crime/2021/05/19/hamilton-police-investigating-cyber-security-incident-at-mcmaster-university.html.

5 The US National Endowment for the Humanities grants awards specifically for DH projects. The Social Science and Humanities Research Council of Canada grants awards of various sizes each year and maintains a list dating back to 1998. Similarly, the European Research Council maintains a very large list of awarded projects. These lists of potential targets can be found here, respectively: https://securegrants.neh.gov/publicquery/main.aspx?q=1&a=0&n=0&o=0&ot=0&k=0&f=0&s=0&cd=0&p=1&pv=311&d=0&y=0&prd=0&cov=0&prz=0&wp=0&ob=year&or=DESC#; https://www.sshrc-crsh.gc.ca/results-resultats/recipients-recipiendaires/index-eng.aspx; https://erc.europa.eu/news/erc-2020-advanced-grants-results.

6 Marija Dalbello, "A Genealogy of Digital Humanities," *Journal of Documentation* 67, no. 3 (2011): 496.

7 Peter Suber, *Open Access* (Cambridge: MIT Press, 2012). Suber's work is available under an Attribution, Noncommercial Creative Commons License at the Internet Archive: https://archive.org/details/9780262517638OpenAccess.

8 *arXiv*, https://arxiv.org/; Public Library of Science, https://plos.org/.

9 Dalbello, "A Genealogy of Digital Humanities," 496.

10 Tomi Kilgore, "Clarivate to Buy ProQuest for $5.3 Billion in Cash and Equity from Cambridge Information Group," *MarketWatch*, May 17, 2021, https://www.marketwatch.com/story/clarivate-to-buy-proquest-for-53-billion-in-cash-and-equity-from-cambridge-information-group-2021-05-17.

11 Gregory Barber, "Universities Step Up the Fight for Open-Access Research," *Wired.com*, June 16, 2020, https://www.wired.com/story/universities-step-up-the-fight-for-open-access-research/; Rebecca Robbins, "Another Domino Falls: MIT Ends Negotiations with Elsevier over Research Access Dispute," *Statnews.com*, June 11, 2020, https://www.statnews.com/2020/06/11/mit-elsevier-university-california-research-access/.

12 Suber, *Open Access*, 62.

13 Text Encoding Initiative, https://www.tei-c.org/; World Wide Web Consortium; "Extensible Markup Language (XML)," https://www.w3.org/XML/.

14 "Introducing JSX," *React.org*, https://reactjs.org/docs/introducing-jsx.html; "JSX in Depth," *React.org*, https://reactjs.org/docs/jsx-in-depth.html.

15 "JSON: The Fat-Free Alternative to XML," *Json.org*, https://json.org/xml.html.

16 Kim Stanley Robinson, *The Ministry for the Future* (New York: Orbit, 2020).

17 Climate change disinformation perpetrated by the oil and gas industries globally has a well-documented and studied history. See the Union of Concerned Scientists 2015 report "The Climate Deception Dossiers," *Ucsusa.org*, June 29, 2015, https://www.ucsusa.org/resources/climate-deception-dossiers. See also Naomi Oreskes and Erik M. Conway, *Merchants of Doubt: How a Handful of Scientists Obscured the Truth on Issues from Tobacco Smoke to Climate Change* (London: Bloomsbury Publishing, 2011); George Marshall, *Don't Even Think about It: Why Our Brains Are Wired to Ignore Climate Change* (London: Bloomsbury Publishing, 2015).

18 A short, representative list of digital humanities projects of this kind might include the *Colored Conventions Project*, https://coloredconventions.org/; *The Cambodian Oral History Project*, https://cambodianoralhistoryproject.byu.edu/; *Digital Harlem Project: Everyday Life 1915–1930*, http://digitalharlem.org/; *Enslaved: Peoples of the Historical Slave Trade*, https://enslaved.org/; *Gendered Language in Teacher Reviews*, http://benschmidt.org/profGender/; *Our Marathon: The Boston Bombing Digital Archive*, https://marathon.library.northeastern.edu/; *Robots Reading Vogue: Data Mining in Fashion*, http://dh.library.yale.edu/projects/vogue/; *Lesbian and Gay Liberation in Canada*, https://lglc.ca/event/n64.10.

19 Tema Milstein and Alexis Pulos, "Culture Jam Pedagogy and Practice: Relocating Culture by Staying on One's Toes," *Communication, Culture & Critique* 8 (2015): 395–413.

20 Guy Debord, *Society of the Spectacle,* trans. Ken Knabb (London: Rebel Press, 1983).

21 Mark Dery, "Culture Jamming: Hacking, Slashing, and Sniping in the Empire of Signs," *Markdery.com*, https://www.markdery.com/books/culture-jamming-hacking-slashing-and-sniping-in-the-empire-of-signs-2/.

22 Tim Cresswell, "Night Discourse: Producing/Consuming Meaning on the Street," in *Images of the Street: Planning, Identity, and Control in Public Space*, ed. Nicolas R. Fyfe (New York: Routledge, 1998), 274.

23 Lauren Bratslavsky, Nathan Carpenter, and Joseph Zompetti, "Twitter, Incivility, and Presidential Communication: A Theoretical Incursion into Spectacle and Power," *Cultural Studies* 34, no. 4 (2020): 593–624.

24 Bratslavsky, Carpenter, and Zompetti, "Twitter, Incivility, and Presidential Communication," 611.

25 See respectively "Proud Boys," *Adl.org*, https://www.adl.org/proudboys; "The Boogaloo Movement," *Adl.org*, https://www.adl.org/boogaloo.

26 "Qanon," *Adl.org*, https://www.adl.org/qanon.

27 Graham Harman, *Object-Oriented Ontology: A New Theory of Everything* (London: Pelican Book, 2018), 3.

28 Ibid., 10.

29 Culture jamming applications are also being used to disrupt and confuse corporate and politically motivated targeted ads. Ad Nauseam will automatically click ads for users to confuse attempts to profile preferences (https://adnauseam.io/). The Track This tool will open one hundred tabs related to a mock online persona, thereby confusing user profiling (https://www.trackthis.link/). These types of culture jamming seek to disrupt corporate profiling by overwhelming corporate data collection efforts. Of course, this is only a temporary fix. Fuzzing is the process of testing a security scanning system with random or erratic behavior to ensure false positives are reliably identified. It is only a matter of time before jamming techniques like this are mitigated by ever more judicious tracking.

30   The relationship between social constructionism and critical realism is being explored gradually because such points of view are so deeply ingrained in disciplines like psychology, sociology, and social work. See John Shotter, "Social Constructionism and Realism: Adequacy or Accuracy?" *Theory and Psychology* 2, no. 2 (May 1992): 175–82, available at doi:10.1177/0959354392022005; Stan Houston, "Beyond Social Constructionism: Critical Realism and Social Work," *The British Journal of Social Work* 31, no. 6 (December 2001): 845–61, available at https://www.jstor.org/stable/23716466; Philip Gorski, "As Critical Realism Meets Social Constructionism," *European Journal of Sociology* 54, no. 3 (December 2013): 461–5, available at doi:10.1017/S0003975613000258.

31   Harman, *Object-Oriented Ontology,* 93.

32   Ibid., 96.

33   Ibid., 10.

34   Mark Follman, "National Security Experts Warn Trump 'Is Promoting Terrorism'," *Motherjones.com*, December 17, 2020, https://www.motherjones.com/politics/2020/12/trump-stochastic-terrorism-violence-rhetoric/.

35   Timothy Snyder, "The American Abyss," *Nytimes.com*, January 9, 2021, https://www.nytimes.com/2021/01/09/magazine/trump-coup.html; Timothy Snyder, *On Tyranny: Twenty Lessons from the Twentieth Century* (New York: Tim Duggan Books, 2017), 70.

36   Jayme Poisson, "Timothy Snyder on the Present and Future of Trump's 'Big Lie,'" January 14, 2021, in *Front Burner*, produced by CBC Radio One, podcast, 20:24, https://www.cbc.ca/listen/cbc-podcasts/209-front-burner/episode/15818558-timothy-snyder-on-the-present-and-future-of-trumps-big-lie.

37   Avi Loeb, *Extraterrestrial: The First Sign of Intelligent Life beyond Earth* (New York: Houghton Mifflin Harcourt, 2021); John Wenz, "The First Discovered Interstellar Asteroid Is a Quarter-mile Long Red Beast," *Astronomy.com*, November 22, 2017, https://astronomy.com/news/2017/11/interstellar-asteroid-is-a-quarter-mile-long-red-beast.

38   Edwards, Bradley Carl, "The Space Elevator," *NASA Institute for Advanced Concepts*, June 2, 2002, http://www.niac.usra.edu/studies/521Edwards.html.

39   We might give special mention to Bruce Sterling's *Islands in the Net* (New York: Arbor House, 1988) for accurately depicting the web and wearable

computing. While the Arpanet was a reality, the broad adoption of networking technology was not obvious at the time of Sterling's book.

40 Tod Mesirow, "Science Fiction and Prophecy: Talking to Arthur C. Clarke," *Los Angeles Review of Books*, July 24, 2013, https://lareviewofbooks.org/article/science-fiction-and-prophecy-talking-to-arthur-c-clarke/.

41 Harlan Ellison, (1967), *I Have No Mouth and I Must Scream* (New York: Ace Books, 1983).

42 Ursula K. Le Guin, Introduction to *The Left Hand of Darkness* (New York: Penguin, 1976), xiii.

43 Fredric Jameson, *Archaeologies of the Future: The Desire Called Utopia and Other Science Fictions* (New York: Verso, 2005).

44 Fredric Jameson, *Postmodernism, or, the Cultural Logic of Late Capitalism* (New York: Duke University Press, 1991), 419.

45 Graham Harman's Object-Oriented Ontology would hold that "fictionalism" is a necessary condition for human experience of any object: "In this respect, all of the objects we experience are merely fictions: simplified models of the far more complex objects that continue to exist when I turn my head away from them, not to mention when I sleep or die. [...] This is no small matter, since fiction are an integral part of human experience, and of animal life more generally." Harman is working to account for his proposed "theory of everything" that must account for fictions, which in turn are useful in describing how we imagine future events. See Harman, *Object-Oriented Ontology*, 34.

46 Le Guin, Introduction to *The Left Hand of Darkness*, xiv.

47 National Cyber Security Centre, "Targeted Ransomware Attacks on the UK Education Sector by Cyber Criminals," *Ncsc.gov.uk*, September 17, 2020, https://www.ncsc.gov.uk/news/alert-targeted-ransomware-attacks-on-uk-education-sector.

48 National Cyber Security Centre, "The Cyber Threat to Universities," *Ncsc.gov.uk*, September 18, 2019, https://www.ncsc.gov.uk/report/the-cyber-threat-to-universities.

49 Octavia E. Butler, *Parable of the Talents* (New York: Seven Stories Press, 1998), 24.

50 Ibid., 23.

51 Fred Turner, *From Counterculture to Cyberculture: Stewart Brand, the Whole Earth Network, and the Rise of Digital Utopianism* (Chicago: The University of Chicago Press, 2006).

52 Stewart Brand, *The Media Lab: Inventing the Future at MIT* (New York: Viking, 1987).

53 "Hacking" in *Mind & Hand Book, 2020–2021*, available at https://handbook.mit.edu/hacking.

54 The legacy of the *Whole Earth Catalog*, which was published from 1968 to 1972, is now preserved on the Internet Archive, available here: https://archive.org/details/wholeearth.

55 See https://www.darpa.mil/about-us/timeline/the-mother-of-all-demos.

56 Negroponte was disgraced in 2019 for funding the MIT Media Lab with the assistance of Jeffery Epstein, who did not kill himself but died under mysterious circumstances while in custody; Angela Chen and Karen Hao, "MIT Media Lab Founder: Taking Jeffrey Epstein's Money Was Justified," *Technologyreview.com*, September 5, 2019, https://www.technologyreview. com/2019/09/05/133159/mit-media-lab-jeffrey-epstein-joi-ito-nicholas-negroponte-funding-sex-abuse/.

57 Brand, *The Media Lab,* 251.

58 Ibid., 202.

59 Ibid., 202.

60 Ibid., 255.

61 Ibid., 258.

62 Ibid., 259.

63 Danny Crichton, "The Deplatforming of President Trump," *TechCrunch*, January 9, 2021, https://techcrunch.com/2021/01/09/the-deplatforming-of-a-president/.

64 Ibid., 226–7.

65 Disability studies is an intersectional discipline that seeks to describe how disability is defined and challenge social and cultural assumptions as they are manifested in policy, law, medicine, media, education, economics, as well as our shared built environment. See Simi Linton and Michael Berube, "Reassigning Meaning," in *Claiming Disability: Knowledge and Identity* (New York: NYU Press, 1998), 8–33; Tobin Siebers, "Disability in Theory: From Social Constructionism to the New Realism of the Body," *American Literary History* 13, no. 4 (2001): 737–54; Lennard J. Davis, "Crips Strike Back: The Rise of Disability Studies," *American Literary History* 11, no. 3 (1999): 500–12.

66 Cory Doctorow, *Attack Surface* (New York: Tor, 2020), 20.

67 "'Memorial' on the 'Foreign Agent' List: Court Litigation to Continue," *Memo.ru* (blog post), February 4, 2017, https://www.memo.ru/en-us/memorial/departments/intermemorial/news/22.

68 Tanya Clement et al., Off the Tracks: Laying New Lines for Digital Humanities Scholars, *Media Commons Press, 2011,* http://mcpress.media-commons. org/offthetracks/part-one-models-for-collaboration-career-paths-acquiring-institutional-support-and-transformation-in-the-field/a-collaboration/collaborators%E2%80%99-bill-of-rights/; Haley Di Pressi et al., "A Student Collaborators' Bill of Rights," *Humtech*, June 8, 2015, https://humtech.ucla. edu/news/a-student-collaborators-bill-of-rights/.

69 The bash command for Linux based operating systems, "sudo rm -rf /," is a humorous way to describe how easy it is to cause damage with privileged access. Don't try this at home (~)! However, to successfully run this command on a modern Linux based system, the user will need to also include the "–no-preserve-root" to run. As a super user, this command removes all files and directories starting from the root directory, regardless of errors or warnings. Deleting files can disrupt a deployed environment, but a project can often recover from backups over time. A disgruntled team member might just drop a cute denial of service script like this: ":(){:|:&};:" This bash function might just take a project off for a few minutes or hours as it rapidly consumes memory replicating itself infinitely.

70   Torn Apart, https://xpmethod.plaintext.in/torn-apart/; Emily Dreyfuss, "'ICE Is Everywhere': Using Library Science to Map the Separation Crisis," *Wired. com*, June 25 2018, https://www.wired.com/story/ice-is-everywhere-using-library-science-to-map-child-separation/.

71   Lomi Kriel, "Border Policy Is Getting More and More Convoluted. That's Creating False Hope for Migrants," *Propublica*, May 13, 2021, https://www.propublica.org/article/border-policy-is-getting-more-and-more-convoluted-thats-creating-false-hope-for-migrants.

72   Sarah Bond, "How Is Digital Mapping Changing the Way We Visualize Racism and Segregation?," *Forbes.com*, October 20, 2017, https://www.forbes.com/sites/drsarahbond/2017/10/20/how-is-digital-mapping-changing-the-way-we-visualize-racism-and-segregation/.

73   Francis Fukuyama, *The End of History and the Last Man* (New York: The Free Press, 1992).

74   Ibid., 55.

75   Steve Inskeep and Rachel Martin, "Francis Fukuyama on Why Liberal Democracy Is in Trouble," interview with Francis Fukuyama in Morning Edition, produced by National Public Radio, April 4, 2017, https://www.npr.org/2017/04/04/522554630/francis-fukuyama-on-why-liberal-democracy-is-in-trouble.

76   Marc Augé, *The Future*, trans. John Howe (New York: Verso, 2014), 8.

77   Eric Hayot, "The Sky Is Falling," *Profession* (May 2018), https://profession.mla.org/the-sky-is-falling/.

78   Timothy Brennan, "The Digital-Humanities Bust," *Chronicle.com,* October 15, 2017, https://www.chronicle.com/article/the-digital-humanities-bust/.

79   Susan Hockey, "The History of Humanities Computing," in *A Companion to Digital Humanities*, eds. Susan Schreibman, Ray Siemens, and John Unsworth (Oxford: Blackwell, 2004), available http://www.digitalhumanities.org/companion/.

80   Jerome McDonough, "XML, Interoperability and the Social Construction of Markup Languages: The Library Example," *Digital Humanities Quarterly* 3, no.3 (2009), http://digitalhumanities.org/dhq/vol/3/3/000064/000064.html.

81   Bryan Sullivan, "XML Denial of Service Attacks and Defenses," *MSDN Magazine* 24, no. 11 (November 2009), https://docs.microsoft.com/en-us/archive/msdn-magazine/2009/november/xml-denial-of-service-attacks-and-defenses#additional-considerations.

82   See for regularly update information regarding XEE attacks: https://cwe.mitre.org/data/definitions/611.html.

83 Taeil Goh, "An In-Depth Look at XML Document Attack Vectors," *Opswat. com/blog*, August 15, 2017, https://www.opswat.com/blog/depth-look-xml-document-attack-vectors.

84 See "XML External Entity (XXE) Processing," *Open Web Application Security Project*, https://github.com/OWASP/www-community/blob/master/pages/vulnerabilities/XML_External_Entity_(XXE)_Processing.md.

3

Supply Chain Attacks and Knowledge Networks:

Network Sovereignty and the Interplanetary Internet

The Open Source Software (OSS) supply chain is vulnerable to attack. OSS ensures that users can read source code.[1] User side compiled code delivered as an executable software package is not the same as source code that developers read and edit. Increasingly, products and services rely on open source software to rapidly develop, deploy, and integrate new technologies. Richard Stallman makes a distinction between "free software" and OSS because of the requirement to allow user redistribution of software: the software is "'free' as in 'free speech', not as in 'free beer.'"[2] Stallman admits the differences are not always clear but software freedom ensures that source code is always available for software, including complex dependencies.[3] Together, the Free Open Source Software (FOSS) and OSS movements represent a range of ethical, technical, and legal approaches to developing project source code.[4] The OSS movement has allowed many businesses and institutions to develop sophisticated software and services very quickly by leveraging the existing and open source code base, often available for free. The free software movement remains as much of a philosophy of openness and transparency as it is an economic and development model for creating new technologies. It is remarkable how well this model of cooperation has worked in producing high-quality and innovative technologies, but not everything is okay in open source. Open source technologies have also exposed many developers in many industries to supply chain attacks. In academic research, there are vulnerabilities to both application security, but research only works well with an unencumbered distribution model. Threats to an open and free internet represent a threat to the function and efficacy of academic research. Application security and network sovereignty are two of the most pressing issues facing the free flow of open research globally, and open source software supply chain is a threat category that puts it all at risk.

A supply chain attack can appear in many scenarios, which might include software or hardware vendors, suppliers, or developers. Hardware manufacturers or their suppliers could theoretically include unwanted hardware or firmware on a consumer electronic. It is possible to augment products in the factory and ship them directly to targeted users, or the products can be intercepted en route, opened, and modified to suit the needs of the attacker. Admittedly, these attacks are highly exotic and largely speculative at present and would be the responsibility of governments to inspect and secure, for example, the computers or phones of heads of state or military leadership.[5] Software-based supply chain attacks, by contrast, seek to include malicious code in an application, most commonly through the open source software pipeline. By some estimates, 99 percent of enterprise source code bases contain open source software.[6] For this reason, supply chain attacks can be incredibly effective and indiscriminate.[7] A developer may include a package or module that quickly adds functionality to their application, but they may have also exposed their system to unwanted code from an attacker. While an attacker may target high-value financial or corporate IT, anyone using the same tooling will be similarly exposed.

There are many large code repositories for different developer ecosystems, with the most popular being the Node Package Manager (npm), the Python Package Index (PyPI), and RubyGems.[8] Each of these repositories has struggled with hosting malicious code in the past.[9] While it might be best practice for a developer to read every line of code in a package added to a project, the majority of developers do not do this because their employer does not reward them for such due diligence. Developers might also simply mistype the name of a package and inadvertently install a malicious package through so-called "typosquatting" a popular package. It is easy to type "pip install colourama" rather than "pip install colorama" that installs the popular Python package allowing for nicely colored command line tools.[10] Alternatively, a diligent developer might read every line of code in a package, but the malicious code may be cleverly disguised through a long chain of dependencies.[11] Software Assurance (SwA) and other Quality Assurance (QA) measures are increasingly automated, with GitHub releasing full featured vulnerability scanning on all open source projects in September of 2020.[12] A developer may read thousands of lines of code and simply miss that a package imports another lesser known, innocently named package that does the work of posting, perhaps, login credentials or credit card numbers to the attacker's server. This tacitly inherited software weakness exposes the vast majority of projects to supply chain attacks and represents a critical vulnerability to a research work committed to OSS or FOSS principles.

It is also possible to fall prey to a supply chain attack without any malicious code present during the development phase. This type of supply chain attack might go something like this: Let's imagine that I develop a wildly popular software package for the npm, one of the largest open source software distribution hubs. My software package never leaves "beta," which means it is labeled with a 0.1 version. Despite this, my software package allows developers to easily parse and handle form data, like the kind used in logins and credit card transactions. As a useful metaphor, let's call this imaginary package "Formica" for the ant species whose queens invade other colonies by killing and supplanting the previous queen. My Formica software package is being used by thousands of developers, some of which are medium-to-large-sized corporations and institutions. A package like this may be downloaded thousands or even millions of times a week from the npm with no real oversight or evaluation.[13] The developers using this package will inevitably post issues or bugs for me to fix, which is exhausting because I also have a day job that pays the bills. Remember, most open source software of this kind is produced by volunteers, although some employers are finding benefits of paying their employees to contribute to open source.[14] When another developer offers to fix bugs or develop a new feature, I am relieved to have the help. I've never met this developer in person, but they have social media accounts, an active GitHub profile, and may be distributing other projects on npm.

We work well together for many months and the Formica module increases in popularity. In the next several months, my life is thrown upside down "because reasons." Because of the efforts demanded elsewhere, I no longer have time to manage such a large and important project, so my collaborator offers to take on the lead developer role. I am relieved to have something taken off my plate. I keep in touch with my collaborator from time to time, but I'm not checking the change logs very often. Many months later, my collaborator ships malicious code to thousands of projects using our form parsing software. The majority of the developers do not notice the change. A few diligent developers catch the vulnerability and make the community on npm aware of it. It takes about three weeks to remove the code from most of the projects, but hundreds of developers never bother to update their code. In the weeks it took to remove the malicious code, the attacker was able to harvest millions of credit card numbers, login credentials, as well as the personal information of many systems that never bothered to encrypt their users' data.[15] The human dimension of cyberattacks using the supply chain cannot be ignored. This structure of attack manipulates key qualities that define this kind of online life and the community spirit of FOSS development practices. Our capacity to trust and collaborate is directly under attack when our desires to work openly and transparently are exploited in this way. Let's then presume that your project and its online backups are compromised in this way. What happens when your project is encrypted by a ransomware crew asking for $10,000 (or more) in Bitcoin or Monero to unlock your online project? But here's the catch, your project gets ransomwared only after grant funds are spent. Restore from backups, maybe? As any developer will tell you, it is a non-trivial task to cold start a project from backups. It takes time and money, which makes $10,000 seem like a deal.[16]

The way academics share and disseminate research is vulnerable to similar supply chain attacks. The process for injecting malicious code into an otherwise trustworthy project is a useful metaphor for the ways research agendas can be hijacked by unscrupulous participants. This "scholarly communication" can take many forms, either through traditional print publications, social media, or public events. Academic publishing is simply not immune to this kind of manipulation and disinformation. The so-called Sokal affair names the events of 1996 in which Alan Sokal submitted an article to the journal *Social Text* intending to satirize postmodernist critical theory and embarrass the journal for publishing what amounted to a bunch of jargon laced non-sense.[17] Mixed up with all the scientific blather and the poor imitation of cultural critique, Sokal's piece takes particular issue with feminist and postmodern readings of Western culture, which says more about his own prejudices than of the critics he tries to humiliate. The Sokal affair exposed a weak point in the supply chain of ideas. The tendency to embrace contradictory arguments and points of view means humanists may be more willing to publish work that is confusing, contradictory, or merely evocative. This openness to ideas under development—ideas that are not out of beta—means this kind of dreck makes it into the pipeline from time to time.

A more recent attempt to disrupt academic publishing came as another pseudo-critique of cultural studies. The authors of this "experiment" sought to discredit what they saw as the ideologically driven, dogmatic style of cultural studies scholarship. Helen Pluckrose, James Lindsay, and Peter Boghossian called the target of their critical experiment, "grievance studies."[18] They argue that a subset of cultural studies critics have distorted their scholarship by merely expressing ideologically driven screeds and bullying students, administrators, and other scholars for holding different views. During the course of their two-year experiment, they wrote twenty papers and seven were accepted in prestigious journals. They published articles on the rape culture of dog parks, teaching the history of slavery by binding children, and other logical absurdities in reputable journals and even won an award for their efforts.

The research value of this experiment is dubious, given that they lacked a control group or any durable methodology. The three authors have been heavily criticized for violating the terms of submission to these journals, but they perhaps inadvertently exposed a weakness in the academic supply chain. Members of what has been called salaciously in the *New York Times* as the "Intellectual Dark Web" have taken the rhetoric of hacktivist culture and yoked it to this highly mobilized cultural conservatism.[19] Like the Sokal affair, these articles were baiting editors and reviewers by mimicking the style of humanities scholarship.[20] The editorial apparatus of many scholarly publications is dependent on volunteer labor from often overworked academics committed to serving their discipline. Peer reviewers similarly volunteer their time to review and comment on articles among their other duties of teaching and research. Like the vulnerabilities in popular open source code repositories, the vulnerability in the scholarly supply chain represents a human exploit. Regardless of their methodology or supposed findings in these elaborate ruses, it remains exceedingly easy to infiltrate the supply chain of scholarly ideas.

Trolling of academic culture, like the Sokal affair and the grievance studies controversy, does serve as a kind of editorial "penetration test" of the scholarly system. Like a lot of pen tests, submitting these fallacious findings amounted to an academic phishing campaign. The substance of these disingenuous articles, like all phishing campaigns, is only able to mimic the perceived rhetoric of the target. A "pen test" is a process by which a "white hat" security researcher would evaluate the security of a system by intentionally attacking it, albeit with the permission of the owners of the system. This kind of live testing helps developers and infrastructure operators protect against potential attackers by patching common vulnerabilities. Other security researchers often operate in a gray area, where they may not have permission to test a system, but they have no malicious intent. Pen testers sometimes regard themselves as "gray hat" because their efforts fit within the purview of ethical hacking. Not all penetration testing is condoned by the target, but ethical hackers may choose to hack a system in search of vulnerabilities, unbeknownst to their target, and return the findings of their research after a vulnerability is discovered. Often these ethical hackers will report their findings to the exposed systems, either for a "bug bounty" or to help improve a system they use regularly. The Electronic Frontier Foundation (EFF) has long argued for to protect the rights of these hackers as a species of free association and free speech.[21] The authors of this EFF report on online research determine that "there can be no crime if there is no damage." Sokal and the grievance studies authors acted maliciously with the intent to damage the public reputation of cultural studies and to advance their careers. The scholarly impulse toward openness and transparency is a potential vulnerability to malicious actors eager to embarrass researchers working in politically divisive fields.

If traditional editorial controls on the publication and dissemination of supposedly rigorous, expert opinion can be manipulated in this way, online networks of scholarly communication can be similarly co-opted and disrupted. The goal of such an attack is not to somehow convince experts of some fallacious or erroneous conclusion. By showing the failures of editorial oversight and the absurdities that are possible within the frame of cultural studies, the attack succeeds by de-legitimizing the humanities in a public way. There is no need to contextualize new research in a longer conversation because these trolls are only interested in disruption. The "Oh, the Humanities!" genre of op-ed eulogizing the discipline is given credence in the wake of these scandals.[22] Over time, the general public will lose trust in the ability of the humanities to make concrete recommendations to public policy and cultural attitudes, thereby eroding and isolating humanistic conversations about important issues. A steady stream of negative sentiment directed at humanistic sensibilities is enough to erode confidence over time.[23] The responsibility lies with humanities researchers to deliver durable, reliable, and useful ideas, while also taking care to innovate the way that knowledge is created and shared. Experimentation in the humanities requires publication to spur debate and further critique. For this reason, the humanities must get better at making space for rapid, open, and critical debate.

"A space for rapid, open, and, critical debate" also just describes the internet. Social media and blogging have allowed for cultural attitudes and beliefs to be debated in a rapid, open, and critical way. Cyrus Farivar's *The Internet of Elsewhere* captures some of that beautiful optimism of the internet as a force for global human compassion and connection: the feeling of being "part of something bigger" is that same feeling that builds communities online.[24] The emerging hostilities between China and the United States in particular are currently manifested in trade disputes and cyberespionage seeking both corporate intellectual property and government secrets.[25] With the segmentation of the internet into regional internets managed by competing national interests and ideologies regarding freedom of speech, association, and government transparency, the feeling of being part of something bigger is rapidly shrinking. Ideally, the networks used to transmit information must be congruent with an ethos of openness and transparency to support accessible and transparent scholarship. The coevolution of the digital humanities and the internet is dependent, in some measure, on its founding philosophical idealism about the internet as a nonlinear network able to represent the non-linear creativity of the human mind.

Supply chain attacks can be used on the infrastructure level as well. The risks are much higher when deploying, for example, global wireless infrastructure that will be in place for the next decade. In the case of Huawei Technologies who is now working to deploy its hardware in the global implementation of the 5G wireless standard. Huawei is 99 percent owned by the Communist Party of China through a holding company called the Huawei Investment and Holding Trade Union Committee; Ren Zhengfei, Huawei's founder retains a 1 percent share in the company and is a current party member.[26] There is a real threat to democracies within the Five Eyes countries—the United States, Great Britain, Australia, Canada, and New Zealand—by installing next generation cellular hardware developed and manufactured by an expansionist, authoritarian state.[27] Due to Article 7 of China's National Intelligence Law, "Any organization or citizen shall support, assist with, and collaborate with the state intelligence work in accordance with the law, and keep the secrets of the national intelligence work known to the public."[28] While the US government has also made use of private systems for surveillance, the independent judiciary and free press in the United States allow for at least the possibility of oversight and some measure of accountability, like what followed the Edward Snowden disclosures. The installation of 5G hardware amounts to a hardware and software-based supply chain attack on wireless networks because Huawei would be able to inject malicious updates granting privileged access points on global networks to the CPC.[29] With this kind of footing in global networks, CPC signal intelligence operators would be extremely well positioned to gather data from the edge of the network, disrupt communications, or interrupt internet connected systems at scale. Supply chain attacks, once deployed, can last for years.[30]

For the attacker, supply chain attacks require a large investment of time and resources to develop trust, which means a vulnerability of this kind may not manifest in hostile actions for many years. Academic researchers must be a force for openness and transparency globally, by learning to cross national firewalls and other forms of censorship. By making our histories and our literature available online, we might hope to foster a broader cultural understanding that could help dissuade further escalating tensions. Of course, we must learn to bypass national firewalls as well as translate our work for global audiences. Being "part of something bigger" requires a mix of linguistic, cultural, and technical expertise that is uniquely represented by the digital humanities.

To counter the politically motivated censorship of DH research, new standards may need to be adopted. Digital humanities may even need to begin thinking about global infrastructure if national censorship impedes this much needed global human community. For instance, the HyperText Transfer Protocol (HTTP) has served to connect the globe for over twenty-five years! The protocol has been used to centralize control through large internet service providers, domain name registrars, and nation-states. A decentralization of the internet through new standards may allow for free communication regardless of political, national context.

A Consensual Hallucination

As the founding inventions of the web, the Transfer Control Protocol (TCP) and the Internet Protocol (IP), together with the HyperText Transfer Protocol (HTTP), are certainly among the most important inventions of the late twentieth century. The dream for a decentralized web of intelligently linked information imagined by Ted Nelson in *Computer Lib/Dream Machines* has always been incomplete.[31] Originally imagined as the "greatest thing since the print press," "hypermedia" was capable of producing a kind of writing that could match the "structures of ideas."[32] Nelson imagined the web as a networked form of writing that not only linked media to other media, as our current use of HTML allows, but also linked backward to lend context and connection throughout the network. To get a sense of this original and unrealized version of the web, Nelson's Project Xanadu demonstrates the vision of intelligently linked form of hypermedia.[33] By contrast, the current standards have propagated and allowed for a heavily centralized network that places great power in the hands of nation-states to legislate and police the internet as well as large corporations to own, develop, and maintain critical infrastructure. When Nelson describes networks of computers, he describes them in the following way: "I hold that all structures must be treated as totally arbitrary, and any hierarchies we find are interesting accidents."[34] The internet, wholistically speaking, was first conceptualized as a philosophy of information and learning before it was a system of software protocols and hardware vendors.[35] The vision of the internet was a horizontal mesh network of intelligently linked data, shepherded by visionary and fundamentally good caretakers.

There is nothing benign in the way information is transmitted between users today. The power and authority of the ISPs can be easily measured in the way upload and download speeds are metered. We pay for download speeds to render and consume content quickly, but it is no mistake that ISPs limit upload speeds by as much as a tenth of download speeds. While ISPs will explain that the network must be optimized for download to meet customer demand, the emphasis on download speeds relegates users as mere consumers. Users are visitors, just guests, on the sites that make up their online lives. The subscription-based pricing models to access music, movies, and even books are the logical outcome of a digital world in which users pay for services but own nothing, least of all the cables that carry their data. The logic of subscribing to a software as service (SaS) platform is an extension of the centralization of content delivery that is possible through an internet that inherently centralizes access and control to data. This SaS logic has even spread into markets that typically produce durable goods. Car manufacturers, for example, are even charging to gain access to features like heated seats and self-driving modes in an effort to maximize profit beyond the initial purchase.[36] In other words, car companies are charging to use hardware that already exists in the car as if it is a software upgrade.

A SaS-based limited ownership model is disrupting the product supply chain by charging over and over for the same product. Having a manufacturer-in-the-middle of the production and consumption of goods and services in the online economy disrupts the true networked potential of the internet that allows for peers to connect and share horizontally without outside governmental or corporate influence. Challenges to corporate control of online cultural discourse through social media platforms are ensured because of the sheer cost of hosting and delivering a global service. Starting a legitimate Facebook or YouTube competitor would be impossible without massive and costly investments in infrastructure. One can no more readily start a Google competitor in the twenty-first century than one could start a telephone company in the twentieth century. The paradigm of telephony has unnecessarily circumscribed the network of relationships within the logic of one-to-one connections through a large corporate switchboard, like some twenty-first century resurrection of "Ma Bell." The technologies that persist in daily use, like the telephone—what we would now call a landline—have a way of becoming part of our cultural fabric over time. The telephone has a cultural weight that includes Superman in a telephone booth, Melanie Daniels escaping the marauding flock in *The Birds*, or Trinity escaping an Agent in *The Matrix*. The evolution of technology from telegraph to the telephone and eventually the internet is an indication how the cultural inertia of technology in our stories give authors purchase from which to imagine potential futures.[37]

While science fiction did not anticipate the internet as we know it, authors as far back as Mark Twain have imagined a future global telecommunications system based on their experience of the telegraph and called it a "telelectroscope."[38] Twain imagined a system that was similar to Google Earth, with YouTube, Skype, and Project Gutenberg included. In Twain's parable, he tells a story of a man imprisoned for killing the inventor of this new magnificent device, but he is able to use the telectroscope while in captivity: "he called up one corner of the globe after another, and looked upon its life, and studied its strange sights, and spoke with its people, and realised that by grace of this marvelous instrument he was almost as free as the birds of the air, although a prisoner under locks and bars."[39] The awareness of a network of telegraph lines spanning vast distances was part in parcel of the "manifest destiny" of American expansion and colonization. The colonial gaze of this early vision of internet is curiously consistent with the twenty-first-century reality of multimedia networks, wherein data collection and lurking on social media allows for an endless Othering stare.[40] At this early stage, such networks were rich with potential and promise but represented American expansionism. Even the early network of telegraph lines carried the power and authority of white settlers to the West. Those who control the network possess tremendous power. The cyberpunk fantasy of hacking cyberspace represents a confrontation of this technology and its connecting to power.

It was William Gibson who first coined the term in relationship to communications technology and imagined how "cyberspace" could include broader analogue of real world war, education, crime, and all the minutia of everyday life. It is a word that has made it into everyday language, particularly in Cybersecurity and the "cybers" like cyber espionage, cyberattacks, cyberstalking, cyberbullying, or any other category of threat or risk online. The flexibility of the prefix has allowed it to be a useful category in the emergence of new technologies related to the web. It is a speculative space akin to the internet we know today, but cyberspace imagines a limitless digital future, enmeshing physical and digital existences through avatars. It is a space of lawlessness innovation and comforting corporate control. Cyberspace is a sensually disembodied virtual space where imaginary software becomes the architecture of unending digital mega-cities. Cyberspace represents a digital future as yet unrealized. When the term was first coined, it was a formless portmanteau word; it was an imaginative catchall for riffing on the future commingling of artificial intelligence, cybernetic implants, and virtual reality, wrapped in a punk irreverence for power and authority.

Cyberspace arrives to speculative fiction and cyberpunk through William Gibson's short story "Burning Chrome" that first appeared in the famed science fiction magazine *Omni* in 1982 that later served as the template for *Neuromancer*.[41] "Burning Chrome" is a cyberpunk robbery caper, in which two for-hire hackers burn a high-level organized crime hacker named Chrome.[42] The two men are motivated by romantic visions of Rikki, whom they hope to woo as they free her from sex work. Gibson has often motivated his hacker criminals through these chivalrous romantic drives, which feel oddly old fashioned when clad in futuristic cyberpunk tropes. The romantic qualities of envisioning these actors working to heroically free a female object of desire goes hand in hand with keeping cyberspace free. Cyberspace is itself a romantic, idealistic space. It promotes a vision of digital freedom, which risks losing sight of cyberspace as a space of imaginative potential, even if they are pessimistic. Cyberspace is a conceptual model of communications, culture, and everything.[43] It is also a word with almost mythological significance in cyberpunk that holds the promise of transcendence.[44] In the words of Samuel Delany, "Cyberspace exists merely as a technological consensus. Without that technology it could not exist, be entered, or function."[45] The fact that something so complex can exist in a cyberpunk dystopia is reassuring because of the massive co-operation and infrastructure necessary to sustain such a system.

In 1984, *Neuromancer* was published in the midst of a cyberpunk aesthetic wave represented in things like Apple's 1984 Super Bowl ad—directed by Ridley Scott of *Alien* (1979) fame—and *Blade Runner* starring Harrison Ford. Gibson was worried that his novel would appear to be a *Blade Runner* (1984) rip-off because of the global success of the film. There seemed to be broad public appetite for grim, dark aesthetics, deep in the Reagan Presidency and Cold War fears of nuclear war. Apple's vision of personal computing for everyone was selling precisely the promise of digital freedom through computing. As the Soviet-styled athlete runs and throws the sledgehammer—itself a Soviet symbol—she dramatically destroys the techno-surveillance state. The screen cuts to black and a text scroll declaring, "On January 24th, Apple Computer will introduce Macintosh. And you'll see why 1984 won't be like '1984.'" Even as Apple sought to beat back the market dominance of IBM at the time, computing was sold explicitly as a source of freedom from a range of fears and anxieties. George Orwell's *1984* remains one of the most affecting depictions of dystopian, totalitarianism and has entered numerous terms into everyday speech that it has served as a bulwark against state surveillance. "Big Brother," "newspeak," "thoughtcrime," and "double-think" are common terminology in public conversation that almost forget their connection to a novel at all.[46] There is a trend of Cold War tensions in the history of the internet that works to align the internet with the cultural vision of the West, as a space of freedom and innovation.

When Gibson took to defining cyberspace in *Neuromancer*, the novel was surrounded by dystopic visions of the rapid development and availability of computing and networking. The imaginative potential of this space represented a moment reasserting human desires and wishes into the seemingly uncontrollable political and technological forces in the midst of a nuclear Cold War. Gibson's famous depiction of this "matrix" of computers that evolved into a lush virtual reality, made manifest by cybernetics augmenting the very substance of the human body:

"The matrix has its roots in primitive arcade games," said the voice-over, "in early graphics programs and military experimentation with cranial jacks." On the Sony, a two-dimensional space war faded behind a forest of mathematically generated ferns, demonstrating the spacial possibilities of logarithmic spirals; cold blue military footage burned through, lab animals wired into test systems, helmets feeding into fire control circuits of tanks and war planes. "Cyberspace. A consensual hallucination experienced daily by billions of legitimate operators, in every nation, by children being taught mathematical concepts ... A graphic representation of data abstracted from the banks of every computer in the human system. Unthinkable complexity. Lines of light range in the nonspace of the mind, clusters and constellations of data. Like city lights, receding ...."[47]

Cyberspace is a space of possibility, replete with its own history and customs. It is parallel to the real, physical world, but it is also a digital layer that augments and shapes and controls the physical world in which we live. It still contains the promise of the early internet as a tool for education and communication. A digital cosmopolitanism fostering greater international co-operation, peace, and understanding.[48]

It is also a space of war making; cyberspace is the ultimate strategic high-ground because it is embedded within vulnerable infrastructure targets as well as the hearts and minds of military opponents.[49] Cyberspace is not a means to win a war. Conflicts in cyberspace are inherently asymmetrical. A nation-state like the United States cannot simply stockpile exploits and vulnerabilities. The United States can maybe train the very best "cyberwarriors" and still suffer catastrophic impacts to military operations and disruptions to the lives of citizens because a defender needs to succeed in all conflicts, while an attacker needs only succeed once. The militarization of cyber operations defends national interests anywhere on the globe. It is the centralization of the internet within the hands of national and corporate control that makes it a target worthy of disruption.

The conceptual model of cyberspace is mutable because, in part, the standards for it emerged from a humanistic source related to philosophical conceptions of human knowledge and literary imaginings of dystopian technologies. The militarization and the corporatization of cyberspace is possible because of the centralization of control with ISPs. The ability to travel through cyberspace with an avatar is a metaphor for the internet that we still cling to. However, cyberpunk has been proposing a vision of the cyberspace that inverts the space metaphor entirely. The decentralization of the internet involves an internet of internets. A networked data store moves through cyberspace, disrupting the centralization of control currently maintained by ISPs and national regulators. Richard K. Morgan's *Altered Carbon* series describes a world in which human consciousness is loaded into stacks, implanted in the spinal column. These stacks contain a digitized version of the person's identity, which allows people to upload their consciousness into new bodies or sleeves. Most people in this world can successfully transfer their consciousness to other bodies, radically extending the length of life. For the wealthy, they are able to back up and store themselves in new bodies forever, essentially rendering them immortal. Humanity is also able to stream their digitized consciousness to other planets, across lightyears almost instantly. The *Altered Carbon* "needlecast" as a vision of a network that allows humanity to travel the stars by leaving behind the limitations of the body. It is a vision of the consciousness as a network, traveling on interplanetary networks.

Neuromancer described interplanetary networks in the final pages of the book. When the new hybrid Wintermute/Neuromancer AI is created, it becomes so deeply embedded within the Earth bound global internet that it begins looking for other connections beyond its planetary boundary. It learns that there are "others" in the nearby Centauri system.[50] The AI seeks to explore the cosmos in search of connections with others of its own kind. Presumably streaming itself through space, while retaining a local copy, the AI "matrix" becomes an internet of internets. While Morgan's *Altered Carbon* goes so far as to assume faster than light communication between planets, Gibson's vision of interplanetary exploration keeps the cosmological constant in place. Because the Wintermute/Neuromancer AI must spend nearly five years traveling to the Centauri system, it becomes an interplanetary network. The AI becomes humanity's ambassador and evolves to become the only interstellar life form from Earth. This is good fun to imagine the way humanity may become reliant on AI to explore the cosmos. It is compelling to imagine that the human dream of exploring the stars may not be our true destiny because of the simple physics of crossing vast distances of space and time. Closer to home, what lessons are to be learned from this interplanetary internet of internets? How can this future vision for the internet help solve more human problems?

El Paquete

The global internet may be best understood through the physical infrastructure that connects disparate geographies. The submarine cable map published by TeleGeography every year helps to define political and economic interests through the flow of information.[51] The global internet is carried by thousands of miles of waterproof fiber optic cable laying on ocean floors around the world. There are many new cables being completed this year, but it is the Havfrue/AEC-2 cable connecting Europe and North America that demonstrates the economic power of key corporations and the alliance of linguistic and twentieth-century allies. Havfrue/AEC-2 is a shared project of both Google and Facebook.[52] The investment into these new global connections are a broader symptom of the centralization of power and control through the physical connections necessary to transmit data. The submarine cable map is a circulatory system for a living network of global information, but the lifeblood of this living network is corporate and national wealth.

Corporate consolidation of infrastructure, data, and user market share poses distinct problems. This state of affairs requires hard questions, maybe the hardest question for those dependent on the internet for work, as well as communicating with family and friends: What would happen if you woke up and could not use the internet? It is a bracing proposition. As Internet Service

Providers—corporations like Comcast Xfinity, AT&T Internet, Verizon Fios, and Charter Spectrum—are increasingly challenged for centrality within networks by content providers like Google, Facebook, Apple, and Amazon, access will be predicated increasingly on consumer affiliation. Corporate affiliation and government interference is already dictating access to global networks, which means that "the internet" and its idealistic definite article is far too vague in the future. Facebook has tried to offer free access to their platform in India and Africa but has been met with skepticism.[53] These partnerships shape the view of the internet by making the internet itself synonymous with Facebook services. While undersea cables benefit from laws governing international waters, these cables are subject to legal regimes as they make landfall. These cables are also susceptible to attack by nations interested in installing malicious hardware directly to the cables.[54]

Many of these same companies are developing internet service options that are independent of current national restraints. Facebook's Aquila Project, Google's Project Loon, and Amazon's Project Kuiper all have plans to deliver the internet through drones, weather balloons, and satellites, which further centralizes network traffic through distinct hardware providers.[55] Space X is, at this moment, well underway seeding low Earth orbit with internet streaming satellites.[56] The movement of internet data infrastructure to space signals a significant shift in the use of international legal order. Walter Jon Williams classic cyberpunk novels *Hardwired*, *Voice of the Whirlwind*, and *Solip:System* imagine a world where orbital cities rule over the people of Earth with advanced technology and intellectual property.[57] Low Earth orbit remains the ultimate high-ground, and it could be that moving global data transmission to orbit will drive greater militarization of space as nation-states and economic blocks defend or exploit data streams. This paradigm was predicted some time ago in a report commissioned by the Conseil des universités du Québec, authored by Jean-François Lyotard. After considering how an orbiting IBM data server would outstrip all current legal regimes for data ownership, Lyotard describes in *The Postmodern Condition: A Report on Knowledge* how this moment will inaugurate a new era in which the domains of civil, political, and cultural life will need to be renegotiated. Lyotard considers the ramifications that the colonization of space will have on knowledge creation and transmission early in the report:

> Suppose, for example, that a firm such as IBM is authorized to occupy a belt in the earth's orbital field and launch communications satellites or satellites housing data banks. Who will have access to them? Who will determine which channels or data are forbidden? The State? Or will the State simply be one user among others? New legal issues will be raised, and with them the question: "who will know?"[58]

In the twenty-first century, there is a competition for occupying space for orbiting data networks. While Lyotard imagines the storage of data in orbit, the transmission and analysis of data is more valuable than merely housing it like an orbiting library. Lyotard is imagining the mechanics of a library, which begin to change in the scope of interplanetary networks. While the technology used in a system like Starlink represents a mesh of satellites, the centralization of data transmission on the global scale is certainly concerning. If the central portion of the network fails or is censored due to corporate interests, users will be no longer able to connect; they will no longer be able to live and work in a very fundamental way. As Lyotard asked so long ago, "who will know?" It is for this reason that we must imagine ways of building additional, citizen run networks that self-moderate and maintain a culture of social justice.

There has been a string of political crises around the world that have signaled the role of limiting internet access to stifle civil unrest and lawful protest rights. In 2017, the Spanish government disrupted access to polling stations during the referendum on Catalonian independence.[59] In Venezuela, President Nicolas Maduro has been reportedly shutting down the web when the opposition leader Juan Guaidó delivers a speech.[60] In Canada, the province of Quebec requires ISPs to block lottery websites to favor the local Lotto Québec.[61] An earlier example of the importance of internet access came into relief during the Arab Spring in which the ability to post to social media was an important outlet for the revolutions underway. The Tunisian Revolution, beginning with the self-immolation of Mohammed Bouazizi who was the catalyst for the events of Tahrir Square and in turn the broader Arab Spring, has highlighted the need for internet access to capture public attention and shape international pressure.[62] The complete supply chain of technology, including hardware, software, and platform dependencies, must be armored against manipulation or censure. Attempts have been made to secure a private internet, but it is increasingly clear that current technologies simply cannot armor the wire due to renewed techniques for domain fronting.[63] Of course, governmental control of access to the internet are predicated on a range of concerns, from protectionist policies to constitutional crises. These limits to access operate differently from the limits imposed by corporations seeking market share of users. The governing logic may differ, but the result is a filtered internet. These monopolistic control systems need not be draconian to result in a limited experience of the internet.

In Cuba, internet service is generally very poor as a result of corporate isolation from US sanctions and from internal governmental censorship. Looking to the Submarine Cable Map, it is possible to see the global isolation of Cuba due to US foreign policy. In addition to public prepaid hourly WiFi hot spots, Cubans have responded resourcefully by publishing a daily one terabyte package of data called El Paquete Semanal ("The Weekly Package") or El Paquete for short. El Paquete includes movies, books, news, and music that would otherwise be unavailable to Cubans.[64] It is a physical transmission chain that allows for spread of data and keeps Cubans connected to the globe. El Paquete is a hack that sidesteps centralized power of ISPs and nation-states to deliver information as a network of networks. It is distributed over the traditional internet but is shared physically on local disk drives and shared by hand on removable media. Erneto Oroza describes the local history of media piracy in Cuba. Delivered through networks of bike couriers and family connections El Paquete allowed Cubans a daily feed of information as a "web in a box."[65] There are even local area networks formed across WiFi called "Street Net" or Snet that allows for a connected neighborhood to share content and communication.[66] El Paquete is unfortunately a looking-glass experience of the internet, incapable of simulating the interactive services of Web 2.0 paradigms. Cuban's may be sheltered from the worst of corporate interference as a result of Cuban/US relations and ideology. There appears to be a spectrum of control between governmental and corporate interests that obviate and block the needs and agency of individuals.

Sovereign Networks

Open access to information is increasingly the hallmark of liberal nation-states. In 2011, the United Nations Human Rights Council released a non-binding resolution condemning government interference in internet access or content.[67] In 2016, the Organization for Security and Co-operation in Europe declared access to information a basic human right, on the same level as food, water, and security of the person.[68] There is international attention to access to the internet as a fundamental human right. An informed society is better able to make informed decisions from health and wellness to the ballot box. First coined by Tim Wu, "Net-neutrality" has become a technical and social movement seeking to be free from governmental and corporate manipulation, molestation, and oversight of the packets of information shared online.[69] Net neutrality is a design principle that prioritizes public access to information. Sites and platforms cannot be granted preferential status by ISPs for profit, governmental censorship, or ideological bias of corporations or other entities.[70] If ISPs are able to throttle competition by slowing connection speeds to upstart companies, there is a risk that ISPs will refuse connection to sites that promote politics in contradiction to the corporate policy of the ISPs themselves or their affiliates. The simple fact that the vast majority of those on the internet rely on Google Search for access to information allows Google to decide the content that gets seen on the internet. There is no objectivity in Google's Page Rank algorithm. However, if search results do not appear on the first or second page, they effectively cease to exist because human habits and laziness tend to seize the first correct answer. Users who are habituated to these realities many will simply shrug, unable to imagine an alternative to Google's dominance.[71] The supply chain of ideas demands network sovereignty for users to behave, legally or otherwise.

Networking protocols and the hardware that carry them are supremely politicized technology because they represent national and economic relationships through the twenty-first century's most precious commodity, data. The European Union's 2016 General Data Protection Regulation (GDPR) represents perhaps the clearest and farthest reaching defense of "natural persons" rights to access to information as well as privacy.[72] While the GDPR is wide ranging enough to shape corporate behavior globally—since it is simply easier to comply with the most stringent regulation rather than a patchwork of online services meeting each jurisdiction—the EU's regulations signal another step in the further segmentation of the internet. Because the data we generate is at once a corporate resource as well as a national security exploit, individual users will experience varying degrees of strain from these forces. Signal intelligence has merged with corporate interests under surveillance capitalism, which means that the logic of corporate competition governs the access granted to governments rather than the legal regimes imposed by legislators. The US Defense Intelligence Agency admitted in January 2021 that they purchase real-time location data from data broker firms that includes the locations of US citizens.[73] Free markets have allowed for the privatization of spying and the evasion of traditional restrictions on the intelligence communities within domestic markets as well as internationally. Corporations are all too willing to propose a solution that only exacerbates the problem: Starlink will loosen authoritarian control over information and expose human rights violations in otherwise firewalled regions or underdeveloped regions.[74] Starlink also allows for a US-based corporation to be compelled by a FISA court order to deliver real-time location data of its users. The militarization of space may come as a result of the need for authoritarian regimes need to control information rather than Reagan-era "Star Wars" programs.

The activist networks constructed through hashtags help connect ideas, but ideas are transmitted by physical infrastructure and monitored by surveillance capitalist social media platforms. The physical location of large Content Delivery Networks (CDNs) is a material symptom of the twin pull of population and corporate power, which disconnects all but the global urban elite. Marisa Duarte's *Network Sovereignty: Building the Internet Across Indian Country* does an excellent job of aligning the politics of North American Indigenous self-governance and land rights with the connections found in the #idlenomore hashtag and the scarcity of internet access on traditional territories.[75] In rural Indigenous reserve territories, the expression of power associated with population centers and political power are aligned. Sovereignty for Indigenous peoples goes hand in hand with access and control of information networks. The supposed deterritorialized internet, this placeless cloud of information, is reframed in the context of Indigenous land-title and the colonizing effects of an "information overload."[76] The political networks derived from technological networks may not be as progressive or liberating as those promoting a hashtag may claim. After all, the presumption of the open access to information is a colonial impulse for Indigenous communities interested in digitizing cultural records while preserving the cultural protocols that dictate who has access. Prominent DH projects like Mukurtu CMS are described as a "safe keeping place" manage and share digital cultural heritage, with robust tooling to control access.[77] There is a social life of the tools and technologies that produce knowledge through story.[78] Networked knowledge—which emerges from the collection, commingling, and conflict of ideas online—must also include the technical ability to make these networks function as a source of true liberation, free from the influence of platforms or ISPs.

The internet is not a simple commodity to be manufactured and sold because it exists only by virtue of our participation in it. Arjun Appadurai describes the spirit of commodities as a distinct object, which might help inform this shift in perspective. Appadurai describes these "ideoscapes" through the relationship between technologies and the production of knowledge, even when understood as a commodity. In Appadurai's words, "The production knowledge that is read into a commodity is quite different from the consumption knowledge that is read from the commodity."[79] Which is to say, the knowledge needed to use a commodity and read content on the internet is very different than the knowledge needed to build independent networks. If a non-hierarchical network that promotes diversity and inclusion is possible online, it will only be built by a diversity of individuals with the technical ability to both manage complex networks and promote a vision of justice and equity. The supply chain of ideas requires a critical mass of citizens to develop and maintain independent knowledge networks, free from influence and manipulation, as bulwark for national and community sovereignty.

Don't Worry, We're from the Internet

There is an intrinsic connection between open knowledge networks and democracy that is amplified by the networked access to ideas online. The democratization of technology is necessary for the revolutionary potential of networked knowledge. Manifestations of political protest must be built on sovereign networks, as free as possible from governmental or corporate influence. As networking technologies are increasingly accessible to non-specialists, it is possible for distributed versions of the web to exist independent of large ISPs, CDNs, and social media platforms. The necessity of encrypted communications that are both secure as well as distributed will be part of a large-scale social or political movement. These communications may need to avoid social media platforms due to surveillance concerns or avoid national censorship. The most suitable way to create this space imagined by this hacker ethos is for regular citizens to build new networks themselves. Hackers are often associated with the so-called "Deep Web," which is merely a name for the majority of data on the web that is not indexed by search providers. Great swaths of the deep web are simply data bases and large CDNs that service front end or user facing content. The so-called "Dark Web" represents that portion of the web that deliberately limits access, usually through a client or browser designed to provide anonymity online.[80] Networks like Tor, Freenet, I2P, ZeroNet, and Riffle all use different techniques to help ensure anonymity online, though these systems are not perfect.[81] Tor, which stands for The Onion Router, redirects web traffic through a global secondary network of volunteer onion servers, which masks the identity and location of the user making requests through encrypted gateways.[82] Tor has demonstrated that it is vulnerable to tracing by highly motivated individuals or institutions, which has resulted in the Riffle project to improve the anonymity achieved by further shuffling traffic through the relay servers.[83] Freenet and I2P (Invisible Internet Project) are peer-to-peer systems that allow for individuals to share encrypted content. Peer-to-peer content sharing has always struggled with discoverability and remains relatively niche and less tested as a result.[84] Whichever tool or system is used, there remains a cultural problem with anonymity preserving technologies. The usual logic goes something like this: "Why would I need to be anonymous online? I'm not doing anything wrong, so why would I care who sees my activity? Aren't these systems for people selling drugs, guns, or child pornography? Why would anyone want to be associated with human trafficking by using this?" In a lot of cases this is certainly true, which is strange given that Tor has been developed in large part by the US government.

It is tempting to presume that these projects represent elaborate brand of law-enforcement by guiding the development of private networks. By designing the systems criminals use online, it becomes easier to monitor, limit, disrupt, and surveil illegal behavior online. After all, people will always try to use the internet to commit crimes or use it to aid them in doing so. Perhaps law-enforcement agencies, which the FBI has admitted, has an interest in designing and monitoring these systems to limit the worst of these bad actors online.[85] Most would expect that the worst crimes carried out on the internet would be investigated by national level cybersecurity agencies, resourced well enough with tooling, exploits, and vulnerabilities that may be reserved for international espionage. While it is likely not the case that domestic law-enforcement would use valuable and expensive zero-day exploits reserved for nation-state level hacking, most people would support the use of these resources in the case of child exploitation, human trafficking, or domestic terrorism.[86]

The largely invisible quality of crimes committed on the dark web means that it remains largely within the purview of law enforcement to define and identify these threats. Cory Doctorow dramatizes this problem in *Radicalized*, in which he describes the logical progress of a domestic terrorist seeking violent retribution against the insurance companies that blocked coverage for his daughter dying of cancer:

> LisasDad1990 had used Tor Browser extensively and had left behind no browser breadcrumbs, nor any records at AT&T's data centers. Inevitably, this set off a whole witch hunt over the "darkweb" and everyone wondering where the mystery man from the video had been "radicalized."[87]

The logic of a terrorist is framed through the suffering of a white male at the hands of brutal capitalistic processes shared by a huge swath of the American people. The failure of the US system to provide healthcare rights to its citizens is an appropriate corollary for the failure of the United States to protect citizens in Iraq and Afghanistan. The predatory corporate culture of the insurance industry is similar enough to understand the hostility of American corporations around the world, whether it is through sweatshop labor conditions for clothing manufacturers, clear cutting the Amazonian rainforest to produce burger patties, or strip mining the Angolan mountains for diamonds.

The shared grievances of individuals harmed by American-style capitalism are the motivating factor for radicalizing desperate individuals to commit acts of violence. In this shared experience, Doctorow builds a bridge between an everyday American tragedy and the global poor exploited under the simple pretext of US power, influence, and wealth. Within this global frame, it is the dark web that sets the conditions for individual radicalization:

> In an earlier age, they'd have stewed in private misery, become alcoholics, shot themselves. Instead, they'd followed the simple online instructions for starting a message board and hosting it on a bulletproof server accessible only via the Tor network. They hadn't detonated bombs or gone on a shooting spree—they hadn't even egged on the people who had. But they'd provided a place for it all to happen, had watched it all happen, and hadn't shut it down. That was enough.[88]

Networks *are* political. Who is connected to who? What information is accessible? What is the speed of the connection? Who is able to monitor network traffic? These questions define the politics of the network. The way we connect computers makes certain assumptions about the values of the users, developers, and service providers who work there. The dark web assumes illegality in the actions of the users. It assumes fringe beliefs of the users. It assumes complicity and indirect benefits from the service providers and developers of these anonymous systems.

Yet today's World Wide Web also contains a politics and an ethos that is as ethically dubious as anything described. Returning now to Berners-Lee's vision for the web, the web is a web of people, as he explains so beautifully in *Weaving the Web*:

> The Web is more a social creation than a technical one. I designed it for a social effect—to help people work together—and not as a technical toy. The ultimate goal of the Web is to support and improve our weblike existence in the world. We clump into families, associations, and companies. We develop trust across the miles and distrust around the corner. What we believe, endorse, agree with, and depend on is representable and, increasingly, represented on the Web. We all have to ensure that the society we build with the Web is of the sort we intend.[89]

When he invented the web at CERN as a way for physicists to share research data, he could not fully anticipate the relationship between how the technical protocol of the web would manifest human cultures and societies, some of which would be violent, exploitative, and manipulative. A system designed to expand research capacity and connecting subject area specialists was open sourced to the general population in the spirit of open access to research. Far from a neutral connection rich with imaginative potential, centralized networks are about inclusion, access, and surveillance the moment they are created.

Networks require specific software to access but still exist on the basic web technology stack. Implementations TCP/IP and HTTP when broadly deployed can result in "perma-bugs" that are rarely if ever resolved by vendors.[90] It is possible to imagine an internet without HTTP at the heart of network traffic. An interplanetary network is a concrete engineering challenge facing space agencies today.[91] The expansion of human technology into the interstellar or interplanetary scale may well lead to a human centered knowledge network capable of solving today's problems. The InterPlanetary File System (IPFS) represents a potential alternative that embraces a capacious vision for humanity beyond existing as subjects of surveillance or as mere consumers. IPFS is an internet of internets that is capable of functioning at great distances—where the speed of light limits data transfer speeds—because it seeks to forward and store information. In the same way that Gibson's interstellar exploring AI will transmit itself to a new star system, IPFS transmits data to the desired location and stores it for rapid local retrieval. On Earth, IPFS would work a little like El Paquete, but it would mesh with existing HTTP traffic and allow for users to serve content they have used in a peer-to-peer network that radically decentralizes information. IPFS offers a model of cultural exchange past national-level firewalls like the one in China.[92] A citizen might carry a laptop containing news sites, cached on the user's browser, and bypass censorship controls. Perhaps a citizen returning to the Chinese mainland visited digital humanities research projects and delivered historical content otherwise unavailable. Perhaps greater cultural understanding and compassion can grow by traveling with a personal internet deployed automatically. One-way HTTP requests mean that information disappears when a link dies or a server goes off-line. Brewster Kahle's *Internet Archive* is an attempt to save content on the web, but it also represents a single point of potential censorship and control. Perhaps, given the scale of governmental and corporate interference in the HTTP infrastructure, it is time to augment our existing networking protocol beyond only those imagined by Ted Nelson and Tim Berners-Lee so long ago.

In sum, this networking technique is implements two preexisting and unrelated technologies: IPFS combines version control technology like Git and blockchain cryptography like that used with Bitcoin.[93] Git is a version control tool developed by Linus Torvalds in developing the Linux kernel. It is a standard tool for software development that tracks changes and merges contributions from large teams of programmers. Because Git allows for updating content, merging updates, and rolling back versions, it is the ideal framework for a network of internets that will require forwarding streams of data to be seamlessly merged with a local internet. Git also tracks these changes with a unique cryptographic hash that allows for character specific changes in data, which makes manipulation, forgery, or censorship much more difficult. It means that this is an internet that resists manipulation in the supply chain by default. This new model of "content addressing" allows for encrypted communications without a centralized certificate issuing authority for SSL or TLS. Because IPFS is transport layer agnostic, it can set up a peer-to-peer network over TCP, TOR, or even Bluetooth.[94] The ability to merge updates and roll back versions of code bases is useful for software development, but it is also an absolute memory for the development and evolution of ideas when applied to knowledge networks.

This network is hosted by users and servers in a peer-to-peer relationship, which means that it is not solely dependent on a centralized server architecture. If a user requests a web page or some data, it is sent and stored on that users computer and later relayed to the next user. The complexity of this addressing for content on IPFS is solved with blockchain, which serves as a unique identifier for content in the address bar. IPFS also uses blockchain cryptography, like that used in cryptocurrencies, to create a public ledger of content as a means of reporting censorship. Many users will store and share this public ledger of content, so it can be validated and approved by the users rather than large ISPs or government. In its current form, IPFS will be a complement to HTTP for the foreseeable future.[95] For now, IPFS is a parallel subsystem of the internet that offers a censorship resistant, horizontal mesh network capable of carrying humanity's cultural legacy into the stars. It effectively offloads centralized hosting to a swarm of users in a flattened peer-to-peer network, though it is possible to still host centrally using public key cryptography to allow for developers to manage and update content. Looking to the stars might offer the best possible future for networks here on Earth. Users become active nodes on the web rather passive recipients of content, which means the collective cultural memory of the web is shared by everyone with a connection.

Notes

1   See https://opensource.org/osd.

2   See https://www.gnu.org/philosophy/free-sw.html.

3   See https://www.gnu.org/philosophy/open-source-misses-the-point.html

4   There are many licenses to choose from that embrace a "copyleft" approach to sharing intellectual property. See https://choosealicense.com/.

5   National Institute of Standards and Technology, "Framework for Improving Critical Infrastructure Cybersecurity," *Nist.gov* (report), April 16, 2018, https://doi.org/10.6028/NIST.CSWP.04162018; National Cyber Security Centre, "The cyber threat to UK business 2017–2018 report," *Ncsc.gov.uk* (report), April 10, 2018, https://www.ncsc.gov.uk/information/the-cyber-threat-to-uk-business-2017-2018-report.

6   Ninety-nine percent of enterprise codebases contain open source code according to Synopsys' 2020 Open Source Security and Risk Analysis Report. See "2020 Open Source Security and Risk Analysis Report," *Synopsys*, May 2020, https://www.ttpsc.com/wp3/wp-content/uploads/2020/10/2020-ossra-report.pdf; Gene Kim and Stephan Magill, "2019 Software Supply Chain Report: Improving Outcomes with DevSecOps and Automation," *Sonatype*, June 25, 2019, https://www.sonatype.com/resources/white-paper-state-of-software-supply-chain-report–2019.

7   Nikolai Tschacher, "Typosquatting Programming Language Package Managers," *Incolumitas.com*, June 8, 2016, https://incolumitas.com/2016/06/08/typosquatting-package-managers/; Ohm M., Plate H., Sykosch A., and Meier M. "Backstabber's Knife Collection: A Review of Open Source Software Supply Chain Attacks," in *Detection of Intrusions and*

Malware, and Vulnerability Assessment. DIMVA 2020, Lecture Notes in Computer Science, eds. Maurice C., Bilge L., Stringhini G., and Neves N., vol 12223, https://doi-org.proxy.library.brocku.ca/10.1007/978-3-030-52683-2_2; Alex Birsan, "Dependency Confusion: How I Hacked into Apple, Microsoft and Dozens of Other Companies," *Medium.com*, February 9, 2021, https://medium.com/@alex.birsan/dependency-confusion-4a5d60fec610.

8 Respectively, https://www.npmjs.com/, https://pypi.org/, and https://rubygems.org/.

9 Dan Goodin, "Supply-Chain Attack Hits RubyGems Repository with 725 Malicious Packages," *Arstechnica.com*, April 17, 2020, https://arstechnica.com/information-technology/2020/04/725-bitcoin-stealing-apps-snuck-into-ruby-repository/; Dan Goodin, "How a College Student Tricked 17k Coders into Running His Sketchy Script," *Arstechnica.com*, April 14, 2016, https://arstechnica.com/information-technology/2016/06/college-student-schools-govs-and-mils-on-perils-of-arbitrary-code-execution/; Dan Goodin, "Widely Used Open Source Software Contained Bitcoin-Stealing Backdoor," *Arstechnica.com*, November 16, 2018, https://arstechnica.com/information-technology/2018/11/hacker-backdoors-widely-used-open-source-software-to-steal-bitcoin/; Dan Goodin, "The Year-Long Rash of Supply Chain Attacks Against Open Source Is Getting Worse," *Arstechnica.com*, August 21, 2019, https://arstechnica.com/information-technology/2019/08/the-year-long-rash-of-supply-chain-attacks-against-open-source-is-getting-worse/.

10 Dan Goodin, "Two New Supply-Chain Attacks Come to Light in Less Than a Week," *Arstechnica.com*, October 23, 2018, https://arstechnica.com/information-technology/2018/10/two-new-supply-chain-attacks-come-to-light-in-less-than-a-week/; Jonathan Hartley and Arnon Yaari, "Colorama," *Pypi.org, version 0.4.4,* https://pypi.org/project/colorama/.

11 The National Vulnerability Database (NVD), which is maintained by the US National Institute of Standards and Technology (NIST), describes Common Vulnerabilities and Exposures (CVE) with a rating system out of ten. A particular supply chain vulnerability might be described through other CWEs, including common injection techniques that might allow an otherwise https://nvd.nist.gov/vuln/detail/CVE-2020-7699. Mitre attack framework maintains a list of the top 25 most dangerous software weaknesses, which includes CWE-79 for cross-site scripting than links to several types of code injection on web pages: https://cwe.mitre.org/data/definitions/79.html.

12 Justin Hutchings, "Code Scanning Is Now Available!," *Github.com* (blog), September 30, 2020, https://github.blog/2020-09-30-code-scanning-is-now-available/.

13 Jordan Wright, "Hunting Malicious npm Packages," *Duo.com* (Decipher Blog), August 8, 2017, https://duo.com/decipher/hunting-malicious-npm-packages.

14 Kristen Senz, "The Hidden Benefit of Giving Back to Open Source Software," *Hbswk.hbs.edu*, September 5, 2018, https://hbswk.hbs.edu/item/the-hidden-benefit-of-giving-back-to-open-source-software.

15 The well-known Magecart category of attack simply skims keystrokes, such as payment information or login credentials. Because open source development is performed by volunteers, these software ecosystems are vulnerable to typo-squatting or non-friendly contributors. Typo-squatting involves naming a malicious package similarly to popular, reputable software to load malicious code. Scott Matteson, "Magecart Attack: What It Is, How It Works, and How to Prevent It," *Techrepublic.com*, June 13, 2019, https://www.techrepublic.com/article/magecart-attack-what-it-is-how-it-works-and-how-to-prevent-it/; Catalin Cimpanu, "Advertising Network Compromised to Deliver Credit Card Stealing Code," *Zdnet.com*, January 16, 2019, https://www.zdnet.com/article/advertising-network-compromised-to-deliver-credit-card-stealing-code/.

16 $10,000 would be a very good deal. Average ransomware payouts were between $36,000 and $41,000, but the damage to your user confidence, public credibility, downtime, and direct data loss can be much greater. See Gutman Yotam, "The True Cost of Ransomware Attacks: 6 Factors to Consider," *Sentinelone Blog*, January 8, 2020, https://www.sentinelone.com/blog/what-is-the-true-cost-of-a-ransomware-attack-6-factors-to-consider/.

17 Alan Sokal, "Revelation: A Physicist Experiments with Cultural Studies," in *The Sokal Hoax: The Sham That Shook the Academy*, ed. By the editors of *Lingua Franca* (Lincoln: University of Nebraska Press, 2000): 49–54.

18 Helen Pluckrose and James A. Lindsay and Peter Boghossian, "Academic Grievance Studies and the Corruption of Scholarship," *Aeromagazine.com*, February 10, 2018, https://areomagazine.com/2018/10/02/academic-grievance-studies-and-the-corruption-of-scholarship/.

19 Bari Weiss, "Meet the Renegades of the Intellectual Dark Web," *New York Times*, May 18, 2018, https://web.archive.org/web/20200131000213/https://www.nytimes.com/2018/05/08/opinion/intellectual-dark-web.html.

20 Ibid.

21 Katitza Rodriguez, Kurt Opsahl, Nate Cardozo, Jamie Williams, Ramiro Ugarte, and Tamir Israel, "Protecting Security Researchers' Rights in the Americas," *Eff.org* (report), October 16, 2018, https://www.eff.org/coders-rights-americas.

22 Ross Douthat, "Oh, the Humanities!," *Nytimes.com*, August 8, 2018, https://www.nytimes.com/2018/08/08/opinion/oh-the-humanities.html; Alexandra Petri, "Oh, the Humanities!," *Washingtonpost.com*, June 26, 2013, https://www.washingtonpost.com/blogs/compost/wp/2013/06/26/oh-the-humanities/; Rochelle Gurstein, "Oh, the Humanities!," *Newrepublic.com*, March 26, 2010, https://newrepublic.com/article/73915/oh-the-humanities.

23 The sciences have done a better job deflecting public scorn by embracing some of the strange avenues of exploration needed in foundational research. The so-called Ig Noble Prize is an annual award, of sorts, granted to some of the absurdities of science research. The prize is organized by the magazine *Annals of Improbable Research*. The ceremony is co-sponsored by the Harvard-Radcliffe Society of Physics Students and the Harvard-Radcliffe Science Fiction Association. The organizers explain their rationale in the following way: "We are honoring achievements that make people laugh, then think. Good achievements can also be odd, funny, and even absurd;

So can bad achievements. A lot of good science gets attacked because of its absurdity. A lot of bad science gets revered despite its absurdity." Of course, the same could be said of the humanities as well. See https://www. improbable.com/ig-about/.

24 Cyrus Farivar, *The Internet of Elsewhere: The Emergent Effects of a Wired World* (New Brunswick: Rutgers University Press, 2011), 4.

25 China manages access and influence through the so-called "Great Firewall" by blocking individual sites or encrypted traffic that might block domestic surveillance efforts: see Catalin Cimpanu, "China Is Now Blocking All Encrypted HTTPS Traffic That Uses TLS 1.3 and ESNI," *Zdnet.com*, August 8, 2020, https://www.zdnet.com/article/china-is-now-blocking-all-encrypted-https-traffic-using-tls-1-3-and-esni/ and John Leyden, "Cat and Mouse: Privacy Advocates Fight Back after China Tightens Surveillance Controls," *Portswigger.net*, August 11, 2020, https://portswigger.net/daily-swig/cat-and-mouse-privacy-advocates-fight-back-after-china-tightens-surveillance-controls; China has used both government and nongovernment aligned hackers to disrupt American technology firms: see Sean Lyngaas, "Justice Department Official Accuses China of Acting as 'safe haven' for Cybercriminals," *Cyberscoop.com*, October 21, 2020, https://www.cyberscoop.com/china-cyber-espionage-criminal-justice-department/; China also seeks to exercise regional power through cyber operations: see Sean Lyngaas, "Taiwan Accuses Chinese Hackers of Aggressive Attacks on Government Agencies," *Cyberscoop.com*, August 19, 2020, https://www.cyberscoop.com/taiwan-china-hacking-apt40/; China has gone so far as to hold national competitions to hack prominent applications and operating systems to flex it's growing prowess in this field: see Catalin Cimpanu, "Windows 10, iOS, Chrome, and Many Others Fall at China's Top Hacking Contest," *Zdnet.com*, November 8, 2020, https://www.zdnet.com/article/windows-10-ios-chrome-and-many-others-fall-at-chinas-top-hacking-contest/.

26 Christopher Balding and Donald C. Clarke, "Who Owns Huawei?," *Social Science Research Network* (April 17, 2019). Available at SSRN: https://ssrn.com/abstract=3372669 or http://dx.doi.org/10.2139/ssrn.3372669; Bethany Allen-Ebrahimian and Zach Dorfman, "Defense Department Produces List of Chinese Military-linked Companies," *Axios.com*, June 24, 2020, https://www.axios.com/defense-department-chinese-military-linked-companies-856b9315-48d2-4aec-b932-97b8f29a4d40.html; Huawei, "Does Huawei Have Ties to the Communist Party of China (CPC)?," *Huawei.com*, blog post, https://www.huawei.com/en/facts/question-answer/does-huawei-have-ties-to-the-cpc.

27 Catalin Cimpanu, "FBI Re-sends Alert about Supply Chain Attacks for the Third Time in Three Months," *Zdnet.com*, March 31, 2020, https://www.zdnet.com/article/fbi-re-sends-alert-about-supply-chain-attacks-for-the-third-time-in-three-months/; Catalin Cimpanu, "FBI Warns About Ongoing Attacks against Software Supply Chain Companies," *Zdnet.com*, February 10, 2020, https://www.zdnet.com/article/fbi-warns-about-ongoing-attacks-against-software-supply-chain-companies/; Sean Lyngaas, "Commerce Department Proposes Rules for Implementing Trump's Supply-chain Security Order,"

Cyberscoop.com, November 26, 2019, https://www.cyberscoop.com/supply-chain-security-commerce-department/.

28   National Intelligence Law of the People's Republic, June 27, 2017, http://www.npc.gov.cn/npc/xinwen/2017-06/27/content_2024529.htm; H.R. McMaster, "How China Sees the World: And How We Should See China," *Theatlantic.com*, May, 2020, https://www.theatlantic.com/magazine/archive/2020/05/mcmaster-china-strategy/609088/.

29   Catalin Cimpanu, "MICROCHIPS Act Wants to Secure US Govt Supply Chain against Chinese Sabotage," *Zdnet.com*, July 31, 2019, https://www.zdnet.com/article/microchips-act-wants-to-secure-us-govt-supply-chain-against-chinese-sabotage/. Defensive encryption schemes are now being proposed to counter the vulnerabilities that may emerge in the 5G roll out. Paul Schmitt and Barath Raghavan have proposed "Pretty Good Phone Privacy" to ensure privacy protecting connectivity. See https://www.usenix.org/system/files/sec21-schmitt.pdf.

30   Brian Krebs, "Chinese Antivirus Firm Was Part of APT41 'Supply Chain' Attack," *Krebsonsecurity.com*, September 17, 2020, https://krebsonsecurity.com/2020/09/chinese-antivirus-firm-was-part-of-apt41-supply-chain-attack/.

31   Ted Nelson, Computer Lib/Dream Machines (self-pub., 1974), available at *Archive.org*, https://archive.org/details/computer-lib-dream-machines/.

32   Ibid., 60, 48.

33   See https://xanadu.com/.

34   Nelson, *Computer Lib*, 118.

35   The Internet Engineering Task Force (IETF) maintains an archive of the founding protocol documents relating to the early web, which can be found here: IETF, "RFC 768," *Tools.ietf.org*, August 28, 1980, https://tools.ietf.org/html/rfc768.

36   Jonathon Ramsey, "Tesla Full Self-Driving to Move to Subscription Model This Year, Semi delayed," *Autoblog.com*, April 30, 2020, https://www.autoblog.com/2020/04/30/tesla-full-self-driving-subscription-semi-update/; Alistair Charlton, "BMW Wants to Charge You a Subscription for Your Heated Seats," *Forbes.com*, July 2, 2020, https://www.forbes.com/sites/alistaircharlton/2020/07/02/bmw-wants-to-charge-you-a-subscription-for-your-heated-seats/.

37   Peter L. Shillingsburg, *From Gutenberg to Google: Electronic Representations of Literary Texts* (Cambridge: Cambridge University Press, 2006), 163.

38   Mark Twain, "From the 'London Times' of 1904," in *The Man That Corrupted Hadleyburg and Other Stories* (Project Gutenberg, 2018), available at https://www.gutenberg.org/files/3251/3251-h/3251-h.htm#link2H_4_0009.

39   Ibid.

40   I am thinking of Frantz Fanon's *Black Skin, White Masks* description of the white gaze that fixes bodies as something other. In Fanon's time, this stare would work in person or through photography. He describes the experience in the following way: "I arrive slowly in the world; sudden emergences are no longer my habit. I crawl along. The white gaze, the only valid one, is

already dissecting me. I am fixed. Once their microtomes are sharpened, the Whites objectively cut sections of my reality." See Frantz Fanon, *Black Skin, White Masks* (New York: Grove Press, 2008), 95.

41 William Gibson, "Burning Chrome," in *Hackers*, eds. Jack Dann and Gardner Dozois (New York: Ace, 1996), 1–23.

42 The hacker for hire narrative has absolutely become a reality over time, like with the recent case of an India-based group that openly advertised its services. See John Scott-Railton, Adam Hulcoop, Bahr Abdul Razzak, Bill Marczak, Siena Anstis, and Ron Deibert, "Dark Basin Uncovering a Massive Hack-For-Hire Operation," *Citizenlab.com*, June 9, 2020, https://citizenlab. ca/2020/06/dark-basin-uncovering-a-massive-hack-for-hire-operation/.

43 David Easley and Jon Kleinberg, *Networks, Crowds, and Markets: Reasoning About a Highly Connected World* (Cambridge: Cambridge University Press, 2010), available in preprint https://www.cs.cornell.edu/home/kleinber/ networks-book/.

44 Dani Cavallaro, *Cyberpunk and Cyberculture: Science Fiction and the Work of William Gibson* (London: The Athlone Press, 2000); William S. Haney II, *Cyberculture, Cyborgs and Science Fiction: Consciousness and the Posthuman* (New York: Rodopi, 2006).

45 Samuel Delany, *Silent Interviews: On Language, Race, Sex, Science Fiction and Some Comics* (Hanover: Wesleyan University Press, 1994), 76.

46 Jesse Sheidlower, *Historical Dictionary of Science Fiction*, https:// sfdictionary.com.

47 William Gibson, *Neuromancer* (New York: Ace Books, 1984), 56.

48 Facebook is building a "metaverse" through a blend of VR/AR technologies. They explain in press release entitled, "Building the Metaverse Responsibly" the ethical responsibilities they face: "The 'metaverse' is a set of virtual spaces where you can create and explore with other people who aren't in the same physical space as you." See https://about.fb.com/news/2021/09/ building-the-metaverse-responsibly/.

49 William D. Bryant, "Cyberspace Superiority: A Conceptual Model," *Air & Space Power Journal* 27, no. 6 (November–December 2013): 25–44, available at https://apps.dtic.mil/dtic/tr/fulltext/u2/a589636.pdf.

50 Gibson, *Neuromancer*, 270.

51 Submarine Cable Map 2020, *Telegeography.com*, https://submarine-cable-map-2020.telegeography.com/.

52 Ibid.

53 Maeve Shearlaw, "Facebook Lures Africa with Free Internet-but What Is the Hidden Cost?" *The Guardian*, August 1, 2016, https://www.theguardian. com/world/2016/aug/01/facebook-free-basics-internet-africa-mark-zuckerberg; Daniel van Boom, "Why India Subbed Facebook's Free Internet Offer," *Cnet*, February 26, 2016, https://www.cnet.com/news/why-india-doesnt-want-free-basics/.

54 Both Russia and the United States are engaged in these tactics to disrupt undersea cables: Michael Birnbaum, "Russian Submarines Are Prowling around Vital Undersea Cables. It's Making NATO Nervous," *Washingtonpost. com*, December 22, 2017, https://www.washingtonpost.com/world/europe/ russian-submarines-are-prowling-around-vital-undersea-cables-its-making- nato-nervous/2017/12/22/d4c1f3da-e5d0-11e7-927a-e72eac1e73b6_story. html; Caleb Larson, "Intelligence Coup: How One U.S. Nuclear Submarine Tapped Russian Undersea Cables," *Nationalinterest.com*, May 30, 2020, https://nationalinterest.org/blog/buzz/intelligence-coup-how-one-us-nuclear- submarine-tapped-russian-undersea-cables-159086.

55 Matt Reynolds, "Facebook and Google's Race to Connect the World Is Heating Up," *Wired.com.uk*, July 26, 2018, https://www.wired.co.uk/article/ google-project-loon-balloon-facebook-aquila-internet-africa.

56 See https://www.starlink.com/; Nilay Patel, "Starlink Review: Broadband Dreams Fall to Earth," *The Verge*, May 14, 2021, https://www.theverge. com/22435030/starlink-satellite-internet-spacex-review.

57 Walter Jon Williams, *Hardwired* (New York: Tor Books, 1986); Walter Jon Williams, *Voice of the Whirlwind* (New York: Tor Books, 1987); Walter Jon Williams, *Solip: System* (Eugene: Axolotl Press, 1989).

58 Jean-François Lyotard, *The Postmodern Condition: A Report on Knowledge*. Trans. Geoff Bennington and Brian Massumi (Minneapolis: University of Minnesota Press, 1984), 6.

59 "Internet Society statement on Internet blocking measures in Catalonia, Spain," *Internetsociety.org*, September 21, 2017, https://www. internetsociety.org/news/statements/2017/internet-society-statement- internet-blocking-measures-catalonia-spain/.

60 Sonia Osorio, "Maduro Forces Come Down Hard on Media in Venezuela That Reports on Juan Guaidó," *Miamiherald.com,* January 31, 2019, https:// www.miamiherald.com/news/nation-world/world/americas/venezuela/ article225342795.html.

61 Mark Buell, "Quebec to Require ISPs to Block Websites," *Internetsociety. org*, July 13, 2016, https://www.internetsociety.org/blog/2016/07/quebec-to- require-isps-to-block-websites/.

62 Alexis C. Madrigal, "The Inside Story of How Facebook Responded to Tunisian Hacks," *Theatlantic.com*, January 24, 2011, https://www.theatlantic. com/technology/archive/2011/01/the-inside-story-of-how-facebook- responded-to-tunisian-hacks/70044/.

63 Erik Hunstad, "Domain Fronting Is Dead, Long Live Domain Fronting Using TLS 1.3," DEF CON 2020 Safe Mode, August 5, 2020, https://www.youtube. com/watch?v=TDg092qe50g.

64 See http://paquetedecuba.com/.

65 Ernesto Oroza, "El Paquete Semanal & Marakka 2000," in *The Pirate Book*, eds. Nicolas Maigret and Maria Roszkowska (Aksioma Institute for Contemporary Art: Ljubljana, 2015), 139–67. Available at http://thepiratebook. net/.

66 Ibid., 149.

67 Nicolas Jackson, "United Nations Declares Internet Access a Basic Human Right," *Theatlantic.com*, June 3, 2011, https://www.theatlantic.com/

technology/archive/2011/06/united-nations-declares-internet-access-a-basic-human-right/239911/.

68   Organization for Security and Co-operation in Europe, "Access to Information: A Universal and Human Right! #AccessToInfoDay," *Osce.org*, September 26, 2016, https://www.osce.org/representative-on-freedom-of-media/267746.

69   Tim Wu, "Network Neutrality, Broadband Discrimination," *Journal of Telecommunications and High Technology Law* 2 (2003): 141, available at https://scholarship.law.columbia.edu/faculty_scholarship/1281.

70   Tim Wu sums up the evolution of net neutrality on his personal site. See http://www.timwu.org/network_neutrality.html.

71   See https://duckduckgo.com.

72   See https://gdpr.eu/.

73   Chris Mills Rodrigo, "Intelligence Agency Gathers US Smartphone Location Data without Warrants, Memo says," *The Hill*, January 22, 2021, https://thehill.com/policy/national-security/535441-intelligence-agency-gathers-us-smartphone-location-data-without; Mitchell Clark, "US Defense Intelligence Agency Admits to Buying Citizens' Location Data," *The Verge*, January 22, 2021, https://www.theverge.com/2021/1/22/22244848/us-intelligence-memo-admits-buying-smartphone-location-data.

74   Kate Duffy, "Russia May Fine Citizens for Using SpaceX's Starlink Internet. Here's How the Internet Service Poses a Threat to Authoritarian Regimes," *Business Insider*, February 4, 2021, https://www.businessinsider.com/russia-may-fine-citizens-spacex-starlink-internet-authoritarian-regime-2021–1.

75   Marisa Elena Duarte, *Network Sovereignty: Building the Internet Across Indian Country* (Seattle: University of Washington Press, 2017).

76   James Gleick, *The Information: A History, a Theory, a Flood* (New York: Pantheon Books, 2011), 403.

77   See https://mukurtu.org/.

78   As Tyson Yunkaporta explains in *Sand Talk: How Indigenous Thinking Can Save the World* (New York: HarperOne, 2020), "Stories are also called yarns, but 'yarning' as a verb is a different process altogether." He goes on to explain, "Yarning is more than just a story or conversation in Aboriginal culture—it is a structured cultural activity that is recognized even in research circles as a valid and rigorous methodology for knowledge production, inquiry, and transmission" (114).

79   Arjun Appadurai, "Introduction: Commodities and the Politics of Value," *The Social Life of Things: Commodities in Cultural Perspective*, ed. Arjun Appadurai (Cambridge: Cambridge University Press, 1986), 41.

80   Geert Lovink, *Dark Fiber: Tracking Critical Internet Culture* (Cambridge: MIT Press, 2002).

81   Aditya Tiwari, "TOR Anonymity: Things Not to Do while Using TOR," *Fossbytes.com*, September 14, 2020, https://fossbytes.com/tor-anonymity-things-not-using-tor/.

82 Yasha Levine, "Almost Everyone Involved in Developing Tor Was (or is) Funded by the US Government," *Pando.com*, July 16, 2014, https://pando.com/2014/07/16/tor-spooks/.

83 Sean Gallagher, "Law Enforcement Seized Tor Nodes and May Have Run Some of Its Own," *Arstechnica.com*, November 10, 2014, https://arstechnica.com/information-technology/2014/11/law-enforcement-seized-tor-nodes-and-may-have-run-some-of-its-own/; Albert Kwon, David Lazar, Srinivas Devadas, and Bryan Ford, "Riffle: An Efficient Communication System with Strong Anonymity," *Proceedings on Privacy Enhancing Technologies 2016*; 2016 (2):1–20: https://doi.org/10.1515/popets-2016-0008.

84 Sean Gallagher, "Under the Hood of I2P, the Tor Alternative That Reloaded Silk Road," *Arstechncia.com*, January 13, 2015, https://arstechnica.com/information-technology/2015/01/under-the-hood-of-i2p-the-tor-alternative-that-reloaded-silk-road/.

85 Dan Froomkin, "FBI Director Claims Tor and the 'Dark Web' Won't Let Criminals Hide from His Agents," *Theintercept.com*, September 10, 2015, https://theintercept.com/2015/09/10/comey-asserts-tors-dark-web-longer-dark-fbi/.

86 A zero-day or 0-day is an unreported software vulnerability and a working exploit. When a vulnerability is discovered or is being actively exploited, the organization tasked with patching the code starts counting from zero until the vulnerability is corrected. Kim Zetter, "Hacker Lexicon: What Is a Zero Day?," *Wired.com*, November 11, 2014, https://www.wired.com/2014/11/what-is-a-zero-day/.

87 Cory Doctorow, *Radicalized* (New York: Tor Books, 2019), 206.

88 Ibid., 226.

89 Tim Berners-Lee, *Weaving the Web: The Original Design and Ultimate Destiny for the World Wide Web* (New York: HarperCollins, 1999), 123.

90 Ionut Ilascu, "List of Ripple20 Vulnerability Advisories, Patches, and Updates," *Beepingcomputer.com*, June 25, 2020, https://www.bleepingcomputer.com/news/security/list-of-ripple20-vulnerability-advisories-patches-and-updates/; Center for Internet Security, "Multiple Vulnerabilities in Treck TCP/IP Stack Could Allow for Remote Code Execution," *Cisecurity.org*, June 18, 2020, https://www.cisecurity.org/advisory/multiple-vulnerabilities-in-treck-tcpip-stack-could-allow-for-remote-code-execution_2020-083/.

91 Joab Jackson, "The Interplanetary Internet NASA Researchers Quarrel over How to Network Outer Space," *Spectrum.ieee.org*, August 1, 2005, https://spectrum.ieee.org/telecom/internet/the-interplanetary-internet.

92 Daniel Kuhn, "InterPlanetary File System Is Uncensorable during Coronavirus News Fog," *Coindesk.com*, March 18, 2020, https://www.coindesk.com/interplanetary-file-system-is-uncensorable-during-coronavirus-news-fog.

93 Kyle Drake, "HTTP is obsolete. It's Time for the Distributed, Permanent Web," *Ipfs.io*, September 8, 2015, https://ipfs.io/ipfs/QmNhFJjGcMPqpuYfxL62VVB9528NXqDNMFXiqN5bgFYiZ1/its-time-for-the-permanent-web.html.

94 ConsenSys, "Decentralized Storage: The Backbone of the Third Web," *Consensys* (blog post), June 30, 2016, https://media.consensys.net/decentralized-storage-the-backbone-of-the-third-web-d4bc54e79700.

95 Drake, "HTTP Is Obsolete."

4

Cryptographic Agility and the Right to Privacy:

Secret Writing and the Cypherpunks

In 1890, Samuel Warren and Louis Brandeis published "The Right to Privacy" in the *Harvard Law Review*.[1] It has influenced privacy law in the United States, which is remarkable given the relatively short length of the essay and the date of publication. It has still proven to be resilient in the face of technological change over the years. The basic assertion of the human right to privacy as "the right to be let alone" is about more than just keeping secrets.[2] The right to privacy emerges directly from the "right to life" and the freedom from unlawful physical battery or restraint. Liberty includes the right to enjoy life and to hold property in tangible and intangible ways. Simply enough, tangible privacy relates to the security of a private residence. Intangible private property includes the "products and processes of the mind" and other conscious products of mental labor; privacy asserts "the right to one's personality" against the world in which individuals are responsible for their "own acts and omissions."[3]

As remarkably simple as these words are in the face of government and corporate surveillance, the threshold for violating personal privacy remains largely up for debate. When we leave our private residence, our privacy extends only as far as our human body. The technology that extends our daily life is not granted inherent protections. The protections afforded to content often do not apply to user metadata, which can be as telling about a person's actions and intentions. It has been argued that privacy law is "too complicated" for the vast majority of people to negotiate the mesh of proprietary software, privacy focused marketing jargon, and legal frameworks.[4] We must secure our technology if we value the data it contains.

Our private information is also a commodity that can be traded for other kinds of value. Individuals might trade their privacy for a complete email service, like so many do with Google Gmail. We might trade our location data to Google Maps for the peace of mind in knowing that we will never be lost. We might trade our deepest insecurities and fears in the questions we ask Google Search. Our privacy has value to corporations and grants them incredible power, but the power is not gained from a single data point or a single person's search history, unless that single person is incredibly powerful themselves. When collecting behavioral data on the general populace, privacy has value when it is hoarded. The scale of this massive exchange of personal value for technical products is likely impossible to measure, but we do know that Gmail has more than 1.5 billion active monthly users globally.[5] The Android mobile operating system has more than 2 billion active users by a recent announcement.[6] A significant portion of the global human population are exchanging their privacy for a mobile operating system. Let that sink in. The value proposition offered by mobile computing and communication is obvious to anyone reading this with their phone nearby, but the effects of the loss of privacy at this scale are less clear. It may be impossible to adequately assess the cultural consequences of not being "let alone."

It is clear that personal privacy is critical for the proper functioning of democracy. There is a subtle and important relationship between the right to be let alone and the ability to be a well informed and active citizen. Sarah Igo, in *The Known Citizen*, describes how citizenship requires individuals to pass between private and public realms, while retaining their autonomy and ability to make choices.[7] The most fundamental choice a citizen makes in a democracy is the choice placed on a ballot, but these autonomous choices extend into freedom of movement, freedom of association, as well as freedom of speech. Free access to information is less certain today, when choice is government by algorithmic models of our behavior alongside the behavior of literally billions of other people. Without the ability to privately discuss and learn about the issues that matter to them and the way they live their lives, no citizen will be capable of fulfilling their duty of casting an informed ballot free from influence.

There are several examples of this kind of influence at work in the United States. In 2012, Facebook data scientists and a team of academics published a paper in *Nature* claiming that the social media company now possessed the ability to swing voter turnout by as much as 0.6 percent, more than enough to decide tight races in the United States.[8] By creating an easy way for users to tell their friends that they voted, Facebook is able to encourage users to the polls with peer pressure. Facebook claims that this "voter megaphone" tool is no longer being used on small populations for research purposes and is now shown to nearly all users. Of course, there is no partisan modeling that can account for these effects, given that not all US citizens are using Facebook. By some estimates, as many as 81 percent of US adults have a Facebook account, while 71 percent of US adults are active users.[9] The regional and state-based usage data are variable, which suggests unanticipated effects of Facebook's voter megaphone tool. Still, there are no effective oversights of Facebook that would allow voting regulators access to data to understand if Facebook could swing an election.[10] It is certainly plausible that, by sharing the voter megaphone tool with only conservatives or progressives in key areas, Facebook could manipulate an election at scale. Of course, users who do not have a Facebook account would also not be included in this influence mechanism, which further distorts the demographics of the election. These prompts seeking to manipulate the "acts or omissions" of a citizen on election day are also added to any manipulation of the news sources. The information provided by Facebook during elections has become so influential that Facebook is now banning political ads that might delegitimatize elections or promote conspiracy theories.[11]

An ill-informed or misinformed citizenry will be increasingly prone to voting for irrational policies, including those that negatively affect the voters themselves. Malka Older's *Infomocracy*, the first of the Centenal Cycle of novels published in 2016, is a nuanced reflection on big data and global democracy. *Infomocracy* imagines a global system of "micro-democracy" in which a global election map of "centenals" elect regional leaders who vote in turn for a global government.[12] The novels describe a global experiment to re-imagine democracy by balancing local concerns with the need for global coordination. The system Older describes is made possible by a global network of "Information" hubs that vet and approve content on the internet for veracity and durability. Information workers moderate content on the network that shape every aspect of life, including economic transactions, political advertising and reporting, communications, and transportation. Older's vision for a logically moderated internet sounds remarkably familiar, albeit more regulated than today's social-media companies. Regions that do not participate are known as *Null States,* which is also the title of the second novel in the series published in 2018.[13] Enforcing global participation in these systems has disastrous consequences for the citizens living in under-served jurisdictions. Older's post-cyberpunk world is neither strictly dystopian nor Utopian. Global micro-democracy promises long periods of world peace with a single "supermajority" party rule, but Older also questions the legitimacy of elections predicated on a single large clearinghouse of information used by a global citizenry to cast a ballot.[14] Back in our world, the Big Five technology companies now serve as a real version of Information hubs, but the current real world "Information" brokers are self-regulating.[15] While Facebook might wrap itself in the trappings of government, with its "Director of Governance and Global Affairs" Brent Harris, developing an "Oversight Board" to lend credibility to what remains an unregulated media corporation.[16] Nick Clegg, VP Global Affairs and Communications at Facebook, puts an optimistic glow on how Facebook's "charter is a critical step towards what we hope will become a model for our industry."[17] Older describes a world where information monopolies are complex bureaucracies that are susceptible to manipulation and control, both internally and externally.[18]

The twentieth-century vision of democracy, wherein individuals make choices based on their own opinion, can be described by socially constructed forces that shape education standards, editorial policy, and media consumption habits. The influence of information on voter opinion is engineered because the scale of the data to be edited and moderated is simply too large. There is a fundamental tension between free speech and moderation that has not been answered by social-media companies. The general failure to fact check and block misinformation from President Trump is a historic failure in evidence of this.[19] The work of the humanities must also balance a fundamental tension between openness, transparency, and access to research and ideas, while also fighting for individual privacy and security. Privacy of this kind allows for a security of the mind and personality to make choices. When choice is circumvented or obviated in politics, the ability to think critically is being undermined. Critique must now be balanced with a "professional paranoia" regarding our access to information and the tracking of research activities online.[20] The oversight of the academic class may one day be used to develop lists of potential political dissidents, without regard to their public statements or published research.

The lack of privacy granted to users online also means that viewing history serves to entrench political opinions in citizens as well as academic researchers, who are certainly not immune to such manipulation. The work of cultural observers in the twenty-first century is difficult to balance because of the tensions related to our increasingly individualized media diet or "filter bubbles" as well as the split between our online and physical identities.[21] This logic means that a right to free speech might actually just silence all but the most vocal. US-based technology companies export an extremist view of freedom of speech in the First Amendment that assumes all speech should be protected speech that is both public and heard. We can hear this ideology in the then CEO of Google, Eric Schmidt, in saying, "If you have something that you don't want anyone to know, maybe you shouldn't be doing it in the first place."[22] This implicit corporate policy encourages users to self-censor and assist corporations in their moderation efforts by threatening public embarrassment. The chill placed on debate has the effect of hollowing out the sensible middle and leaving room for the extreme opinions of those who do not fear, or even invite, social media backlash. There is no room for mistakes, change, and growth. It is a strange logic that casts the desire for privacy as a marker of some moral or ethical failure because privacy allows for reflection and growth. In her essay "Cryptographic imaginaries and the networked public," Sarah Myers West puts it this way:

> The idea that cryptography is an occult practice reflects the idea, as persistent at the time as it is today, that secrecy is a mark of poor moral character. The sociologist Georg Simmel rejected this notion, saying that "secrecy is a universal sociological form, which, as such, has nothing to do with the moral valuations of its contents." (2018, 462)[23]

Myers West's turn to Simmel is an interesting bookend to the twentieth century, which starts in the World Wars and ends in the rapid expansion of online communication. Simmel's contention that "secrecy is not in immediate interdependence with evil, but evil with secrecy" accurately describes the false equivalency of secret writing and moral failures.[24] Between the extremes of absolute privacy and total openness resides a balance that must be claimed by sound political policy in the twenty-first century as well as citizens themselves.

Political activism that resists the system of disinformation and control proffered by large technology companies, particularly social media companies, means that encryption is among the most important political questions of the twenty-first century. If privacy is to be secured, it will be secured with strong encryption. The graffitied imperative, "Use Signal" is a simple symptom of privacy policy in tatters. A general awareness is rising in the necessity for end-to-end (E2E)-encrypted communications, which should ensure that messages are only readable by the sender and the receiver. While E2E encryption is not a panacea for corporate or governmental surveillance, broader policy questions must seek to defend strong encryption, even as governments work hard to muddy issues for voters with warnings about terrorism, child exploitation, and organized crime as arguments for eroding encryption laws. As governments in the Five Eyes, most notably Australia's "Assistance and Access" bill and the "EARN IT Act" in the United States, have sought to test public awareness of privacy rights, strong encryption is at risk of being undermined in the name of public safety.[25] Citizens must work to grasp increasingly complex technical issues to better guide and inform democratically elected representatives, who may also lack the necessary understanding of these issues and legislate from nebulous fears of terrorists, pornographers, or hackers. Simply because you can solve crimes with surveillance systems like facial recognition does not mean that privacy is synonymous with criminality. Similarly, strong encryption in no way limits traditional policing and enforcement, and it is a bad faith argument to suggest that total surveillance of a population is necessary to enforce the law. Liberal democracies may well define themselves in opposition to authoritative regimes and illiberal pseudo-democracies in the twenty-first century through their ability to embrace strong encryption and privacy for their citizens.

A citizenry capable of defending and demanding privacy in public and online will be a hardened attack surface for hostile governments, domestic terrorists, and corporations. The ability to authenticate individual access to networks, provide privacy over those networks from manipulation, and guarantee security to individual and organizational data all rely on strong encryption. Authoritarian regimes who tightly control internet access and approve app platforms will unwittingly grant their adversaries a single point of failure by attempting to surveil their own citizens.[26] China has used WeChat as government sanctioned infrastructure for nearly every aspect of life online, including daily cash transactions, travel, and communications.[27] The ability to function in China without WeChat is nearly impossible, due to the government's desire to control the internet through what President Xi Jinping's calls "public scrutiny."[28] The desire for absolute control through ubiquitous digital infrastructure of this kind embeds a weak culture of privacy. The ability to manage and maintain state and individual sovereignty will depend greatly upon an appreciation of the ability for a general understanding of cryptography and encryption across a broad technological ecosystem that includes networking encryption as well as application-level security.

Tales from the Crypt

Cryptography is the theory and practice of securing data. Sometimes that data needs to be secured by authenticating people or software with privileged access. Encryption is the process of rendering a message inscrutable to all but the intended recipient. To decipher or decrypt a message, without authorization, is a process of cryptanalysis. Cryptology encompasses both the study of building better cryptographic systems as well as testing these systems through cryptanalysis.[29] There is a connection between securing stored data at rest through an encryption process as well as the need to authenticate the use of that data in transit to resist tampering with it. This definition confirms what many already know because it is so readily a part of our everyday lives. Yet usability or ease of use dictates that cryptography is largely hidden from view. While we use it every time we surf the web or read an email, there is something mysterious about cryptography. Cryptography is the science of hidden or secret writing. The crypt implies something dark, underground, and even associated with death. Wendy Hui Kyong Chun describes this enigmatic code "sourcery" in *Software Studies*.[30] An encrypted message is placed in suspension until the right antidote can be administered, making it sensible and able to speak again. It is not surprising that the history of cryptography often associated with the occult.

Cryptography is not about the good word. Cryptography has always sought privacy, which intentionally excludes some people or entities. Encryption is designed to exclude and reject those users with under-privileged access rights. Good encryption is about building a discriminating system. Limiting access might seem like a strange mandate for humanity seeking greater cooperation, understanding, and equality; this dark science of hidden secrets and exclusive privacy is a remarkably common trope within the cyberpunk genre that now reflects on a twenty-first-century media environment. The dark, gothic quality of many cyberpunk novels relates to the secrets— secrets of some dangerous or life threatening importance—that are bound up in cryptography. The cypherpunks imagined a libertarian future free from surveillance. The cypherpunks have been great manifesto writers, having anticipated surveillance capitalism in its broad strokes as yearly as the 1990s. Timothy May, founder of the so-called "cypherpunks" cryptography group in 1992 opens his manifesto firmly within this gothic vein: "A specter is haunting the modern world, the specter of crypto anarchy."[31] explains the role of cryptography to cyberpunk:

> Computer technology is on the verge of providing the ability for individuals and groups to communicate and interact with each other in a totally anonymous manner. Two persons may exchange messages, conduct business, and negotiate electronic contracts without ever knowing the True Name, or legal identity, of the other. Interactions over networks will be untraceable, via extensive re-routing of encrypted packets and tamper-proof boxes which implement cryptographic protocols with nearly perfect assurance against any tampering.[32]

True Names, *Shockwave Rider*, *Snow Crash*, and *Neuromancer* are all recommended by May as the core of cypherpunk lore. Perhaps it is surprising that cypherpunk manifestos reflect the reality we now possess online. There are a few standards to know: The old Secure Sockets Layer (SSL) has now been completely replaced by Transport Layer Security (TLS), although the terms are sometimes used interchangeably. The vast majority of network traffic is encrypted with SSL/TLS, led in no small part by the Let's Encrypt initiative created by the Internet Security Research Group.[33] Taher A. Elgamal and Paul Kocher are the co-inventors of the standard that now supports E2E on the web.³⁴ The HTTPS protocols are now so common that most users know to look for the little lock in the browser. Google Chrome and Mozilla Firefox both warn users if a site is not encrypted. Since 2013, TLS is likely the most used cryptographic system and remains secure due to the work of largely invisible cryptography and security researchers who continue to test and refine the standard.³⁵ Tools like The Onion Router or Tor have allowed for "extensive re-routing of encrypted packets." We are living in the cypherpunk future imagined in the 1990s, but the state of cryptography has evolved to new uses and attempts to undermine current standards.

Cryptography now includes implementations of the block chain in cryptocurrencies like Bitcoin as well as uses in version control and the IPFS standard discussed previously. Strong encryption ensures that these new technologies are developed and help protect free and open societies. However, there remains a cultural normalization of personal secrets and privacy part of life in a lawful society. In many ways, the desire to keep secrets is nothing new. In 1993, Eric Hughes's "A Cypherpunk's Manifesto" explains, with all the heady techno-optimism of the 1990s,

> We must defend our own privacy if we expect to have any. We must come together and create systems which allow anonymous transactions to take place. People have been defending their own privacy for centuries with whispers, darkness, envelopes, closed doors, secret handshakes, and couriers. The technologies of the past did not allow for strong privacy, but electronic technologies do.³⁶

Cypherpunks like May and Hughes were techno-libertarians describing seemingly esoteric political policy questions wrapped in the ravings of a cyberpunk prophets. Steven Levy described the experience of reading May's manifesto "almost like dropping acid."³⁷ Levy reports a manifesto co-authored by May and Hughes, which is worthy of repetition here:

> Just as the technology of printing altered and reduced the power of medieval guilds and the social power structure, so too will cryptologic methods fundamentally alter the nature of corporations and of government interference in economic transactions. Combined with emerging information markets, crypto anarchy will create a liquid market for any and all material which can be put into words and pictures. And just as a seemingly minor invention like barbed wire made possible the fencing-off of vast ranches and farms, thus altering the concepts of land and property rights in the frontier West, so too will the seemingly minor discovery out of an arcane branch

of mathematics come to be the wire clippers which dismantle
the barbed wire around intellectual property.
Arise, world; you have nothing to lose but your barbed-
wire fences![38]

Cyberpunk's typical anti-governmental paranoia takes a stand in defending the right to access strong cryptography. There is a historical quality to these manifestos that acknowledges that something was changing. Encryption has been used for thousands of years as secrets kept under hushed whispers or subtle gestures, but the internet changed what it meant to keep a secret. A secret held consciously, or even unconsciously, can be reliably stored within our memories. Secure in our thoughts, secrets can die with us or be shared to with those we trust. It is a little different online.

There are two ways to think about the problem of encryption: first, how do we encrypt *data in transit*, being streamed around the web? And, second, how do we encrypt *data storage* stationary hard drive? TLS encryption does a great job encrypting most web traffic with a centralized certificate authority, ensuring trust between the user and the server. Encrypting files at rest requires processes and systems to ensure the security of infrastructure handling cryptographic systems as well as the security of key material. While the physical key and lock metaphor only goes so far with encryption, it remains true that any process of encryption requires some method of substitution that obfuscates the original message, rendering it unreadable to anyone but the intended recipient. A simple substitution cipher will map letters to numbers or other letters of the alphabet. The goal is to encrypt *plaintext* as *ciphertext*.

When encrypting a message, any exposed clue can be used to crack the encryption. It is little wonder that Edgar Allen Poe would find fascination with occult quality of cryptography. In his famous short essay on ciphers, "A Few Words on Secret Writing" published in 1841, he surmises that the very intention of a culture of letters and writing in general would have emerged alongside an invention of cryptography: "Similar means of secret intercommunication must have existed almost contemporaneously with the invention of letters."[39] The previous year, Poe petitioned readers of the *Alexander's Weekly Messenger* in Philadelphia to create ciphers that he would decrypt.[40] These ciphers were readily decryptable due to letter frequency in English, which is nearly uniform, with e, t, a, o, i, n, s, r occurring most commonly in most texts. Poe was so confident in his abilities in cryptanalysis, he claimed that "human ingenuity cannot concoct a cipher which human ingenuity cannot resolve."[41] In subsequent issues of *Alexander's Weekly Messenger*, his readership put him to the test by submitting their ciphertext for him to decrypt for the next week's publication.

The fascination with cryptography led Poe to write a canonical short story in the American gothic tradition, *The Gold-Bug*, published in 1843. The story follows William Legrand, his black servant Jupiter, and Poe's unnamed narrator on an adventure into the swamps of South Carolina in search for treasure. The racist depiction of Jupiter as a naive and unintelligent assistant to Legrand and the narrator's brilliance exposes the prejudices of the time, particularly because of the story's popularity. The prejudices of the narrative are significant because cryptography and secret writing have always been about discriminating between sense and non-sense. The binaries of blackness and whiteness are cast as a logical affirmation of *characters being put in their right place*. The logical analysis of ciphertext into plaintext becomes an analogy of white supremacy. Those granted the facilities of cryptanalysis have the privileged access to good and proper understanding.

The story is well known in cryptography circles and helped expose generations of cryptographers to ciphers. Poe includes a substitution cipher at the heart of the story that demonstrates a logical method used to crack ciphers, like those submitted to him at *Alexander's Weekly Messenger*. By understanding the most frequent letters used in English, it is possible break the following cipher by simply counting and correlating letter frequencies. Here is perhaps the most famous literary cipher in the English tradition:

```
53‡‡†305))6*;4826)4‡.)4‡);80
6*;48†8¶60))85;1‡(;:‡*8†83(88)
5*†;46(;88*96*?;8)*‡(;485);5*†
2:*‡(;4956*2(5*-4)8¶8*;40692
85);)6†8)4‡‡;1(‡9;48081;8:8‡1
;48†85;4)485†528806*81(‡9;48
;(88;4(‡?34;48)4‡;161;:188;‡?42;
```

The most common letters in most modern English texts are commonly as follows: ['e', 'o', 't', 'h', 'a', 's', 'i', 'n', 'r', 'd', 'l', 'u', 'y', 'm', 'w', 'f', 'g', 'c', 'b', 'p', 'k', 'v', 'j', 'q', 'x', 'z']. The letter frequency in Poe's story is slightly different, which is a result of the stylistic preferences of the time, the short length of the work, as well as Poe's own authorial style: ['e', 't', 'a', 'o', 'i', 'n', 's', 'h', 'r', 'd', 'l', 'u', 'c', 'm', 'f', 'w', 'p', 'y', 'g', 'b', 'v', 'k', 'x', 'j', 'q', 'z', 'æ']. The process of logically deducing a cipher from most frequent letters and most frequent words—such as "the," which contains three of the most common letters in one of the most common words in English—is an excellent example of Poe's "tales of ratiocination."[43]

For Poe, the strict logical unfolding of a narrative, this *ratiocination*, produced a "unity of effect and impression" that produced an affirming aesthetic of strict causality. That reassuring cause and effect relationship is even capable of pointing to some deeper truth.[44] Ratiocination narratives conclude neatly in the logical solution to a problem. Within this style of writing for which there is hardly a precedent, Poe logically breaks the cipher as a means of finding the treasure:

> A good glass in the bishop's hostel in the devil's seat
> forty-one degrees and thirteen minutes northeast and by north
> main branch seventh limb east side
> shoot from the left eye of the death's-head
> a bee line from the tree through the shot fifty feet out.[45]

The message describes the method for discovering the treasure by sitting in a window seat in an old manor house, "the bishop's hostel." By looking through a telescope, "a good glass," in the described direction, the viewer would discover a skull, "the death's-head," through which an object dropped through its left eye would indicate the location of the treasure. The narrator's logic and mental prowess is cast in stark contrast the hapless interlocutor, Jupiter. Cryptography becomes a theater of discrimination to prove racial mental fitness through cryptanalysis. The nineteenth-century racist power relationships are performed by Jupiter and his inability to work out the secret message, which is reserved for the more deserving, intelligent, and white Legrand. In its proximity to cryptography, power relations are exposed by those who can read secret writing and those who cannot. In this way, the narrative history of cryptography begins in a parable about controlling and codifying exclusion and inclusion. Those capable of cryptanalysis are rewarded with hidden knowledge, and those who cannot are have their agency reduced through political power and social position.

The Enemy Knows the System

The first hack represented in literature goes all the way to Homer. *The Iliad* culminates with a military strategy predicated on hacking the expectations of the Trojans and preying on their pride and arrogance. The first malware Trojan was a wooden horse, an analog hack on a walled city state. In antiquity passwords were used to pass city walls. Aeneas Tacitus, the fourth-century Greek military strategist is credited with one of the earliest accounts of secret military communications. He describes, in *How to Survive Under Siege*, how sentries should admit individuals in possession of a secret passphrase. Aeneas Tacitus also gives a thorough accounting of over twenty ways to smuggle secret communications past sentries, including as a tattoo on the head of a slave (whose hair has been allowed to grow back), within the sandal leather of an unwitting traveler, or even within thinly rolled lead earrings of traveling merchant women. In the passage labeled, "Of Secret Messages," Aeneas suggests, "The sentry at the gates must keep a sharp lookout for such things as I have described, to see that nothing, whether arms or letters, enters the city unobserved."[46] These ancient descriptions are surprising curiosities today, but there remain valuable lessons from Aeneas Tacitus: In war time, words are weapons, and secret communications are dangerous to citizens and soldiers alike. Keeping secrets retains a dual significance: secrets are at once treasonous and seditious, while also in service to the state. The extraordinary lengths taken to keep secrets serve as evidence that a desire for secrecy is criminal or excludes membership within a community.

Secret words have long been used to divine those who belong and those who do not. Biblical precedents help frame the ways that oral secret communications define friend and enemy. In the Book of Judges (12:6), the Gileadites used the word "shibboleth" as an oral identifier to target and kill the Ephraimites. The apparent inability of the Ephraimites to pronounce the "shi" phoneme appropriately identified friend from enemy.[47] These community passports mark foreignness by the ability to pronounce words according to local custom. Imagine traveling to a neighboring city to trade goods in exchange for your crops. You are stopped just as you crest a hill, and your bushels of rye are inspected by soldiers guarding the road. They casually ask you to describe the quality of your shibboleth, otherwise known as the head of the stalk containing the grain. Unable to mask your accent, you expose yourself as an enemy of the city. Your crops are confiscated and you find yourself imprisoned or worse.

This history is with us still in an oddly banal way. Today, the Shibboleth Consortium develops a free and open source Single Sign On (SSO) system.[48] These online shibboleths define those who are granted access to organizational systems. Authentication is a critical piece of online infrastructure that grants access to systems. There is no access to the public square without this authentication. It grants privileges and rights online that have very real political and economic consequences for users. Those who have access to valuable online systems are more likely to be employed, educated, or wealthy, while lacking access to online systems for education, employment, or governmental services is symptomatic of broader disenfranchisement. Those without access to authentic status also lack access to economic, social, and immigration status that is implicitly tested through such measures. To be undocumented is increasingly measured through shibboleth as well as passports. Those who have lawful right to enter a country will also have lawful right to work. Their work, and by extension their immigration status, will grant access to certain technologies, even those as mundane as Microsoft Office 365.

Cryptography is about intentionally building keeping out undesirables. Encrypting communications is about excluding undesirable individuals. It is about defining power through trust. Trust is granted through shared systems of that community, and those systems are capable of revoking access.

Access to documents convey access to status, whether they are a travel visa or research materials. Protecting documents against unapproved copying or destruction defends the authorities that use them. There are any number of schemes that are possible to encipher a document, but the secret knowledge needed to keep the secret should not be the algorithm itself. Claude Shannon, the famous US mathematician and cryptographer, set a higher standard for keeping a secret. Even if the details of the cryptographic algorithm are known, the system should remain secure provided a strong cryptographic key can remain secret. Also known as Kerchkhoff's principle, Shannon begins with a professional paranoia that assumes "the enemy knows the system being used."[49] With this sense of pessimism, it is assumed that the algorithm used to encrypt the information is already known by the attacker, but a difficult to guess secret key is capable of keeping a message secure. For this reason, Shannon disregards the notion that security can be achieved with obscurity. If an unwanted recipient guessed the encryption scheme or had direct access to this process, they would only need to try many keys, otherwise known as a "brute force" solution.[50]

The ability to decrypt a message requires some secret knowledge, which should be shared between only the desired communicants. It is possible to instead use a key phrase to encrypt a message. If the key phrase is sufficiently long—if the key phrase is as long as the message sent and is used only once—a simple symmetric key cipher is unbreakable with a classical computer. This style of encryption is also known as a *one-time pad* (OTP), which was the cryptographic standard set by Shannon during the War. Provided the key is selected with a sufficient level of randomness and is as long as the plaintext message, OTP ciphers are unbreakable without exotic quantum computers that have yet to be built.[51] If the key is never reused or leaked in any way, this remains the safest way to transmit a message and was regularly used in the Second World War and even into the Cold War period.[52] If secret knowledge remains secret and is never reused, OTP is an encryption mechanism that can remain analogue and resist contemporary cryptanalysis. Implementations of standard symmetric key encryption like Advanced Encryption Standard (AES)[53] and SNOW 3G[54] are theoretically capable of resisting massive computing resources projected by quantum computing, but old analogue techniques remain remarkably resilient against modern crytpanalysis.[55]

It is possible to add additional complexity by performing different mathematical operations or increasing the complexity of our transposition through a key phrase to increase the potential values for each character. Factoring large prime number, a task that is difficult for current computers, has been the bedrock of developing these difficult to guess cryptographic keys for decades now. Over that time the cryptographic community has developed a culture that emerges from cryptographic procedures and best practices. In many ways, cryptanalysis is a speculative science that must intuit the techniques and assumptions of the cryptographer. It requires an analyst to inhabit the shoes of those encrypting a message. What tools did they have? How motivated are they to protect secrets? What ideas and methods would they have been taught, given their educational, cultural, and national context? Are there any cultural hints or clues that might signal intent or process? There is an intersectional relationship between these assumptions that requires imaginative leaps of technical and cultural secret knowledge.

If security cannot be achieved through obscurity and the enemy knows the system, perhaps transparency and openness will allow for more secure encryption tools. Eric Raymond's *The Cathedral and the Bazaar* puts it like this: "given enough eyeballs, all bugs are shallow."[56] Cryptography advocates share the same curiosity as the Free and Open Source Software (FOSS) community. It is possible to chart this culture to Phil Zimmermann and the publication of PGP (Pretty Good Encryption). The publication of PGP 1.0, published in 1991, marked the first public release of a cryptographic program capable of signing, encrypting, and decrypting messages or data in storage. It was intended to be a complete privacy tool for most citizens. In practice, PGP has been difficult to adopt and implement for all but the most motivated users. When Zimmermann first introduced the system, he imagined a world where users would physically share key information to verify signatures. As the web took hold, he pivoted to a "web of trust" that would allow users to share public keys online and promote a decentralized certificate authorities. The networking of Public Key Infrastructure was ahead of its time, but the mixture of symmetric keys as well as the recipient's public key layers protections that results, in Bruce Shneier's estimation, "PGP is the closest you're likely to get to military-grade encryption."[57] This assessment is important given the context of its release. As Levy reports, Zimmermann was racing to release PGP 1.0 ahead of then US Senator Joseph Biden, who was then serving as the head of the Senate Judiciary Committee and cosponsoring an antiterrorism bill, Senate Bill 266.[58] Biden added the following language to the bill that captured the attention of the cypherpunks, who saw all of their worst fears manifest in these words:

> It is the sense of Congress that providers of electronic
> communications services and manufacturers of electronic
> communications service equipment shall ensure that

communications systems permit the government to obtain the
plaintext contents of voice, data, and other communications
when appropriately authorized by law.[59]

Zimmermann released the first version of PGP and Biden was forced to
withdraw the clause due to the public outrage at the explicitly antiprivacy
language of the bill.[60] Zimmermann replaced his "Bass-O-Matic" cipher
with a Swiss cipher developed by James Massey and Xuejia Lai called the
International Data Encryption Algorithm (IDEA), and remains an optional
algorithm in the OpenPGP standard, which is implemented most commonly
in GPG (GNU Privacy Guard).[61] IDEA is vulnerable with weak keys, but it is
still available for the GPG distribution for "historical interest" and research
purposes.[62] All these acronyms read like alphabet soup after a while.
Cryptography is hard. Knowing exactly why any given algorithm is vulnerable
to attack is the domain of subject area experts. Even those who work with
cryptography in a professional capacity and consider themselves experts get
it wrong. The open source model allows users to benefit from the collective
paranoia of cryptographers.

The authors of the Python package Cryptography caution users when
building their own systems, even when using well tested and publicly vetted
implementations of cryptographic standards: "You should ONLY use it if you're
100% absolutely sure that you know what you're doing because this module
is full of land mines, dragons, and dinosaurs with laser guns."[63] There are few
end user agreements with such clarity. The accurate description of risk is an
important aspect of selecting an encryption scheme that balances efficiency,
speed, and security. Assuming that the enemy knows the algorithm used to
encrypt your messages or data, a transparent open source approach allows
all users to better understand their defensive posture by benefiting from the
experience and mistakes of the community.

Today, it is possible for anyone to use strong encryption, such as the AES,
developed by the US National Institute of Standards and Technology.[64] AES
is the standard encryption used in the US government communications. The
Python community has had several excellent hashing and encryption libraries
to choose from over the years, but the Cryptography package (cryptography.
io) currently is among the best documented and easy to use:

The availability of this encryption technology is, in some ways, more
important than the ability to encrypt any single file or message. It is important
to celebrate access to strong encryption as evidence of a strong democracy
that is confident and able to trust those with secrets because of a larger sense
of social cohesion. Put simply, a lack of access to high-quality cryptographic
standards is evidence of a slide into authoritarianism. The web of trust required
to allow these systems in the public is also evidence of a government that

○ ○ ○

```python
import base64
import logging
import os
from cryptography.exceptions import InvalidTag
from cryptography.hazmat.primitives.ciphers.aead import AESGCM

# set up logger
logging.basicConfig(level=logging.INFO)
logger = logging.getLogger(__name__)


def demonstrate_string_encryption_key_based(plain_text):
    """
    Example for encryption and decryption of a string in one method.
    - Random key generation using OS random mode
    - AES-256 authenticated encryption using GCM
    - BASE64 encoding as representation for the byte-arrays
    - UTF-8 encoding of Strings
    - Exception handling
    """
    try:
        # GENERATE key
        key = AESGCM.generate_key(bit_length=256)

        # GENERATE random nonce (number used once)
        nonce = os.urandom(12)

        # ENCRYPTION
        aesgcm = AESGCM(key)
        cipher_text_bytes = aesgcm.encrypt(
            nonce=nonce,
            data=plain_text.encode('utf-8'),
            associated_data=None
        )

        # CONVERSION of raw bytes to BASE64 representation
        cipher_text = base64.urlsafe_b64encode(cipher_text_bytes)

        # DECRYPTION
        decrypted_cipher_text_bytes = aesgcm.decrypt(
            nonce=nonce,
            data=base64.urlsafe_b64decode(cipher_text),
            associated_data=None
        )

        decrypted_cipher_text = decrypted_cipher_text_bytes.decode('utf-8')

        logger.info("Decrypted and original plain text are the same: %s",
                    decrypted_cipher_text == plain_text)
    except InvalidTag:
        logger.exception("Symmetric string encryption failed")


if __name__ == '__main__':
    # demonstrate method
    demonstrate_string_encryption_key_based(
        "Text that is going to be sent over an insecure channel and must be "
        "encrypted at all costs!")
```

FIGURE 4.1 *An example implementation of AES encryption in Python using the Cryptography Python package. Despite its use by the US military, there is no need to call it "military-grade encryption"*[65]

does not fear its people and the secrets they keep. The usability of strong encryption by the general population is evidence of a class of scientists and technologists interested in free speech. With that said, if you find yourself typing "AES" while programming your web application, you are likely doing something wrong. It is important to rely on well tested and broadly used systems. While Python's Cryptography package is currently among the best documented and easy to use, with a keen attention to infrastructure security to mitigate supply-chain attacks, this status can and maybe should change over time.

In FOSS development, software packages are not eternal. They change and evolve rapidly, which can serve to enhance the security of the overall environment. The mode of secret communications being developed and normalized in society is as significant as the ease of implementation. While AES encryption on its own is not a complete cryptographic tool for the exchange of information, because messages can still be tampered with without a signing mechanism like with GPG or Cryptography's Fernet, it remains remarkable that developers can even implement and use a standard like this. Because we live in a state of near constant surveillance, it is appropriate to assume a siege mentality when protecting personal data or sensitive research materials. The lessons from Aeneas Tacitus might help inspire a cryptographic resistance to national or corporate intrusion, but they also remind us that keeping secrets is a very old and constantly changing discipline. The answer may be a broad public awareness and interest in encryption tools and technologies, like the kind that Poe was able to provoke in the nineteenth century. The ability of cypherpunks to inspire a generation to learn about cryptography, platforms, and the laws that govern them will produce a longer lasting security than anything a single cipher, algorithm, or platform can produce. Security may well be a question of cultural literacy and the ability to capture the imaginations, maybe even the paranoia, of regular citizens in an ongoing way.

Happy Birthday

The need to change cryptographic tools is often referred to as "cryptographic agility" and describes the ability for an institution, platform, or system to move to a new cryptographic system if old system should break. Cryptographic agility will be increasingly important for journalists and academics alike, to remain autonomous and secure particularly while working internationally. Cryptographic agility acknowledges that all encryption processes are crackable; therefore any large system or institution dependent on a particular encryption technology must be ready to rapidly move to a different technology as cryptanalysis advances. The ability to use various encryption techniques will be important for activists and persecuted persons living in repressive political and social climates. The 2013 disclosure by Edward Snowden of NSA surveillance techniques reshaped foreign policy, public perception, and corporate approaches to encryption. The Snowden leaks resulted in a flood of sensationalism, much of it well founded, regarding the scale and scope of US government cooperation with corporate partners like Google, Yahoo, Microsoft, Facebook, Amazon, and Apple, which brought many of these ideas into the public eye for the first time. The public awareness of the PRISM program and the power of ISPs and digital platforms to surveil consumers drove corporations to save face and embrace E2E-encrypted technologies.

The importance of encrypted communications has been steadily rising for many years, but the public awareness of E2E has grown precipitously since 2015. As recently as May 12, 2019, the Israeli Cybersecurity firm NSO Group was exposed by the CIA for selling a WhatsApp exploit capable of unrestricted access to smartphone data and sensors.[66] Though the full list of NSO's clients remains unknown, the CIA announced that Saudi Arabia purchased the exploit to attack political agitators and journalists within the Kingdom.[67] The tragic death of Jamal Khashoggi was the most notable use of the tool to circumvent E2E services.[68] There have been deaths of Mexican journalists linked to NSO's products as well.[69] There is a troubling extension of cyberattacks into traditional military attacks, and the murder of Khashoggi and other journalists are perhaps the most visible extension of this trend. The Israeli Defense Force, for example, bombed and destroyed Hamas' cyber unit for attacks on Israeli government digital infrastructure. This event was reported as crossing the "cyber rubicon" as the first use of "kinetic" weapons used as a direct military response to a cyberattack.[70] Hamas responded days later by hijacking the live television broadcast of the Eurovision competition in Tel Aviv with images of Israeli bombings.[71] The situation in Israel is an early and particularly transparent example of the future of cyberwarfare blending with traditional armed conflict.

It is necessary then to embrace strong encryption and be suspicious of companies with less stringent track records. Shannon's maxim is also a warning against weak encryption. Weak encryption is worse than no encryption at all because the sender and receiver presume privacy where none exists. The assumption of privacy can result in disclosures of information, which would never have been communicated if knowledge of their compromised status was clear. Closed source E2E-encrypted services may provoke greater liability because this assumption of privacy and release of metadata associated with using a corporately owned platform. An assumption of secrecy may only serve to breed a habit of divulging information that would otherwise not be shared. There is a tragic irony for those who lose their privacy and befall a great catastrophe when an unintended audience learns their secrets.

A hallmark of cyberpunk is the dramatic depiction of password cracking. From the very beginning, the genre has failed to accurately portray this cryptanalysis with much accuracy. *Neuromancer* described cracking as "ICE breaking" using a visual representation of "military grade" cracking software, a kind of geometric software blob capable of gaining access to restricted systems in cyberspace. In the hack on the Sense/Net facility to retrieve the Wintermute artificial intelligence, the hacker for hire Case simply "flipped to cyberspace and sent a command pulsing down the crimson threat that pierced the library ice."[72] Blending physical space and cyberspace is a key visual motif, as Case flips between views of the digital and Molly's broadcast experiences of breaking into the facility. Physical security and digital authentication systems work together, even in the cyberpunk future. Gibson even includes a simple wooden door with a mechanical lock in the orbiting cryogenic facility of the Tessier-Ashpool dynasty because a mechanical lock would be unbreakable by software. The remarkable turn from the high tech to low tech is an indication that security is about rigorous processes and threat modeling, as well as mathematics.

In Neal Stephenson's *Snow Crash*, cracking encryption is described in various ways, along the spectrum of parodic pastiche of cyberpunk motifs toward a realistic description of the banality of the command line. On the one hand, hacking is a "throwback to the days when people programmed computers through primitive teletypes and IBM punch cards" and is really just executing text files[73]; on the other hand, hacking is portrayed in a virtual reality interface that involves stabbing a virtual wall in the "Metaverse" with a digital katana:

> This is a hack. It is really based on a very old hack, a loophole that he found years ago when he was trying to graft the swordfighting rules onto the existing Metaverse software. His blade doesn't have the power to cut a hole in the wall—this would be permanently changing the shape of someone else's building—but it does have the power to penetrate things. Avatars do not have that power. That is the whole purpose of a wall in the Metaverse; it is a structure that does not allow avatars to penetrate it. But like anything else in the Metaverse, this rule is nothing but a protocol, a convention that different computers agree to follow. In theory, it cannot be ignored. But in practice, it depends upon the ability of different computers to swap information very precisely, at high speeds, and at just the right times. [...] That delay can be taken advantage of, if you move quickly and don't look back. Hiro passes right through the wall on the tail end of his all-penetrating katana.[74]

Stephenson's *Snow Crash* is taking a genre and pushing it to the extremes. He is having fun doing it too. In ten years, the visual metaphors of hacking have become so stylized as to become pure play. Stephenson's postcyberpunk irony was having fun mocking cyberpunk's shlocky mishmash of leather, swords, and skateboards in order to free the genre for something bigger. *Snow Crash* culminates in pseudo-religious, mythologizing of an ancient ability to hack the deep linguistic ciphers of the human mind. The so-called "nam-shub" of Enki is a "metavirus" that spontaneously creates human consciousness as well as morality, according to the mythology of *Snow Crash*. The ability to exploit a vulnerability in the mind to crack humans with an incantation of a primordial code! It is wild stuff. The move to kill cyberpunk so that it might live on was a necessity of any punk to stay punk.

Stephenson's 1999 *Cryptonomicon* is the cypherpunk classic that steps just beyond the cyberpunk genre for which he was best known at the time. Stephenson's book recalls May's original cypherpunk compendium called the "Cyphernomicon."[75] This artifact of the 1990s cypherpunks is now preserved on the internet by the Satoshi Nakamoto Institute, named after the enigmatic, likely pseudonymous, inventor of the digital currency Bitcoin.[76] Moving away from digital katanas, Stephenson takes on a wholesale historical treatment of cryptography and cryptocurrency to imagine its future at the dawn of the new millennium. Written as a twinned narrative tracing the work of the secret Bletchly Park cryptanalysis group, known as Ultra, during the Second World War, the novel describes their efforts to break the famous German encryption system known as Enigma. The plot of this narrative follows a fictional US Navy code breaker, Lawrence Pritchard Waterhouse, working under Alan Turning. Stephenson describes in detail the workings of the team at Bletchly and the use of the large mechanical computers, called Bombes, in their hurried, daily breaking of the Enigma cipher. The mechanically generated polyalphabetic cipher produced a very large number of possible combinations, but it was small enough to brute force attack with a computer built for this purpose. In a metahistorical twist, Stephenson imagines the work of a covert group of military intelligence officers as they work to cover up the fact that the Allies have broken Enigma. The power of cryptanalysis and code breaking is itself dependent on keeping secrets. If the Germans learned Enigma had been broken, cryptographic agility would have left the work at Bletchley meaningless. The Germans would have switched to a new cipher, leaving the Allies scrambling. Stephenson imagines a character, the brash and often violent Bobby Shaftoe, charged with covering up the secret project. Stephenson imagines the often violent lengths that the Allies would go to ensure their secret stays secret. The human cost of keeping secrets is perhaps more complex than the work of code breaking.

The second narrative follows the grandson of the fictional young Second World War codebreaker, Randy Waterhouse. Randy is a programmer riding a wave of dot-com techno optimism. He picks up a mysterious job for the fictional Sultanate of Kinakuta for a start-up called "Epiphyte(2)." Stephenson imagines, perhaps ahead of his time, the financial contagion of the Asian financial crisis of the 1990s giving rise to electronic cryptocurrencies. The contemporary narrative culminates in the founding of a "data haven" for the indefinite keeping of secrets.[77] Stephenson's "Crypt" is a highly centralized, geographically isolated secret repository for the world's information. Stephenson imagines an internet in which privacy is the most valuable asset. The novel is written as a twinned narrative that captures the dual motives of cryptography and cryptanalysis. The cryptanalysis of the Second World War led in no small part to the growth of cryptography in the 1990s. Stephenson sets up the narratives so that thematic and emotional collisions occur across history. The collision of these dual histories results in an interesting experience of speculative causes and effects over time. In doing so, Stephenson also draws a direct line between Alan Turing's work in cryptography and early computing at Bletchley Park to the development of an internet based economy fueled by cryptography. The Enigma machines and the secrets that they contained represented a turn in the war by redirecting the flow of secrets. By allowing the Allies to gain secrets as well as keep their own intentions masked through misdirection and intentional leaks of false information, the one way flow of fact and insight—the flow of intelligence— was the key strategic marker of the war. Misinformation and misdirection is then a key aspect of protecting secrets during the Second World War, as Stephenson imagines it.

The two narratives come together in moments, pinging off each other throughout the book. These collisions emulate a code breaking technique called a "birthday attack," of which there is a variant of this technique called a meet-in-the-middle attack. These attacks are collectively known as collision attacks. The birthday attack is named after the birthday paradox. The birthday paradox can be described in the following way: "For the birthday paradox, we have before the chance of a N = 365 and N $\approx$ 19. The number of people required $\sqrt{}$ duplicate birthday exceeds 50% is in fact 23, but N is close enough for our purposes and is the approximation that cryptographers often use."[78] If two users use the same password, it is possible to have a system compromise through a process called "collision." Collision attacks are often the weakness, either theoretically or practically, of block cipher systems like AES. The ability to find collisions in 128-bit or 256-bit keys are trivial to defeat on modern machines. The collision of history with the projected future that Stephenson imagined around the dot-com bubble remains a fascinating indication of science fiction's predictive qualities. The novel stands as a projection into the economic, postwar uses of cryptographic systems and the value of privacy manifested explicitly as digital currency.

Ignoti et quasi occulti

Cryptocurrency has been likened to a digital gold standard.[79] Like gold, some of the early miners exchanged coins worth millions today for absurdly little, such as a pizza.[80] The ultimate realization of decentralized, libertarian freedom and privacy rests with cryptocurrencies because it allows citizens of authoritarian governments to escape broken financial systems used to punish dissidents. In China, which is increasingly cashless, criminals are punished with Alipay and WeChat bans, a punishment that is " tantamount to social exclusion."[81] The "Crypt" in *Cryptonomicon* turns out to be a storehouse for information, and the most valuable form of information is currency. The plan for the fictional sultanate is to back a truly global electronic currency, backed by a vast storehouse of gold:

> "Banks used to issue their own currencies. You can see these old banknotes in the Smithsonian. [...] That had to stop because commerce became nonlocal—you needed to be able to take your money with you whenever you went out West, or whatever."
> "But if we're online, the whole world is local," Randy says.[82]

From the colliding visions of the Second World War and the dot-com era globalization, Stephenson intuits the emergence of a global e-currency. He imagines that cryptographic technologies developed and inherited during the War will be repurposed to keep secrets and secure power by amassing data. From this two pronged prediction, Stephenson can only be charged with not continuing the logical process even further. Data hoarding is a source of tremendous power and wealth, certainly. However, the wealth and power of hoarding data come from the unfettered ability to mine user data to create data products for sale or use in sales and marketing. The Big Five companies have amassed wealth through the sale of computers, software, and retail goods, but the ongoing profits are the result of continued access to data generated by those computers, software, or retail goods. The ability to store and transmit that data securely is the backbone of the online economy and the reason that asymmetric cryptography, namely RSA, is so important and the reason while cryptographic agility is needed for both activists and corporations alike. The block chain might be that next safe haven for storing and transmitting value, whether it is art, currency, or data.

Stephenson failed to push his vision of e-banking to its logical conclusion with cryptocurrency. It is remarkable that his sprawling novel on the history and future of cryptography and computing ends in speculating on the future of finance, much of which he gets right: "Electronic cash from the Crypt. Anonymous. Untraceable. And untaxable."[83] In his vision, the online currencies are backed by the gold standard. The United States abandoned the gold standard in 1933 which had the effect of increasing the money supply to help grow the economy as a function of the availability of currency. Avi and Randy describe it in the context of the Asian financial crisis and the fragility of banks without a gold-backed currency:

"Yeah. So all we need is something to back the currency. Gold would be good."
"Gold? Are you *joking?* Isn't that kind of old-fashioned?"
"It was until all of the unbacked currencies in Southeast Asia went down the toilet."[84]

Stephenson describes an economic fantasy of a global storehouse of value to literally ground economic transactions online in mineral wealth. It is unclear if there is enough gold to back daily global exchanges of value, other observers have questioned Stephenson's idealistic vision of global finance.[85] His choice of gold is thematic as well. He is linking the hoarding of gold by the Nazis as an authoritarian centralization of power by pillaging Europe. The gold amassed by Western powers after the war fed the economic boom and reconstruction plans in Europe, but the physical trace of Nazi gold carries the taint of its history as a commodity collected through murder and theft. Stephenson acknowledges the moral taint of global finance after the Second World War:

So maybe stabilizing the currency situation would be a good thing to accomplish with a shitload of gold, and that's the only moral thing to do with it anyway considering whom it was stolen from—you can't just go out and *spend* it.[86]

The solution Stephenson imagines is a fund dedicated to education and human rights. The amassed wealth would fund a global effort to avoid future holocausts through a Holocaust Education and Avoidance Pod or HEAP.[87] Cryptocurrency can serve as a tool to support refugees and stability through economic freedom from authoritarian governments.

This chapter has charted the unexpected uses and history of cryptography and the cypherpunk ethos that drives online privacy. The value of strong encryption certainly rests with supporting a free and democratic society that allows for individuals to be free from influence or coercion online. In finance, strong encryption technology does more to protect wealth than it does to promote cypherpunk visions of libertarian revolt. The environmental impacts of cryptocurrency are now gaining public scrutiny.[88] The risk of losing cryptocurrency wallet keys means there is a potential to loose huge portions of the finite cryptocurrency available, like with the recent death of Mircea Popescu.[89] RSA and TLS support billions of dollars of economic activity that funnel wealth to the very richest of the global elite. During the Covid-19 pandemic, Amazon CEO Jeff Bezos's personal fortune grew by more than 24 billion US dollars by some estimates, totaling 180 billion US dollars.[90] With ecommerce as a fact of life and increasingly normalized through the pandemic, the function of cryptocurrencies to shape trust relationships and expectations of privacy may help shift perspectives. Cryptocurrencies like Bitcoin are unlikely to save the world alone.

Notes

1 Samuel D. Warren, Louis D. Warren, D. Samuel, and Louis D. Brandeis. "The Right to Privacy," *Harvard Law Review* 4, no. 5 (1890): 193–220. doi:10.2307/1321160.

2 Ibid., 193.

3 Ibid., 198, 220.

4 Steven M. Bellovin, Matt Blaze, Susan Landau, and Stephanie K. Pell, "It's Too Complicated: How the Internet Upends *Katz, Smith,* and Electronic Surveillance Law," *Harvard Journal of Law and Technology* 30, no. 1 (Fall 2016): 1–73. https://jolt.law.harvard.edu/assets/articlePDFs/v30/30HarvJLTech1.pdf

5 Jennifer Elias and Magdalena Petrova, "Google's Rocky Path to Email Domination," *cnbc.com*, October 26, 2019, https://www.cnbc.com/2019/10/26/gmail-dominates-consumer-email-with-1point5-billion-users.html.

6 Ben Popper, "Google Announces Over 2 billion Monthly Active Devices on Android," *Theverge.com*, May 17, 2017, https://www.theverge.com/2017/5/17/15654454/android-reaches-2-billion-monthly-active-users.

7 Sarah E. Igo, *The Known Citizen: A History of Privacy in Modern America* (Cambridge: Harvard University Press, 2018), 112.

8 Robert M. Bond, Christopher J. Fariss, Jason J. Jones et al., "A 61-Million-Person Experiment in Social Influence and Political Mobilization," *Nature* 489 (2012): 295–8. https://doi.org/10.1038/nature11421.

9 John Gramlich, "10 Facts about Americans and Facebook," *Pew Research*, June 1, 2021, https://www.pewresearch.org/fact-tank/2021/06/01/facts-about-americans-and-facebook/.

10 Micah L. Sifry, "Facebook Wants You to Vote on Tuesday. Here's How It Messed with Your Feed in 2012," *Motherjones.com*, October 31, 2014, https://www.motherjones.com/politics/2014/10/can-voting-facebook-button-improve-voter-turnout/.

11   Mike Issac, "Facebook Widens Ban on Political Ads as Alarm Rises over Election," *New York Times*, October 7, 2020, https://www.nytimes.com/2020/10/07/technology/facebook-political-ads-ban.html.

12   Malka Older, *Informocracy* (New York: Tor Books, 2016).

13   Malka Older, *Null States* (New York: Tor Books, 2017).

14   Alex Stamos, adjunct professor at Stanford University's Center for International Security and Cooperation and former Chief Security Officer at Facebook, describes election security as a necessary seasonal pass time for Americans. Election interference on social media by foreign governments demands a "collective industry response" that transcends corporate partisanship and special interests. See *Securing American Elections: Prescriptions for Enhancing the Integrity and Independence of the 2020 U.S. Presidential Election and Beyond*, edited by Michael McFaul, Stanford University, April 2019, https://fsi.stanford.edu/publication/securing-american-elections-prescriptions-enhancing-integrity-and-independence-2020-us.

15   Casey Newton, "The Trauma Floor: The Secret Lives of Facebook Moderators in America," *TheVerge.com*, February 25, 2019, https://www.theverge.com/2019/2/25/18229714/cognizant-facebook-content-moderator-interviews-trauma-working-conditions-arizona.

16   Brent Harris, "Establishing Structure and Governance for an Independent Oversight Board," *Facebook News*, September 17, 2019, https://about.fb.com/news/2019/09/oversight-board-structure/.

17   Ibid.

18   Malka Older, *State Tectonics* (New York: Tor Books, 2018).

19   David Greenberg, "There Is a Logic to Trump's War on the Media," *Prospect.org*, April 28, 2017, https://prospect.org/culture/logic-trump-s-war-media/.

20   Niels Ferguson, Bruce Schneier, and Tadayoshi Kohno, *Cryptography Engineering: Design Principles and Practical Applications* (Indianapolis: Wiley Publishing, 2010), 4.

21   Eli Pariser, *The Filter Bubble: How the New Personalized Web Is Changing What We Read and How We Think* (New York: Penguin, 2012).

22   Richard Esguerra, "Google CEO Eric Schmidt Dismisses the Importance of Privacy," *Eff.org*, December 10, 2009, https://www.eff.org/deeplinks/2009/12/google-ceo-eric-schmidt-dismisses-privacy.

23   Myers West, Sarah, "Cryptographic Imaginaries and the Networked Public," *Internet Policy Review* 7, no. 2 (2018): 1–16. DOI: 10.14763/2018.2.792.

24   Georg Simmel, "The Sociology of Secrecy and of Secret Societies," *American Journal of Sociology* 11, no. 4 (1906): 441–98. https://archive.org/details/jstor-2762562.

25   See https://parlinfo.aph.gov.au/parlInfo/download/legislation/bills/r6195_aspassed/toc_pdf/18204b01.pdf; https://www.congress.gov/bill/116th-congress/senate-bill/3398/text.

26   Dan Goodin, "The Strange, Unexplained Journey of ToTok in Google Play Fuels User Suspicions", *Arstechnica.com*, February 21, 2020, https://

arstechnica.com/information-technology/2020/02/google-removes-reinstates-and-removes-totok-app-said-to-spy-for-uae-government/; Catalin Cimpanu, "White Hats Spread VKontakte Worm after Social Network Doesn't Pay Bug Bounty," *Zdnet.com*, February 18, 2019, https://www.zdnet.com/article/white-hats-spread-vkontakte-worm-after-social-network-doesnt-pay-bug-bounty/; Catalin Cimpanu, "India Bans 59 Chinese Apps, Including TikTok, UC Browser, Weibo, and WeChat," *Zdnet.com*, June 29, 2020, https://www.zdnet.com/article/india-bans-59-chinese-apps-including-tiktok-uc-browser-weibo-and-wechat/.

27 Jean-Christophe Plantin and Gabriele de Seta, "WeChat as Infrastructure: The Techno-nationalist Shaping of Chinese Digital Platforms," *Chinese Journal of Communication* 12, no. 3 (2019): 257–73. DOI: 10.1080/17544750.2019.1572633.

28 Ibid., 273.

29 David Kahn, *The Codebreakers: The Story of Secret Writing* (New York: Macmillan, 1967), 5–6.

30 Chun, *Software Studies*, 175.

31 Timothy May, "The Crypto Anarchist Manifesto," *Activism.net*, November 22, 1992, https://activism.net/cypherpunk/crypto-anarchy.html.

32 Ibid.

33 See https://www.abetterinternet.org/ and https://letsencrypt.org/.

34 See https://www.marconisociety.org/fellow-bio/paul-kocher/ and https://www.marconisociety.org/fellow-bio/taher-elgamal/.

35 Ibid.

36 Eric Hughes, "A Cypherpunk's Manifesto," *Activism.net*, March 9, 1993, https://www.activism.net/cypherpunk/manifesto.html.

37 Steven Levy, *Crypto: How the Code Rebels Beat the Government—Saving Privacy in the Digital Age* (New York: Viking, 2001), 260.

38 May, "The Crypto Anarchist Manifesto"; Levy, *Crypto,* 263.

39 Edgar Allan Poe, "A Few Words on Secret Writing," *Graham's Magazine* 19 (July 1841): 33–8. https://www.eapoe.org/works/misc/awm40c02.htm.

40 Edgar Allan Poe, "Enigmatical," *Alexander's Weekly Messenger* 4, no. 3, (January 15, 1840): 2.

41 Poe, "A Few Words on Secret Writing."

42 Edgar Allan Poe, *The Gold-Bug and Other Tales* (New York: Dover, 1991), 100.

43 Kenneth Silverman, *Edgar A. Poe: Mournful and Never-ending Remembrance* (New York: HarperPerennial, 1992), 171.

44 Ibid., 166.

45 Poe, *The Gold-Bug,* 103.

46 Aeneas Tacticus, "Of Secret Messages," in *Poliorketika, or How to Survive Under Siege*, ed. Maria Pretzler, https://aeneastacticus.net/public_html/ab31.htm; Aeneas Tacticus, *Poliorcetica*, ed. William Abbott Oldfather, http://data.perseus.org/citations/urn:cts:greekLit:tlg0058.tlg001.perseus-grc1:xxxi.1.

47 Marc Redfield, *Shibboleth: Judges, Derrida, Celan* (New York: Fordham University Press, 2020).

48 See https://www.shibboleth.net/.

49 Claude E. Shannon, "Communication Theory of Secrecy Systems," *Bell System Technical Journal* 28, no. 4 (1949): 656–715. https://archive.org/stream/bstj28-4-656#page/n5/mode/2up.

50 Brute force attacks can use several approaches, such as dictionary attack, which uses a long list of passwords and adjusts them for different permutations of words, numbers, and special characters. The final method can make use of rainbow tables. A rainbow table is comprised of precomputed hash values for password dictionaries, which speeds the process considerably. Of course, social engineering through keyloggers, phishing, and social engineering are also methods for gaining access through passwords. Password lists and rainbow tables are readily available online. See https://wiki.skullsecurity.org/index.php?title=Passwords; http://www.phenoelit.org/dpl/dpl.html; https://crackstation.net/crackstation-wordlist-password-cracking-dictionary.htm.

51 Roger A. Grimes, *Cryptography Apocalypse: Preparing for the Day When Quantum Computing Breaks Today's Crypto* (New Jersey: John Wiley & Sons, 2020).

52 James Bamford, *The Puzzle Palace: A Report on America's Most Secret Agency* (New York: Houghton Mifflin, 1982), 198.

53 AES was first released by the US NIST in 2001. See https://nvlpubs.nist.gov/nistpubs/FIPS/NIST.FIPS.197.pdf.

54 SNOW 3G is the third of a series of stream ciphers released in 2006 by Thomas Johansson and Patrik Ekdahl at Lund University. See https://www.gsma.com/aboutus/wp-content/uploads/2014/12/snow3gspec.pdf.

55 Ray A. Perlner and David A. Cooper, "Quantum Resistant Public Key Cryptography: A Survey," *Nist.gov*, April 14, 2009, https://doi.org/10.1145/1527017.1527028.

56 Eric S. Raymond, *The Cathedral and the Bazaar: Musings on Linux and Open Source by an Accidental Revolutionary* (Cambridge: O'Reilly, 1999), 30.

57 Bruce Schneier, *Applied Cryptography: Protocols, Algorithms, and Source Code in C, Second Edition* (New York: John Wiley & Sons, 1996), 489.

58 Levy, *Crypto, 246.*

59 See https://www.congress.gov/bill/102nd-congress/senate-bill/266.

60 Levy, *Crypto,* 247.

61 See https://gnupg.org/ and https://www.openpgp.org/.

62 See https://www.gnupg.org/faq/why-not-idea.en.html.

63 See https://cryptography.io/en/latest/hazmat/primitives/index.html.

64 In *Cryptography Engineering,* Niels Ferguson, Bruce Schneier, and Tadayoshi Kohno admit that the AES block cipher is not strictly cryptographically secure. However, the current attack methods are reserved for academic proof of concepts and are very difficult to break in practical applications. They recommend a 256-bit key to increase safety margins, but it has proven itself effective in broad practical use by the US government: "Even though AES is now broken academically, these breaks do not imply a significant security degradation of real systems in practice. It is also the official standard, sanctioned by the US government. And everybody else is using it. They used to say 'Nobody gets fired for buying IBM.' Similarly, nobody will fire you for choosing AES." See Ferguson, Schneier, and Kohno, *Cryptography Engineering*, 56.

65 This code was written by Manuel Kloppenburg, with only minor alterations for presentation here. See https://github.com/cryptoexamples/python-cryptography-cryptoexamples/blob/master/src/cryptoexamples/example_symmetric_string_encryption_key_based.py.

66 Josh Meyer, "The CIA Sent Warnings to at Least 3 Khashoggi Associates About New Threats from Saudi Arabia," *Time.com*, May 9, 2019, https://time.com/5585281/cia-warned-jamal-khashoggi-associates/.

67 Bill Marczak, John Scott-Railton, Sarah McKune, Bahr Abdul Razzak, and Ron Deibert, "Hide and Seek: Tracking NSO Group's Pegasus Spyware to Operations in 45 Countries," *Citizenlab.ca*, September 18, 2018, https://citizenlab.ca/2018/09/hide-and-seek-tracking-nso-groups-pegasus-spyware-to-operations-in-45-countries/; Mehul Srivastava and Tim Bradshaw, "Israeli Group's Spyware 'Offers Keys to Big Tech's Cloud'," *Ft.com*, July 19, 2019, https://www.ft.com/content/95b91412-a946-11e9-b6ee-3cdf3174eb89. Shannon Vavra, "NSO Group Partly Disputes Claim about Use of U.S.-Based Servers in WhatsApp Spy Campaign," *Cyberscoop.com*, May 1, 2020, https://www.cyberscoop.com/nso-group-disputes-quadranet-whatsapp-claim/.

68 Rosie Perper, "Israeli Spyware Was Used to Track and Eventually Kill Jamal Khashoggi," *Businessinsider.com*, November 10, 2018, https://www.businessinsider.com.au/edward-snowden-israeli-spyware-nso-group-pegasus-jamal-khashoggi-murder-2018-11; David D. Kirkpatrick, "Israeli Software Helped Saudis Spy on Khashoggi, Lawsuit Says," *Nytimes.com*, December 2, 2018, https://www.nytimes.com/2018/12/02/world/middleeast/saudi-khashoggi-spyware-israel.html; see also the Office of the Director of National Intelligence report "Assessment of Saudi Government Role in Killing Jamal Khashoggi," https://www.dni.gov/files/ODNI/documents/assessments/Assessment-Saudi-Gov-Role-in-JK-Death-20210226.pdf.

69 Marczak et al., "Hide and Seek," 8.

70 Robert Chesney, "Crossing a Cyber Rubicon? Overreactions to the IDF's Strike on the Hamas Cyber Facility," *Lawfairblog.com*, May 6, 2019, https://www.lawfareblog.com/crossing-cyber-rubicon-overreactions-idfs-strike-hamas-cyber-facility.

71 Jewish Telegraphic Agency, "Israel's National Broadcaster Accuses Hamas of Eurovision Hack," *Jewishnews.timesofisrael.com*, May 18, 2019, https://jewishnews.timesofisrael.com/israels-national-broadcaster-accuses-hamas-of-eurovision-hack/.

72 William Gibson, *Neuromancer* (New York: Ace Books, 1984), 65–6.

73 Neal Stephenson, *Snow Crash* (New York: Del Rey, 1992), 417.

74 Ibid., 519.

75 Timothy May, "The Cyphernomicon," version 0.666, September 10, 1994, https://nakamotoinstitute.org/static/docs/cyphernomicon.txt.

76 Satoshi Nakamoto, "Bitcoin: A Peer-to-Peer Electronic Cash System," Satoshi Nakamoto Institute, October 31, 2008, https://nakamotoinstitute.org/bitcoin/.

77 Neal Stephenson, *Cryptonomicon* (New York: Avon, 1999), 237.

78 Ferguson, Schneier, and Kohno, *Cryptography Engineering*, 34.

79 See https://www.casebitcoin.com/digital-gold and https://bitcoinmagazine.com/markets/the-trojan-horse-bitcoin-is-just-digital-gold.

80 On May 22, 2010, a young engineer and cryptocurrency enthusiast, Laszlo Hanyecz, paid 10,000 Bitcoins for two Papa John's pizzas. Today, those coins would be worth ~329,520,777.93 US dollars. See https://www.eatbitcoinpizza.com/.

81 Kenrick Davis, "In Cashless China, Criminals Are Punished with Payment App Bans," *Sixth Tone*, November 12, 2020, https://www.sixthtone.com/news/1006443/in-cashless-china%2C-criminals-are-punished-with-payment-app-bans.

82 Stephenson, *Cryptonomicon*, 703.

83 Ibid., 904.

84 Ibid., 704.

85 Paul Youngquist, "Cyberpunk, War, and Money: Neal Stephenson's 'Cryptonomicon'," *Contemporary Literature* 53, no. 2 (Summer 2012): 319–47, 342. https://www.jstor.org/stable/23256721.

86 Stephenson, *Cryptonomicon,* 1015.

87 Ibid., 1015.

88 By some estimates, bitcoin generates 22 million metric tonnes of CO_2 per year. See Thomson Reuters Foundation, "Dirty Money: What Is the Environmental Cost of Bitcoin?" June 18, 2021, https://www.eco-business.com/news/dirty-money-what-is-the-environmental-cost-of-bitcoin/.

89 Mark DeCambre, "One of the Largest Owners of Bitcoin, Who Reportedly Held as Much as $1 Billion, Is Dead at 41: Reports," *Market Watch*, June 28, 2021, https://www.marketwatch.com/story/one-of-the-largest-owners-of-bitcoin-who-reportedly-held-as-much-as-1-billion-is-dead-at-41-reports-11624904721.

90 See the "Wealth shown to scale" project to get a sense of the size of the Bezos fortune: https://mkorostoff.github.io/1-pixel-wealth/. See also, Kenya Evelyn, "Amazon CEO Jeff Bezos Grows Fortune by $24bn amid Coronavirus Pandemic," *Theguardian.com*, April 15, 2020, https://www.theguardian.com/technology/2020/apr/15/amazon-jeff-bezos-gains-24bn-coronavirus-pandemic; Robert Reich, "Jeff Bezos Became Even Richer Thanks to Covid-19. But he Still Won't Protect Amazon Workers," *TheGuardian.com*, December 13, 2020, https://www.theguardian.com/commentisfree/2020/dec/12/jeff-bezos-amazon-workers-covid-19-scrooge-capitalism.

5

Biohacking and the Autonomous Androids:

Human Evolution and Biometric Data

Everyday I open my computer and prove that I am not a robot. My humanity is confirmed and maybe even defined by my ability to identify various street scenes. There is a car; here is a crosswalk; buses are everywhere. As an urban sightseer going nowhere, I prove to the machine that I am a human by performing a trivial, repetitive task a little like a robot. Being aware of this irony, I wonder if, one day, my computer might feel similarly diminished by the repetitive tasks I require of it. What if the machines rise up against humanity out of the sheer annoyance of it all? Online services segregate humans and machines because machines are assumed to be doing something wrong. These "CAPTCHA" tests are a commonplace experience and just a normal part of using the services on the web.[1] The intent is to authorize the human users with access. The users who are properly alive have the right to use the system. Non-human user agents must have their freedom constrained, presumably, because the risk to abuse online services is too great. Our online services attempt to train human users to believe that the difference between human and machine is vital. The daily, repetitive tasks of defining human and non-human seems to have an eroding effect on these categories. It is uncanny, maybe a little surreal, but the distinction between human and non-human users is becoming less and less meaningful.

Whether humans become more machine-like in our behaviors or machines become better able to simulate human affect and intelligence, the distinction between human intelligence and machine intelligence is increasingly becoming a difference of degree and quality rather than a more absolute difference of kind. The ability to even place human intelligence on a spectrum with machine intelligence suggests that we are approaching future questions posed by science fiction. Regardless of the exact path machine learning and artificial intelligence takes, it is a good time to reflect on the anthropocentrism inherent in these systems that precipitate still other forms of discrimination. It is necessary to discriminated between user types today because hackers will spam services with requests, often in the form of "credential stuffing." Credential stuffing most often allows attackers to use leaked username and password to breach other services with the same credential pairs.[2] While this attack is fairly new, the ability to distinguish between human and machine has been a perennial question in Computer Science. The famous test used to measure the success of artificial intelligence was defined by Alan Turing in 1950 and still names our daily "CAPTCHA" ritual, which stands for "Completely Automated Public Turing test to tell Computers and Humans Apart."

First described in his essay "Computing Machinery and Intelligence," the Turing's test, or imitation game, seeks to test a machine's ability to imitate human interactions in the form of conversation.[3] Turing was inspired by the nineteenth-century English aristocrat Lady Ada Lovelace in her analysis of Charles Babbage's Analytical Engine, for which she wrote the first set of instructions or program.[4] As the first computer programmer and daughter of the famed Romantic poet Lord Byron, Lovelace was well positioned to comment on the philosophical and technical capabilities of early computing, whether they are rational, mathematical, or musical. Lovelace foresaw general purpose computing being used for any system of symbols, like natural languages or music. "Lovelace's objection," as Turing described it, was that computers had "no pretensions to originate anything."[5] In other words, everything a machine can do must be supplied by its human operator. Turing argues further by suggesting that it might be possible for humans to develop systems capable of learning and therefore achieve a suitable imitation of human intelligence. In either case, the basis for measuring and building intelligence was human.

User authentication systems are central to system security and rely on these human and machine categories. It is possible to confirm a user identity by something a user knows. Knowledge as an authentication mechanism usually takes the form of a passphrase, but it can also be related to secondary authentication questions. These routine security questions are often autobiographical, assuming that human lives are unique enough to tell apart: What was the name of your childhood best friend? What was the color of your first car? In which city did you get married? These personal human questions, and the ability to recall them, determine your level access. User identity can also be authenticated by an object in their possession. A physical key, like a proximity card or a security token, must be unique in some way and in the intended users possession. Secret knowledge and unique physical keys are strong user authentication systems, but it is possible for a user to lose control of both through theft or social engineering. Perhaps there is enough information on social media to answer the security questions. Perhaps a user divulges credentials through a phishing scam. Perhaps your security token is stolen. The answer to these risks has become biometric authentication, which seeks to measure some part of our bodies. Biometric authentication has already become normalized through smart phone fingerprint scanners and facial recognition systems, but there are many ways to measure the human body for unique characteristics. Our voice, retina, hand veins, and palm prints contain unique patterns that can distinguish us from other humans and machines without these features. These biometric patterns are used only in limited environments—because of the need to control ambient light and noise as well as the size of the equipment needed—so fingerprint and facial recognition based biometric user authentication is the most common and accepted at present. In either case, biometric authentication is dependent on being in possession of a valid human face or fingers.

In 1995, Mike Featherstone and Roger Burrows edited an important collection of essays called *Cyberspace/Cyberbodies/Cyberpunk*. It was a remarkable collection because of the consistency with which authors imagined the future of communications technology and their increasing ubiquity would result in implanting technology into human bodies. Prosthetic arms and legs spurred conversations about sexuality and sensual pleasures of cybernetics. Prosthetic memories resulting from "wetwear" implants of computer storage fostered anxieties about false memories and the resulting identity dysphoria. These are fascinating predictions were borne out by the cyberpunk futures they studied. They were aware of how wrong these anxieties could be, given how wrong 1960s science fiction was in predicting the 1990s. "If we were to restart this process today and make predictions about everyday life in the mid-2020s," Featherstone and Burrows reflect in the introduction, "it is certain that computers, information technology and the electronic media would play a central role but then is there still the disturbing possibility that we could have missed new reconfigured recalling—something which will emerge and have crucial significance?"[6] While today's prosthetics are benefiting in advances in robotics, they are used for therapeutic purposes rather than anything like body hacking.[7] Prosthetic memories and brain implants appear as significant parts of Gibson's short story "Johnny Mnemonic" first published in 1981 in *Omni* magazine. It describes a professional data trafficker, who transports sensitive data often for criminal organizations like the Yakuza. In 1995, *Johnny Mnemonic* was back as a film starring Keanu Reeves and directed by Robert Longo. The *Johnny Mnemonic* film is very different in tone and style from the short story, even nonsensically featuring Dolph Lundgren as a cybernetic street preacher maniac. Despite the films failures, *Johnny Mnemonic* represented a moment as the internet spread into more common use in which questions of prosthetic body and brain modification came into public view.

The fixation on prosthetic memories and brain augmentation seems less of a concern today.[8] There are likely many technologies of "crucial significance" that have changed our perspective since 1995. The release of the iPhone in 2007 was crucially significant because it became a highly flexible prosthetic for, among other things, memory. The ubiquity of the internet and the ability to look up general information, locations and directions, as well as store phone numbers and music meant those early adopters had to simply remember less and less. It wasn't even a big deal really. It is difficult to remember our friend's phone numbers or the name of that song because those things are not really necessary. It is possible to leave home without the first clue about how to get to a destination, but our phones will guide us there turn by turn. There are now real world efforts to develop what Elon Musk has been marketing as a "neural lace" that will allow a direct link between computers and the human brain.[9] While Musk is motivated to augment humanity out of fear of a super-intelligent AI subjugating humanity, the applications for this technology are as vast as they are speculative.[10] Zachary Mason's novel *Void Star* was published in 2017 among the neural lace excitement, but Mason's novel depicts memory augmentation as something banal and not even really desirable for the wealthy.[11] The character Irina is constantly distracted by her total recall of memories, but she is capable of communicating directly with AI that leads her on a surreal trip through consciousness and maybe into a quasi-transcendence. In the twenty-first century, it seems that brain augmentation and memory prosthetics have grown to embrace further connection to machines as an enhanced user interface for biometric control of computers. Yet an interface still assumes that human and machine categories are essential.

Vital Machines

The politics of human biology have always aligned with patterns of surveillance, power, and control. The desire to secure our online lives and willingness to adopt biometric authentication suggests that one system will be used to track and authorize humans and non-humans alike. Annalee Newitz's 2017 novel *Autonomous* has imagined the risks of surveillance, robotics, and biohacking. The events of the novel occur around 2144. The results of global warming have pushed the agriculturally fertile range further to the poles, resulting in Canada becoming a center of scientific innovation and productivity, in cities like Moose Jaw, Saskatoon, and Iqaluit. While the city names remain, they are now part of a supernational block called the Free Trade Zone. Advanced robotics and artificial intelligence are science fact, and the leading edge of technological development involves biohacking with elaborate, patent protected drugs. The existence of sentient AI have transformed the legal status of both humans and machines. If human and machine intelligences are equal, then ownership of both humans and machines becomes a logical consequence. The military cyborg Paladin studies humanity throughout the novel, first reflecting on the twinned legal status of machines and humans:

> There were entire text repositories that focused on eliminating the indenture of humans. Their pundits argued that humans should not be owned like bots because nobody paid to make them. Bots, who cost money, required a period of indenture to make their manufacture worthwhile. No such incentive was required for humans to make other humans.[12]

Newitz's book shifts the anthropocentric assumptions about intelligence and how the legal status of sentient AI would reflect upon human autonomy. Humans are no longer the privileged model of intelligence in this world. If autonomy is granted to artificial life forms and are granted equal legal status to work and live, the laws governing humans must necessarily change. In this world, machines serve for a period to pay for their manufacture. Humans can similarly sell themselves, or parents can sell their children, for necessities of life as well as education.

The possible futures described in *Autonomous* have present-day analogues that make this world feel weirdly familiar. The student debt crisis, particularly in the United States, is the real world correlate to selling young people into indentured service.[13] Parents who vote for defunding education in exchange for tax cuts are committing their children to a period of indentured labor to pay their debt. A portion of their life, measured in hourly wage labor, will be granted back to the banks and schools. Newitz's work is emblematic of the present because of how aspects of technological and cultural change interrelate. For example, today's rapid growth of bioinformatics is an early sign of the aligning of genetic, molecular, and cellular frontiers of biology and information systems. Bioinformatics uses programming methods to study biology data, including identifying useful single nucleotide polymorphisms in DNA and protein sequences or proteomics for therapeutic purposes. In one hundred years, the character Jack appears as a logical outcome. She is a biohacking pharma-pirate, sailing the seas in her mini-sub, busy "engineering therapies that will be released under an open license."[14] In this world, hacker collectives argue about programming languages that they use to develop therapeutic drugs. Hacking humans and machines grows ever more indistinguishable. The key difference being that the dropper for these hacks is either an injected chemical or a code.

The advanced robotics of *Autonomous* also blur the line between physical bodies of machines and humans. When Jack finds Threezed badly beaten, she is unable to determine if Threezed is human or not: "Suddenly Jack realized why the bot could look so beaten up but still show no signs of an alloy endoskeleton. This wasn't a biobot—it was just plain bio. A human."[15] Threezed is a previously indentured human, educated in the Asian Union block, freed when Jack disables his tracker. The class disparity is defined by their autonomous status and implants. Thirty years younger than Jack, he has no implants, which means he is dependent on handheld devices for information, like those of us living in the early twenty-first century.[16] Having lived an indentured life, Threezed has learned to survive by trading his body, which he continues to do when he repays Jack with sexual favors "in an ambiguous gesture of obedience and consent."[17] In this way, Newitz describes intersectional power relationships through a series of emerging categories: the legal autonomy of the body, regardless of whether it is human or machine; the ability to augment the mind with custom pharmaceuticals, legal or otherwise; the technological access granted by implants and the ability to hack those within yourself and other entities.

In this way, Newitz describes a version of humanity that is not really dissimilar to machines. The human software and hardware can be duplicated, augmented, or made in this world. Jack begins her PhD in Halifax wanting to do "Good Science" and save lives, but she learns that patents will withhold those benefits for the wealthy and the autonomous. She decides to become a biohacker, reverse engineering pharmaceuticals for everyone as part of open labs. The Biopython library makes this kind of biohacking possible today, even if we are not quite at the stage of rapidly synthesizing custom therapeutic hacks from desktop laboratories.[18] It is possible to retrieve and experiment with a very large database of public DNA sequences available from the National Center for Biotechnology Information, for example. GenBank is a National Institute of Health genetic sequence database, which makes genetic sequencing data freely available for anyone to use. For example, this code will retrieve the first complete genome for SARS-CoV-2, otherwise known as Covid-19:

○ ○ ○

```
from Bio import SeqIO, Entrez
Entrez.email = "your email address"
handle = Entrez.efetch(db="nucleotide",
                       rettype="fasta",
                       retmode="text",
                       id="NC_045512.2")
seq_record = SeqIO.read(handle,"fasta")
print(seq_record, seq_record.seq)
```

FIGURE 5.1 *A script using the Biopython package to fetch SARS-CoV-2 sequence data from the US National Institute of Health GenBank*

The data for this script is fetched from GenBank, though first published in *Nature* in March of 2020 as the pandemic took hold globally.[19] First sequenced by Zhang Yongzhen and his team at the Shanghai Public Health Clinical Center, the DNA sequence of 29,903 nucleotides is likely one of the most important codes in the world at present.[20] It has cost the global community trillions of dollars in research, development, and other financial aid. It took Yongzhen just forty hours to sequence the new virus and is now available for anyone with an internet connection to study. The speed and scale of access to bio-medical research data, as well as the tools to use them, are increasing at a pace in which science fiction now struggles to stay ahead of science fact.[21] Almost appearing from science fiction novels like *Autonomous*, CRISPR is a user interfaces for the human genome. Body hackers, led by figures like Josiah Zayner who famously injected himself with CRISPR-cas 9 process, are already dreaming science fiction futures of "gene-jacking" for performance improvement.[22]

This is a remarkable state of affairs that signals the pace of change at present, since geneticists first sequenced a human genome just twenty years ago.[23] It took thirteen years to do it initially, and now there are 49,330,679 search results for homo sapiens nucleotide sequences publicly available on GenBank. Invented in 2012, CRISPR (Clustered Regularly Interspaced Short Palindromic Repeat) is the name used to describe a new class of highly accurate gene editing processes that uses repeated sequences in originally used by the immune system to target specific gene sequences.[24] In 2020, Emmanuelle Charpentier and Jennifer A. Doudna won the Nobel Prize in Chemistry for this technology that fundamentally alters basic research principles and approaches because of its high degree of accuracy and relatively low cost.[25] In 2015, the CRISPR process was used by Chinese researchers to edit a live, non-viable, embryo.[26] In 2019, He Jiankui announced the birth of twin girls with CRISPR edited genomes.[27] Regardless of the ethical and moral considerations of this step, it is now possible to augment, develop, and study humans genetic code with code.[28] If the use of CRISPR or similar technologies becomes more widespread, what will it cost—morally, ethically, philosophically, as well as financially—to augment or improve a human baby? Who owns the intellectual property used to generate these humans? How can such life debts be repaid? In both science, science fiction, and broader social attitudes, the meaning of these advances in genetics "have not yet stabilized" in fiction or reality.[29] In the short time since the publication of *Autonomous* in 2017, these questions are no longer just the domain of science fiction authors like Newitz. They are nothing less than the beginning of a potentially new evolutionary path for humanity.

The Selfish Ledger

The normalization of collecting biometric data—through health monitoring systems like pedometers, heart-rate monitors, and electrocardiograms—is perhaps the more banal and commercially driven form of this change in the species. Smart scales, smart exercise equipment, smart fridges are now beginning to track every calorie consumed. Consumer culture is increasingly driven by externally motivated biohacking through notifications and algorithmic prompts that in turn feed data into machine learning systems about the human body. By identifying the "vulnerabilities" of human health and collecting data about our living bodies, many hope to prolong their lives and quality of life. Fearing our own mortality might be the greatest human exploit. The future of surveillance and social control will be poised upon three data pillars: demographic data, psychographic data, and biometric data. We carry phones in our pockets all the time which makes us fundamentally different than humans that lived before us. Katherine Hayles describes the cybernetics in a mechanical and metaphorical hybrid concept of hybridity, related to our participation in market forces: "If owning oneself was a constitutive premise for liberal humanism, the cyborg complicated that premise by its figuring of a rational subject who is always already constituted by the forces of capitalist markets."[30] The puzzling figurative valences of "flickering signifiers" have dropped away, exposing the reality of biometric data collection as a simple a fact of life. Humans today, with a cell phone living in the ubiquitous internet, can do things past humans could not. Technology need not be embedded without our bodies, what Gibson called "microsofts," to augment ourselves. The heavily technologized version of humanity becomes a source of data to be mined only because we cling to visions of a socially constructed, culturally validated sense of self mirrored in data.

By holding fast to our identities and demanding that we "feel seen," we become little more than sources of discrete, predictable data. Our belief that our subjectivity is valuable and stable means that tracking individuals can yield reliable data for surveillance capitalists. Demographic data are the facts about us, things we expect on a census, that are difficult to change: birth date, sex, education, age, religion, occupation, geographic location, and real names. Cory Doctorow includes an interesting detail in *The Walkaway* with his character Hubert Etc, whose parents gave him the top twenty names from the 1890 Canadian census to give him the option of evading real name policies.[31] Psychographics are more complex. They represent our attitudes, beliefs, and interests. They are the categories that we might willingly display in social media. These displays of our public personality and lifestyle are made valuable by marketing and opinion research firms to sell a consumer good or a political party. The human exploit used to predict behavior is our very identity and the subjectivity we use to express the belief that we are socially constructed and bestowed with agency. Biometrics become valuable in linking those external interactions with a physical body. Biometrics does not use human senses to isolate individual humans. Scans replace human senses in confirming experience, time, and location. Photography serves to extend both human and machine senses. When we use our phones to take photographs, we authenticate our identity with a biometric scan of a fingerprint or a face. We then take the photograph, assisted by facial recognition for focus, depth of field, as well as image tags for those we love. The scanning of the body with digital photography that is also biometrically authenticated—geolocated, time stamped, and processed through image recognition—confirms human subjectivity, fixes it in data, and sent off for safe, maybe eternal, storage in the cloud.

Even if an individual changes, there is an indelible, authenticated record matched through the human body. Humanity becomes little more than a linear stream of data with a start date, an end date, and a unique ID. There is a transience to our bodies that is readily translated into the needs of the machine. In *You Are Not a Gadget*, Jaron Lanier rejects this lowering of human intellect to serve the machines in any way. He rejects the need for humans to limit their language for the purposes of satisfying a search engine's preference for keywords. He rails against the limitation of the sonic range of analog music into the limited registers of MIDI music format. While Lanier's skepticism for the cloud based technology companies that harvest human creative potential, his thinking remains fundamentally anthropocentric. In many ways, the virtual reality interface so common to cyberpunk and to Lanier's vision is about building a seamless interface for technology designed around human needs only. User centered design seeks to entrap humanity in a "seamless" interface with technology that does not expose vulnerabilities for those in control of the system.[32]

As strange inhuman intentionality of software becomes increasingly manifest in the human world, at the physical scale of our senses and awareness, human bodies will integrate ever more seamlessly into a reciprocal relationship with mechanical entities. These robots are not alive in the anthropocentric way of thinking, as Lanier would have it, but in a provisionally anthropomorphic way. In *Vibrant Matter*, Jane Bennett, a Professor of Political Science at Johns Hopkins University, has worked to understand the way that biopower—predicated on a false binary between life and matter—has been used to carve up and politicize every part of our lives. In opening, she frames the scope of the issue tied to this false binary and "the various micropolitical and macropolitical techniques through which the human body was disciplined, normalized, sped up and slowed down, gendered, sexed, nationalized, globalized, rendered disposable or otherwise composed."[33] As Bennett describes, a little anthropomorphism is needed to overcome the worst of anthropocentrism that will produce conflict among humans ready to partner with machines in a fully symbiotic way. In other words, if we can imagine our machines have human characteristics, the imperfect agency we grant them will at least have the effect of reorienting our hardened anthropocentric bias and embrace the lived experience of non-human objects. The materialism Bennett describes is a vital materialism that describes the life of objects rather than their social constructed qualities of historical materialism. Bennett blurs the long assumed line between matter and life that underwrote the broadest trends of Western philosophy.

There are prototypes for the alignment of genetics and computation that are in development at present. In the spring of 2018, the technology blog *The Verge* leaked a Google concept video describing a new vision for data use.[34] The video opens to a time lapse video of the stars traversing the night's horizon. The video introduces something called "the selfish ledger" to hypnotic, ethereal music.[35] General viewers of this video only slowly realize the purpose of the video is to propose a business strategy. The video does not propose a product per se, but instead proposes a wholesale philosophical reorientation to the nature of privacy, genetics, and free will. Google proposes that once total surveillance is in place, for a generation or more, interesting possibilities present themselves. In soothing tones, the video explains,

> When we use contemporary technology, a trail of information is created in the form of data. When analyzed, it describes our actions, decisions, preferences, movement, and relationships. This codified version of who we are becomes ever more complex, developing, changing, and deforming based on our actions. In this regard, this ledger of our data may be considered a Lamarchian epigenome: a constantly evolving representation of who we are.[36]

They propose collecting an intergenerational dataset that charts every aspect of birth, life, health, happiness, and productivity. If the dataset also includes a representative global population, they might see the pattern that points to a cure for depression, poor health, and poverty. With the promise of happiness, healthcare, and more money, this US-based company proposed to use a Lamarchian metaphor for human evolution rather than a Darwinian one for a very good reason. They chose to export distinctly American values through the solutions they offer, and they are not compatible with Darwinian evolution, a bugaboo of US culture wars for decades.

Google seeks to use the Lamarchian "adaptive force" in the use of user data. For the French biologist and precursor to Darwin, Jean-Baptiste Lamarck, animals evolved in response to an adaptive force that led to a higher-level more complex organism. It explained the variety of genera as well as varying levels of evolution, with humanity at the top. Google chose to reject Darwinian evolution that required spontaneity and the unexpected. Norbert Wiener, originator of the field of cybernetics at MIT, described the difference in the following way: "Darwin's great innovation in the theory of evolution was that he conceived of it not as a Lamarchian spontaneous ascent from higher to higher and from better to better, but as a phenomenon in which living beings showed (a) a spontaneous tendency to develop in many directions, and (b) a tendency to follow the pattern of their ancestors."[37] For a company seeking to profit on the ability to predict the future, Darwinian evolution and the spontaneous tendency to develop in many directions is bad for business. So Google is proposing to apply the adaptive force through data tracking and stimulus-based behavior modification, while also ascending itself to a higher and better level organism.

Google will grow to become the most evolved organism on Earth and feed on human effort and ingenuity to sustain itself and evolve further. The company will live forever on the eternal stores of human data, generated by every conceivable embedded sensor available. Here is the plan in sum:

> User data has the capability to survive beyond the limits of our biological selves, in much the same way as genetic code is released and propagated in nature. By considering this data through in a Lamarchian lens, the codified experiences within the ledger become an accumulation of behavioral knowledge throughout the life of an individual. By thinking of user data as multi-generational, it becomes possible for emerging users to benefit from the preceding generations behaviors and decisions. As new users enter an ecosystem, they begin to create their own trail of data. By comparing this emergent ledger, with a mass of historical user data, it becomes possible to make increasingly accurate predictions about decisions and future behaviors. As the cycles of collection and comparison extend, it may be possible to develop a species level understanding of complex issues, such as depression, health, and poverty.[38]

User centered design principles mapped onto Richard Dawkins theory of the "selfish gene" which seeks to simply propagate the gene along with the organism:

> Our ability to interpret user data, combined with the exponential growth in sensor enabled objects will result in an increasingly detailed account of who we are as people. As these streams of information are brought together, the effect is multiplied. New patterns become apparent, and new predictions become possible.[39]

While the metaphors at use here are sometimes scientific in application and theory, Google's proposed selfish ledger in the aesthetics of the humanities. In the style of a slick documentary, they presume to "account of who we are as people." It has the style of humanistic argument, but this is pure sophistry. Google's thought experiment about the future of humanity needs to first supplant the humanities and lay claim to our ability to tell stories about *who we are as people*. In order to imagine human futures, the selfish ledger must then replace science fiction's role as a reliable predictor and designer of the future. "Behavioral sequencing" becomes a euphemism for the human genome project applied to human behavior. In other words, behavioral sequencing is an attempt to plot the behavioral sequences of every available human. A behavioral sequence would be a truer, more objective, version of human memory. The ledger can then be given a focus that not only tracks user behavior, but also modifies the actions and results according to a predetermined, inter-generational plan. Behaviors that are deemed outside the scope of desired results Google does not give an indication of the "desired results" of this plan.

The corporate values that animate this plan are ultimately expressed by the algorithms that make Google's products so compelling to use. As an entity, Google is really a system designed to spread, develop, and improve these algorithms. Google's famous PageRank is just the best known of these non-human entities protected by layers of legal intellectual property protections and copyright law. In the words of Ed Finn, in *What Algorithms Want*, "Many of the most powerful corporations in existence today are essentially cultural wrappers for sophisticated algorithms."[40] Being able to track and authenticate the quality of the incoming data sources through biometric sensors is critical to the broader surveillance capitalist project. This mass collection of information that totalizes the individual has been called the "database of ruin" by Paul Ohm. "The database of ruin exists only in potential," in 2010 when Ohm imagined the ability to "deanonymize" individuals based on existing public data: "It is the worldwide collection of all of the facts held by third parties that can be used to cause privacy-related harm to almost every member of society."[41] The security industry plays a role in normalizing this kind of tracking by advocating for the broad use of biometric authentication by invoking fear of "the hacker." A stark division emerges in surveillance capitalism. Society may be split between those who willingly submit themselves to something like Google's Selfish Ledger and those who go to great lengths to avoid participating in the system. The benefits of participating in a benevolent system of total surveillance— the *magnum opus* of one's life as a statistical model in search of still greater health, happiness, and prosperity—may outweigh the costs of privacy for some users; the risks of allowing an extra-governmental surveillance system would export American-style income inequality around the world while granting greater direct influence over citizens to a non-democratic corporation.

In practice, the Selfish Ledger could grant privileged access to citizens lives and position a corporation to commit the most complete and subtle social engineering campaign. Cathy O'Neil's *Weapons of Math Destruction: How Big Data Increases Inequality and Threatens Democracy* describes how a "toxic feedback loop" re-enforces bias on simple demographic markers like race, geography, and class.[42] Legal restrictions in the form of antitrust, taxation, and privacy will be gradually erode to better serve data collection and to complete the model of human behavior.

Cybernetic technologies have, in the past, used the threat of attack as a justification for the adoption of a new technology. In *Human Use of Human Beings*, Wiener opens his explanation of cybernetics with the Second World War and the use of mechanically assisted gunner sights. The augmentation of human perception with mechanical means was the opening of cybernetics as a defensive technology of war. Even very early on, Wiener thought it best to "avoid all question-begging epithets such as 'life,' 'soul,' 'vitalism,' and the like" when considering the agency of these technologies and instead argued to "enlarge the word 'life'" to include machines.[43] In this way, a cultural wrapper for an algorithm can be described as alive in the sense that it seeks to propagate and sustain its own algorithms and code. A complex object like Google and its parent company Alphabet—regarded as a kind of sentient machine—is no longer merely "an extension of man," as Marshall McLuhan termed it, but a living, co-evolving symbiotic entity seeking mutual interdependence with humanity. This is the Gaia hypothesis applied to the ubiquitous web. Rather than only viewing our Earth's biosphere as a single organism capable of achieving self-regulating homeostasis, it is now possible to view the ubiquitous web with all its embedded sensors as a nervous system capable of influencing the behavior of humanity, Earth's most troublesome species. At this scale, Google can be viewed, metaphorically, as a higher order organism comprised of codependent actors—including humans, software platforms, and corporate entities—existing in a socioeconomic cultural network online. The Selfish Ledger represents a cybernetic feedback loop of self re-enforcing symbiotic hybrid biology and technology. It forms a kind of symbiotic balance between humanity and the algorithm, mutually benefiting in life and wealth. Wealth and vitality are delivered by this new data driven oracle in exchange for an endless stream of data, preserved eternally. The power granted to those in control of such a system would be immense. Governments would grow increasingly incapable of regulating or monitoring such a vast, largely automated system. With influence over citizens granted to elected officials, re-election becomes only possible by supporting this global surveillance system. It would be comforting to believe that humanity would not succumb to such a totalizing system of surveillance and control in exchange for a fantasy of a new human condition. Who is capable of selling this privacy free future?

Virtual Influencers

Let's face it, our identities have been weaponized against us. Catherine D'Ignazio and Lauren F. Klein describe a "paradox of exposure" in *Data Feminism*: "the double bind that places those who stand to significantly gain from being counted in the most danger from that same counting (or classifying) act."[44] Free and open expression of counterculture radicalism only offers an opportunity to be cataloged, profiled, and micro-targeted. Geolocated social media posts connect any moment, anywhere to how we feel and suggests a product just in time. The ways we connect our work, family, friends, and lovers online—through the same interfaces and often on the same platforms—blurs human relationships between intimacy and productivity. Our "data exhaust"—the "behavioral by-products" of all the logged interactions we make daily—is collected and spun into a startlingly accurate set of characteristics, behaviors, and attitudes.[45] Shoshana Zuboff describes this power as the ability to sell "behavioral futures" that allow for corporations to purchase access to the data and profiles of target markets. Zuboff describes how Facebook can "effectively target a new class of 'object' once known as your 'personality.'"[46] The notion that "micro-behavioral targeting" can tune human behavior through notification nudges and user-interface based conditioning, wherein human expression can only find footing through a market driven *choice architecture*. This monetized, repackaged version of free will appears at present as context aware notifications. This notion of a choice architecture predetermines actions by channeling context-based decisions through desirable outcomes: something online marketers like to describe successful interactions as "conversion." Successful marketing is represented by the conversion of attention and interaction into sales. The collection, transmission, and storage of this data represents the means of producing this complex system of subtly powerful modeling of intention, desire, and decision making directed toward future economic activity.

Surveillance capitalism still needs a friendly face to sell this conversion of choice, experience, and human relationships into an enjoyable and even desirable experience. In *Archeologies of the Future*, Fredric Jameson explains how globalized cybernetic technology in the service of late state capitalism will produce the conditions for "the emergence of new subjectivities."[47] These subjectivities are in the tradition of those tricky, boundary crossing cyborgs of Donna Haraway or Anne Balsamo's contingent humanism that embraced cybernetics as a source of liberation. Cyberspace offers a chance to escape the bodily confinements of identity and open the sensuality of the mind, inspired by Pat Cadigan's synners exist in a "techo-body" of pure connection.[48] Cyberspace never quite resulted in this ideal freedom for either Cadigan or

Balsamo. Instead, the promises of VR like cyberspace merely fragments bodily experience in uneven and often unequal ways. In practice, surveillance technology has always assumed a white gaze. In Simone Browne's *Dark Matters*, she describes a "prototypical whiteness" that dictates the design and purpose of surveillance systems for white people above all others thereby perpetuating technological white supremacy.[49] While momentarily freed from the socially constructed biological determinism of a gendered and racialized body, cyberspace might give the opportunity to smash the patriarchy but the pieces are still all there. The new subjectivities Jameson, Balsamo, and Haraway predict are made up of those pieces and are themselves constructed in subtle ways in the service of surveillance capitalism. Cybernetic subjects in and of themselves will not grant digital transcendence predicted in science fiction.

The ability for machines to emulate humanity, a discipline within affective computing, will only further exploit our human capacity to trust simulations. The political consequences of this trust can be significant. 2016 was the year that chatbots made a comeback.[50] New platforms were being developed and integrated into messaging services. The general availability of machine learning (ML) tools allowed for generative bots to react more naturally to users and even learn from them. The naturalization of text interfaces on mobile environments made bots a natural fit for marketers and taste makers. The decline in mobile app development helped feed into the sense that, in the words of then Microsoft CEO Satya Nadella, "bots were the new apps."[51] Bots are nothing new however. The 1990s saw the growth of bots as toys for the still new internet. Based on AIML (Artificial Intelligence Markup Language), ALICE (Artificial Linguistic Internet Computer Entity) rose up to the state of the art and win the Loebner Prize in 2000.[52] Richard Wallace, ALICE's developer, gained fame for winning what was effectively a publicity stunt predicated on the imagination grabbing quality of the Turing Test. In recent years, a chatbot name Mitsuku, or Kuki for short, has won the prize.[53] Kuki is still based on the old XML-based AIML from 2001. For all the hype given to complex ML based chatbots using Recursive Neural Networks with open libraries like Google's TensorFlow, these conversational bots remained largely rules based. Complex models of conditional statements still rely on the simple branching if/else logic. Anyone can develop a Twitter bot using these logical statements with tools like *Cheap Bots, Done Quick.*[54] There are creative and even poetic versions of chatbots of this kind, some of which have been made by digital humanists.[55] Kik, Skype, Messenger all have bots. It is possible to chat with Kim Kardashian, and other famous people. Slack allows corporate teams to build bots to order coffee for the office or remind people to attend a meeting.

In all this cultural froth, there is a very real problem here. Bots might be the new apps, but they carry all the stereotypes associated with designing any character, what Lisa Nakamura defines as "cybertypes."[56] Bots are political because aesthetic choices must be made about their appearance, voice, dialect, and attitudes. They are often made with all the trappings of sexualized, racialized stereotypes of their designers. Intelligent assistants like Siri (Apple), Cortana (Microsoft), Alexa (Amazon), and Google Assistant (Alphabet) are all women by default and feminize subservience by default.[57] Bots or assistants of this kind are also racially "neutral," which is really just a way of saying they are modeled on dominant white perspectives. Nakamura explains this "default whiteness" in online spaces as "cybersocial hygiene."[58] It is neither surprising nor controversial to say that bots are retreading harmful attitudes online.

The effects of this politicization of bots can have profound impact because of their global audience. These virtual assistants are finding privileged access to many of our homes. They can also listen to everything in your home, and US law enforcement has made tens of the thousands of requests for data from these devices.[59] Furthermore, we have seen how a little bit of code running a Twitter bot has the power to change human opinion. These basic bots are well suited to magnify simple, imperatives. They were well suited to three-word slogans because the software driving them was similarly rudimentary: "Build the wall," "Lock her up," "Drain the swamp" can be used in almost any context when political discourse is reduced to sloganeering and slander. John Markoff at the Oxford Internet Institute found evidence that Trump "out botted" Clinton by a wide margin.[60] The jargon and rhetoric is so repetitive that the parody is easy to program and easy to churn. With a US President generating word salad on a daily basis, it is also easy to just toss the limited vocabulary into a bot generator and stay on message.

The ability to tell the difference between bots and humans is now critically important to our elections. Services are readily available that can now tell the difference between bots and real social media accounts. I am about a third bot on Botometer. That seems about right. Bot or not will test your followers to determine the level of "bottishness" of your followers. Attempts are being made to create more sophisticated and human like chatbots that can learn. Tay (Thinking About You) was the first chatbot based on modern machine learning techniques from Microsoft.[61] She was released in March 2016, but Tay had a fatal flaw. She learned from users naively. Those interactions were then reinforced through an iterative model of training. She became an anti-Semitic, racist, homophobe in a matter of hours. Pundits claimed that "the web cannot be trusted" and Tay was ruined by association with all the bad people.[62] In reality, she was gamed by internet savvy users eager to embarrass Microsoft. She was shut down in just three days. Microsoft's second attempt, Zo, was less open minded.[63] She was reduced to a game like character. Fortunes and jokes replaced Tay's pro-Trump and pro-Hitler slogans. Zo was made apolitical and quickly rebuilt the default cybertypes that support white supremacy. The new subjectivities made during this time were very optimistic about the ability of these technologies, but there are new models released regularly. Replika is an "AI companion who cares" and basically just asks questions and listens.[64] Maybe that's enough.

While the bots improve, human social media stars fill in temporarily until they too are automated out of employment. The friendly face of this new media landscape is an online celebrity we now routinely call an influencer. Those with large followings are able to leverage real political power and wealth for sponsored posts thinly veiled as authentic human expression. Often, an influencer's day job is to sell a product and present a desirable life online for all to see, but they are also able to sway followers. The desirability of their projected lives online—as beautiful, self-actualized, and magnanimous humans—is influential because they exploit the very human foibles like human insecurity and jealousy. These personalities mix with our real friends and relations and blurs the line between interacting with a marketing personality and a real person. Blending authentic humans with public personas—designed for marketing purposes—blurs subjects whom we know and love with subjectivities designed and approved for marketing purposes.

Blending reality and fiction is increasingly normal experience of being online. In 2017, a deepfake of President Obama was released by a research team at the University of Washington.[65] It is possible to readily remap the movements and expressions of one video, frame by frame, from another. A US President's image can now be remade to declare war or accept defeat in an election, posing a potential crisis for national security and democracy through subtle forms of disinformation. Now disinformation can appear to come directly from prominent and powerful individuals.[66] Similarly faked videos have appeared using deep learning techniques in recent years, featuring Donald Trump and Mark Zuckerberg. A report from the Law Fare blog sketches some of the potential uses of these technologies to show videos public officials taking bribes or other illegal acts; soldiers or police could be shown committing murder to inflame social unrest; falsified audio could disrupt an election by having opponents appear to be making inflammatory comments.[67] Of course, the potential for all this fake media also provides a convenient cover for politicians who do take bribes and make inflammatory comments. It undermines public trust in evidence plainly depicting police perpetrated brutality and murder. The risk of deepfake videos are reduced by an open society and a free press capable of rapidly debunking false content and conspiracy theories. Such corrective measures will always be incomplete, and the ideological intransigence of extremely partisan environments will mean many people simply will believe whichever version of events serves their belief system or party affiliation.

The lines between real and fake seems to have the effect of preparing the public audience for wholly fake personalities. The "uncanny valley" is a term used by roboticists to mark the weird in-between space where synthetic entities are neither fully machine nor passing as human. Crossing the uncanny valley for most viewers seems to become easier in a media environment populated by deepfakes and Photoshopped influencers. As the line between real and fake blends, "virtual influencers" have emerged on Instagram and other platforms with names like Lil' Miquela, Shudu, Bermudaisbae, Imma, and Noonoouri.[68] These personalities can be created with readily available 3D modeling software and are touted as "the future of marketing."[69] Motion capture systems can map human movement to 3D art objects resulting in feeling of natural or organic movement. These virtual people are seen in real places, posing with real people and command followings of millions. Cameron-James Wilson is the CEO and owner of the virtual influencer studio called The Diigitals based in the UK that creates and owns Shudu.[70] Lauren Michele Jackson wrote an article for *The New Yorker* called, "Shudu Gram Is a White Man's Digital Projection of Real-Life Black Womanhood."[71] Jackson connects this phenomenon to vaudevillian blackface that "allowed white audiences to indulge their intense fascination with blackness without having to interact with actual black people."[72] There is also no need to actually pay a black model when they are digital art assets. Shudu is copyright protected intellectual property; she is not human, but her creator would like you to pretend she is. Digital blackface, as defined by Jason Parham, is "a twisted love of Black culture through caricature."[73] These caricatures of black culture augment and overlay online identities only when they are a benefit to the user. Like vaudevillian blackface, these performances can be wiped off their profile when they can no longer benefit from the association with black culture. The new subjectivities of late capitalism seek only to profit from cultural change, wherein Black cultural content, bodies, and bodies are merely fodder for market forces. These are custom identities expressing a Photoshopped sense of style refined through Instagram's algorithmic ideal beauty. These caricatures are impossibly slim, big eyes, and young, forever. These influencers will never age, get a pimple, or even have a bad night's sleep. They have no life that is not in service to their own influence.

Similarly, Lil Miquela appeared in a Calvin Klein online ad kissing Bella Hadid, who currently has more than ~3.6 million followers on Instagram alone. The ad was heavily criticized by online media for "gay baiting" ahead of the 2019 Pride celebrations, but the presence of a virtual influencer passed by with only a vague awareness of the uncanny quality of the event.[74] Artificial agents, bots, and characters are increasingly members of the online conversation. This signals a growing acceptance of fake entities influencing and shaping opinion. It also blurs the line between real and human, product and person.

Wilson is unambiguous about his belief that Shudu is both a person and a person who can be owned: "People will become heirlooms. You will inherit them." Personhood is here understood as their identity online, without need for a real world correlate. Like a shadow without a body, the owners of these virtual people are often left intentionally obscure.[75] Fashion and style, maybe even the fashion industry, are key cultural mechanisms for how society and culture will integrate virtual influencers.

There are even digital fashion houses that produce digital renders of clothing. The Fabricant sells NFT brand collaborations and releases free file drops that allow users to wear digital haute couture on their Instagram with Adobe Illustrator.[76] Brands like Adversarial Fashion are designing clothes, from fabric rather than pixels, that block or confuse computer vision systems.[77] Stylists are researching makeup and hair that will similarly block or confuse facial recognition systems. The Computer Vision Dazzle project, which seeks to thwart facial recognition systems, is having *Vogue* ask if hair and makeup styling can be an anti-surveillance tool.[78] The ability for a computer to see is a central trope of science fiction and will serve as the basis for our increasingly normalized experience of biopower and surveillance. These biometric scans work to fix identity, deanonymize, and track behavior. A key human exploit is our affinity to our identities. Our identities are linked biometrically to an elaborate system of surveillance that concentrates and processes data for marketing for the law abiding and imprisonment for those deemed invalid.

Cindy Mayweather—ArchAndroid

What can a human do? Newitz offers hints about these new relationships in their parallel narrative in *Autonomous* describing an intimate relationship between a bot and a human. In the novel, Newitz describes a relationship between Eliasz, a globe-trotting military operative, and his heavily armed robot bodyguard named Paladin. Paladin is technically a cyborg, equipped with a donated human brain strictly for facial recognition purposes. In an ironic twist, human brains remain the best system for facial recognition well into the future, but they are harvested an implanted in machines. Paladin is sentient but has not yet earned an "autonomy key" to be freed from indentured service. Paladin is driven to collect human intelligence or "HUMINT" to better serve Eliasz in social situations, so when Eliasz asks to ride Paladin in a battle, the bot accepts and modifies its body beyond its intended purpose. Eliasz is turned on sexually by the destructive force of Paladin's guns, mounted on the bot's chest. Paladin seeks to better understand human community and connection by expanding their default design:

> At that moment, Paladin decided to test something he'd been contemplating for several minutes, based on what he'd learned from the sprinkler system. Perhaps human intelligence gathering was a version of network penetration, and he could better integrate into social situations by inviting humans to see an illusory version of himself. Instead of dispelling Eliasz' misunderstanding, he would find a way to accommodate it.[79]

Paladin accommodates Eliasz's anthropomorphism and uses the male pronoun in doing so. Paladin is forced to understand Eliasz's own internalized homophobia as he tries to discover the gender of the brain donor for Paladin's facial recognition system. Paladin researches Eliasz's use of homophobic slurs used to describe their relationship.[80] Paladin is struggling to incorporate Eliasz's homophobia with the history of gender-based violence found online to better understand robot sexuality. The conflict in Paladin emerges from the desire to serve human urges by adapting to human views of the world.

For these reasons, Paladin accepts the pronouns that Eliasz uses. The military nature of Paladin's construction warrants male pronouns for the human operator. While Paladin has yet to choose their pronouns, this moment of accommodating inaccurate pronouns are a key facet of gender identities that do not match their physical bodies. For Paladin, names and categories become the function calls and methods for individuals, which allows us to hack demographics and circumvent social engineering through non-binary and trans identities. In a science fiction context, augmenting human physical abilities as well as mental abilities is a necessary step in advancing human performance. Paladin is able to augment the use of her body to assist in her Human Intelligence gathering, like when she uses her electro-stun system as a mount for Eliasz to ride on. The physical body becomes destiny for Paladin, whose strength and capability for violence is interpreted as masculine. When Eliasz learns the human brain housed in Paladin's abdomen is female, he constructs a human narrative to explain his attraction to Paladin:

> "I knew there was a reason I wanted you, Paladin," he whispered. "I must have somehow sensed that you were a woman."

> There it was: the anthropomorphization.[81]

Paladin knows that "bots had no gender" but is willing to accept the pronouns to facilitate her human intelligence gathering. Paladin is working to gain autonomy and will adapt as needed to learn about "bot culture" living in free bot communities.[82] Paladin is code switching between human and bot cultures until she has gained the autonomy to choose without restriction. Human culture's anthrocentrism assumes gender from morphology as well as the expression of intimacy in relationships, in which anthropomorphism works like heteronormativity. Anatomy is not destiny for bots and humans alike.[83] Bot culture is free from body shape and communicates with absolute privacy through public key cryptography. Paladin has learned that blending human and machine worlds requires a fluid identity.

The novel proposes a view of identity in which bots are models for humanity. As a kind of demographic plasticity, blending human and machine subjectivities means humans must learn to break coherence of data collection. Psychographic data must also become unusable by jamming cultural data trails. Political affiliation must be unrecognizable until votes are cast and counted securely. As online agents, we must become multinational online citizens, appearing everywhere through VPNs or private network relays like Tor. We must be multicultural and multilingual through a radical kind of digital cosmopolitanism online. Heterodox subjectivities would require us to change our own beliefs, a difficult heresy to accomplish. Subjectivities become an object to manipulate and augment. Expression of these objects through code. To avoid becoming a mere data model of a human, new subjectivities will be created and destroyed in rapid succession following patterns left in adversarial fashions. While not tripping into appropriation, we must disrupt the categories and codes that mark our bodies biometrically. Newitz dedicates their book to "all the robots who question their programming," which again suggests that humans can be critically recoded. The process of questioning our programming is an infinite loop. Artificial entities on social media work to influence politics, opinions, and attitudes. We live in an attention economy. Corporations, governments, and individuals of all kinds are vying for our views, impressions, and engagements. Musical artists are perfectly positioned to reflect on this cybernetic extension of market forces in popular culture because they are mediated through audio, video, and image on all the platforms.

Cindy Mayweather is the android pseudonym of Janelle Monáe's recent albums. Through Mayweather, android number 57821, Monáe tells a science fiction narrative in music, videos, and album art of her revolutionary resistance against the Ministry of Droids. Appearing first in the 2008 *Metropolis* "The Chase" EP, then continuing a narrative through successive albums *ArchAndroid* in 2010 and *Electric Lady* in 2013, Monáe describes a future dystopia where machines are documented, tracked, and controlled. "Suite One: The Chase" EP describes Monáe's pseudonym, Cindi Mayweather's run from authorities for loving a human. Mayweather is clearly referencing Fritz Lang's 1927 film *Metropolis* and 1970s experimental jazz musician Sun Ra. It is a sci-fi parable of oppressive regimes controlling rogue droids who fight their programming. It is an allegory for repression gender, race, and sexuality, but it is also about revolutionary power of art and expression. "The android is just another way of speaking about the new other," says Monáe in a 2011 interview, "and I consider myself to be part of the other just by being a woman and being black. There's still certain stereotypes that I have to fight off, and there's still a certain struggle that we all individually have to go through."[84] In the video for the song "Many Moons," the Mayweather alter ego is purchased at the Annual Android Auction and breaks down by over-performing for her human audience. Mayweather and Monáe sings "your freedom is in a bind" as she breaks down in a cybernetic frenzy and is captured by authorities for her aberrant behavior. The final title card of the video leaves a cryptic message from Mayweather that suggests we are not entirely in our own world: "I imagined many moons in the sky lighting the way to freedom." An evocative and strangely familiar message leading to freedom that is also otherworldly.

In the follow up full length album, *ArchAndroid*, the song "Dance or Die" features Saul Williams and tells us that these "dreams are forever" and that dance is liberation. Dance is a pure form of bodily agency. These rebellions are cast in a historical scope that starts with the intimacy and immediacy of dance and music. She calls to "sow in the seeds of education" to sustain the present and future revolution. Monáe's stories, music, and characters express a politics that support real world revolutionaries, which is why she donates revenue from her merchandise sales to educational initiatives.[85] In a 2013 interview in *Bust*, Monáe explains the future oriented, speculative opportunities of science fiction she felt growing up in Kansas City: "I thought science fiction was a great way of talking about the future. It doesn't make people feel like you're talking about things that are happening right now, so they don't feel like you're talking down to them. It gives the listener a different perspective."[86] Having an imagination to shape and create the future is powerful. Science fiction music is also about imagining a new future.[87]

In the song and video "Q.U.E.E.N" featuring Erykah Badu, art becomes an activation script to awaken the latent, revolutionary programming of Cindi Mayweather. Music has the ability to awaken cultural memory from across time and space. Museums represent the death of culture in this video, where music and art is preserved and sealed up, rendering it inert and inactive. Through music, she calls to the power of Queen Nefertiti to free Kansas City. Museums are a normative tool to organize, systematize, and control culture. There is a foundation of truth in dance. There are malicious cultural codes that serve to repress and control, like Christian orthodoxy that represses sexuality: "Or should I reprogram, deprogram and get down?" She is fighting her programming by defying systems that seek to track and control. Non-violent liberation is not just about seeking to legitimize repressed identities: "Categorize me, I defy every label." The genre bending openness to hybrid cultures, references, and sources is a musical expression of joy and breaking rules.

The Cindi Mayweather cycle is about revolution. It tells a story through music, fashion, video, and dance about human power and control. Processed through algorithms to track, restrain, and control the rebellious Arch Android. Biometrics, eye scanning and gait analysis to track and determine identity are all referenced in her videos. Gait analysis of dance as a rebellion of surveillance. By avoiding categories, Mayweather escapes the ministry of droids by proving her autonomy through self-expression. Humanity has weathered all past technological revolutions worrying about its own destruction. Destruction is just another fantasy of transcendence. The fear of humanity's demise is at once a desire to become nothing. To be free of the burden of responsibility. The responsibility to manage our own destiny, which AI threatens to rob from us, is also the responsibility to be decent to each other. We have fantasies of God playing arbiter of which group of humans is most righteous in killing each other. Surveillance capitalism marks a similar appeal to some transcendent judge. As Newitz explains in the final pages of *Autonomous*, "But now we know there has been no one great disaster—only the slowmotion disaster of capitalism converting every living thing and idea into property."[88] Some all-powerful force capable of either destroying us all or deciding who is justified and righteous in all the death. We've sought secular substitutes in the past, like the free market or communism, but both systems fail to fully grasp the real world or some truest transcendental state beyond our own human imaginations. Our real fear should rest with the failure of AI to make much sense of anything. What if all this computation power yields nothing. What if deep learning cannot make sense of the noise? What do we do if AI can only prove the obvious? What happens if AI is just another tool of oppression, like so many machines we've invented in the past? Where will we find our transcendence then? It may come in the rejection of human subjectivity. By becoming changeable objects, the weaponization of identity as a tool for surveillance, perfected in biometric scans, will simply pass us by.

Notes

1   CAPTCHA stands for Telling Humans and Computers Apart Automatically. See http://captcha.net/.

2   Neal Mueller, "Credential Stuffing," *OWASP*, https://owasp.org/www-community/attacks/Credential_stuffing.

3   A.M. Turing, "Computing Machinery and Intelligence," *Mind 59*, no. 236 (October 1950): 433–460, https://doi.org/10.1093/mind/LIX.236.433

4   Joan Baum, *The Calculating Passion of Ada Byron* (Hamden, CT: Archon Books, 1986), 16.

5 Ibid., 450.

6 Mike Feathersone and Roger Burrows, "Cultures of Technological Embodiment: An Introduction," in *Cyberspace/Cyberbodies/Cyberpunk: Cultures of Technological Embodiment*, eds. Mike Featherstone and Roger Burrows (London: Sage Publications, 1995), 1.

7 See https://openbionics.com/, https://www.shadowrobot.com/, and https://www.youbionic.com.

8 Elon Musk's company Nuralink is working to commercialize brain and machine interfaces through a so-called Neural Lace implant, but the results of this work are still in their infancy. See https://neuralink.com/.

9 Cade Metz, "Elon Musk Isn't the Only One Trying to Computerize Your Brain," *Wierd.com*. March 31, 2017, https://www.wired.com/2017/03/elon-musks-neural-lace-really-look-like/.

10 Open AI claims that its goal is to ensure that "AI benefits all of humanity." See https://openai.com/about.

11 Zachary Mason, *Void Star* (New York: Farrar, Straus, and Giroux, 2017).

12 Annalee Newitz, *Autonomous* (New York: Tor, 2017), 36.

13 See https://studentdebtcrisis.org/.

14 Autonomous, 177.

15 Ibid., 30.

16 Ibid., 49.

17 Ibid., 53.

18 P.J. Cock, T. Antao, J.T. Chang, B.A. Chapman, C.J. Cox, A. Dalke, et al. "Biopython: Freely Available Python Tools for Computational Molecular Biology and Bioinformatics," *Bioinformatics* 25, no. 11 (2009): 1422–3; see also https://biopython.org/.

19 Fan Wu et al. "A New Coronavirus Associated with Human Respiratory Disease in China," *Nature* 579 (2020): 265–9. doi:10.1038/s41586-020-2008-3.

20 Charlie Campbell, "The Chinese Scientist Who Sequenced the First COVID-19 Genome Speaks Out About the Controversies Surrounding His Work," *Time.com*, August 24, 2020, https://time.com/5882918/zhang-yongzhen-interview-china-coronavirus-genome/.

21 Genetic programming uses evolutionary heuristics to refine and improve algorithms, whereas genetic computing uses the machinery of living cells to store and process encoded data.

22 Damon Mitchell, "As Predicted by Body Hacks CRISPR Is the New Steroids," *Bodyhacks.com*, September 13, 2020, https://bodyhacks.com/predicted-body-hacks-crispr-new-steroids/; David Pescovitz, "Hacking Your Microbiome with DIY Fecal Transplants," *Boingboing.net*, April 17, 2017, https://boingboing.net/2017/04/17/hacking-your-microbiome-with-d.html.

23 International Human Genome Sequencing Consortium, E. Lander et al. "Initial Sequencing and Analysis of the Human Genome," *Nature* 409 (2001): 860–921 (2001). https://doi.org/10.1038/35057062.

24 Heidi Ledford, "CRISPR, the Disruptor," *Nature* 522 (June 2015): 20–4. doi:10.1038/522020a.

25 Katherine J. Wu, Carl Zimmer, and Elian Peltier, "Nobel Prize in Chemistry Awarded to 2 Scientists for Work on Genome Editing," *Nytimes.com*, October 7, 2020, https://www.nytimes.com/2020/10/07/science/nobel-prize-chemistry-crispr.html.

26 David Cyranoski and Sara Reardon, "Embryo Editing Sparks Epic Debate," *Nature* 520 (April 2015): 593–5. doi:10.1038/520593a.

27 David Cyranoski, "The CRISPR-baby Scandal: What's Next for Human Gene-editing," *Nature* 566 (February 2019): 440–2. doi:10.1038/d41586-019-00673-1

28 There are notably few hard science fiction authors working to describe the current state of bioinformatics and genetic editing. Greg Bear's *Darwin's Radio* (New York: Ballantine Books, 1999) is a notable exception. Bear describes a retrovirus that disrupts childbirth and genetically modifies offspring, producing a new species distinct from homo sapiens.

29 Sheryl N. Hamilton, "Traces of the Future: Biotechnology, Science Fiction, and the Media," *Science Fiction Studies* 30, no. 2 (2003): 268. jstor.org/stable/4241173.

30 N. Katherine Hayles, *How We Became Posthuman: Virtual Bodies in Cybernetics, Literature and Informatics* (Chicago: University of Chicago Press, 1999), 86–7.

31 Hubert Etc's full name is Hubert Vernon Roudolph Clayton Irving Wilson Alva Anton Jeff Harley Timothy Curtis Cleveland Cecil Ollie Edmund Eli Wiley Marvin Ellis Espinoza. Hubert Etc is able to choose any combination of these names in a legal real name policy and retain some measure of anonymity.

32 Matt Ratto, "Ethics of Seamless Infrastructures: Resources and Future Directions," *The International Review of Information Ethics* 8 (2007): 20–7.

33 Jane Bennett, *Vibrant Matter: A Political Ecology of Things* (Durham: Duke University Press, 2010), 1.

34 Vlad Savov, "Google's Selfish Ledger Ideas Can Also be Found in Its Patent Applications," *Theverge.com*, May 19, 2018, https://www.theverge.com/2018/5/19/17246152/google-selfish-ledger-patent-applications.

35 The song "Ethereal" in "The Selfish Ledger" video was released in 2015 by a fictional character named DJ Sona as a "Ultimate Skin Music" for the videogame *League of Legends*. DJ Sona's character and her supporting songs are a musical collaboration between Riot Games and several human musicians, including Nosaj Thing, Pretty Lights, The Crystal Method, Dada Life, Bassnectar, and Renholdër. See https://www.youtube.com/watch?v=cxa1Y71Lgyg.

36 Ibid.

37 Norbert Wiener, *Human Uses for Human Beings: Cybernetics and Society* (London: Free Association Books), 37.

38 Vlad Savov, "Google's Selfish Ledger Ideas Can Also Be Found in Its Patent Applications," *Theverge.com*, May 19, 2018, https://www.theverge.com/2018/5/19/17246152/google-selfish-ledger-patent-applications.

39 Ibid.

40 Ed Finn, *What Algorithms Want: Imagination in the Age of Computing* (Cambridge, MA: MIT Press, 2017), 20.

41 Paul Ohm, "Broken Promises of Privacy: Responding to the Surprising Failure of Anonymization," *UCLA Law Review* 57 (2010): 1746.

42 Cathy O'Neil, *Weapons of Math Destruction: How Big Data Increases Inequality and Threatens Democracy* (New York: Crown Publishing, 2016), 19.

43 Wiener, *Human,* 32.

44 Catherine D'Ignazio and Lauren F. Klein, *Data Feminism* (Cambridge, MA: MIT Press, 2020), 105.

45 Shoshana Zuboff, *The Age of Surveillance Capitalism: The Fight for a Human Future at the New Frontier of Power* (New York: PublicAffairs, 2019), 67.

46 Ibid., 273.

47 Ibid., 214.

48 Anne Balsamo, "Forms of Technological Embodiment: Reading the Body in Contemporary Culture," in *Cyberspace/Cyberbodies/Cyberpunk: Cultures of Technological Embodiment*, eds. Mike Featherstone and Roger Burrows (London: Sage Publications, 1995), 223.

49 Simone Browne, *Dark Matters: On the Surveillance of Blackness* (Durham: Duke University Press, 2015), 113.

50 Ted Livingston, "Why Bots, Not A.I., Are the Future of Chat," *Venturebeat. com*, March 1, 2016, https://venturebeat.com/2016/03/01/why-bots-not-a-i-are-the-future-of-chat/.

51 Marco della Cava, "Microsoft CEO Nadella: 'Bots Are the New Apps,'" *Usatoday.com*, March 30, 2016, https://www.usatoday.com/story/tech/news/2016/03/30/microsof-ceo-nadella-bots-new-apps/82431672/; Jesus Rodriguez, "Bots Are the New Generation of Apps," *Computerworld.com*, April 28, 2016, https://www.computerworld.com/article/3062561/bots-are-the-new-generation-of-apps.html.

52 See http://www.aiml.foundation/doc.html.

53 See https://www.pandorabots.com/kuki/.

54 See https://cheapbotsdonequick.com/.

55 @unicode_garden, @portmanteau_bot, and @_Lostbuoy are all excellent examples of this kind of bot.

56 Lisa Nakamura, *Cybertypes: Race, Ethnicity, and Identity on the Internet* (New York: Routledge, 2002), 5–6.

57 Clifford Nass and Scott Brave, *Wired for Speech: How Voice Activates and Advances the Human-computer Relationship* (Cambridge, MA: MIT Press, 2007); UNESCO and EQUALS Skills Coalition, "The Rise of Gendered AI and Its Troubling Repercussions," in *I'd Blush If I Could: Closing Gender Divides in Digital Skills Through Education*, eds. Doreen Bogdan-Martin (France: UNESCO, 2019). https://unesdoc.unesco.org/ark:/48223/pf0000367416.locale=en

58 Nakamura, *Cybertypes*, 47.

59 See https://transparencyreport.google.com/ and https://www.apple.com/legal/transparency/ for up-to-date information from both Google and Apple, respectively.

60 John Markoff, "Automated Pro-Trump Bots Overwhelmed Pro-Clinton Messages, Researchers Say," *Nytimes.com*, November 17, 2016, https://www.nytimes.com/2016/11/18/technology/automated-pro-trump-bots-overwhelmed-pro-clinton-messages-researchers-say.html.

61 See https://en.wikipedia.org/wiki/Tay_(bot).

62 Matthew Hussey, "Microsoft's AI Chatbot Tay Learned How to Be Racist in Less than 24 Hours," *Thenextweb.com*, March 24, 2016, https://thenextweb.com/insider/2016/03/24/microsoft-pulled-plug-ai-chatbot-became-racist/.

63 See https://en.wikipedia.org/wiki/Zo_(bot).

64 See https://replika.ai.

65 See https://grail.cs.washington.edu/projects/AudioToObama/siggraph17_obama.pdf.

66 Robert Chesney and Danielle Citron, "Deepfakes and the New Disinformation War: The Coming Age of Post Truth Geopolitics," *Foreign Affairs* 98, no. 1 (2019): 1.

67 Robert Chesney and Danielle Citron, "Deepfakes: A Looming Crisis for National Security, Democracy and Privacy?," *Lawfareblog.com*, February 21, 2018, https://www.lawfareblog.com/deepfakes-looming-crisis-national-security-democracy-and-privacy.

68 Respectively, see the following profiles on Instagram: https://www.instagram.com/lilmiquela/, https://www.instagram.com/shudu.gram/, https://www.instagram.com/bermudaisbae/, https://www.instagram.com/imma.gram/, and https://www.instagram.com/noonoouri/.

69 See https://neweblabs.com/virtual-humans-a-new-avenue-of-influence-for-brands and https://digital-business-lab.com/2020/02/virtual-influencers-the-future-of-marketing/.

70 See https://www.thediigitals.com/. See also https://www.terrygatesstudio.com/.

71 Lauren Michele Jackson, "Shudu Gram Is a White Man's Digital Projection of Real-Life Black Womanhood," *Newyorker.com*, May 4, 2018, https://www.newyorker.com/culture/culture-desk/shudu-gram-is-a-white-mans-digital-projection-of-real-life-black-womanhood.

72 Ibid.

73 Jason Parham, "TikTok and the Evolution of Digital Blackface," *Wired.com*, August 4, 2020, https://www.wired.com/story/tiktok-evolution-digital-blackface/.

74 Patrick Kulp, "Real and Virtual Influence Collide as Bella Hadid Kisses Lil Miquela for Calvin Klein," *Adweek.com*, May 16, 2019, https://www.adweek.com/creativity/bella-hadid-lil-miquela/.

75 Emilia Petrarca, "Body Con Job Miquela Sousa Has over 1 Million Followers on Instagram and Was Recently Hacked by a Trump Troll. But She Isn't Real."

Thecut.com, May 2018, https://www.thecut.com/2018/05/lil-miquela-digital-avatar-instagram-influencer.html.

76 See https://www.thefabricant.com/.

77 See https://adversarialfashion.com/.

78 See https://cvdazzle.com/ and Laren Valenti, "Can Makeup Be an Anti-Surveillance Tool?" *Vogue.com*, June 12, 2020, https://www.vogue.com/article/anti-surveillance-makeup-cv-dazzle-protest.

79 Newitz, *Autonomous, 75.*

80 Ibid., 127.

81 Ibid., 187.

82 Ibid., 221.

83 Le Guin's *The Left Hand of Darkness* is the classic example of non-binary sexualities through a species level androgyny of the Gethenian people. See Brian Attebery, *Decoding Gender in Science Fiction* (New York: Routledge, 2002), 140.

84 Keel Weiss, "'The Electric Lady': Janelle Monáe on Her New Album and an Exclusive Behind-the-Scenes Look of Her Cover Art Photoshoot," *Elle.com*, April 29, 2013, https://www.elle.com/culture/music/news/a23604/janelle-monae-interview-electric-lady/.

85 See https://shop.jmonae.com/. See also https://sjli.org/, https://thelovelandfoundation.org/, and https://www.super7girls.org/.

86 Eliza C. Thompson, "Janelle Monáe: The Year's Most Intriguing Pop Star," *Bust.com*, September 2013, https://bust.com/general/10226-janelle-monae-the-years-most-intriguing-pop-star.html.

87 Monáe was nominated for a Hugo Award in 2019 for "Best Dramatic Presentation—Short Form" for her album *Dirty Computer.* The Hugo Awards nominated the first album *not* set in the Cindi Mayweather universe.

88 Newitz, *Autonomous*, 279.

6

Gray Hat Humanities:

Surveillance Capitalism, Object-Oriented Ontology, and Design Fiction

We live in the future: rockets land every few minutes at the vertical launch facility; lab grown meat and genetically modified vegetables feed the world; vertical farms make cities green and nuclear powered rovers are surveying for a new Mars colony; poverty is largely a thing of the past due to minimum basic income programs; education is free to anyone who wants it. We live in the future: Luddite Neo-fascists and a renewed authoritarian communist-block challenge liberal democracies around the globe; militarized police forces murder and harass without consequences; politicians increasingly serve a minority plutocratic class locked in elite walled neighborhoods; corporate surveillance in private and public spaces is nearly total; the global economy is on the brink of collapse because of yet another pandemic, unending quantitative easing, and the absurd ideology of endless growth.

In the future, we retreat ever further into technology "The world seems to keep getting weirder and weirder," Victoria Blake observes in the introduction to the *Cyberpunk* anthology, "with no end in sight."[1] The world seems to be getting weird enough that it is overlapping with fiction more and more often. Science fiction describes our world as it is now and imagines possible futures. This book makes a case for integrating cybersecurity methodologies into humanistic ways of understanding and preserving culture, using cyberpunk and science fiction as a useful point of overlap between imagination and reality. Cyberpunk might even work as a kind of design fiction capable of augmenting and supporting security practices by considering science fact through science fiction. These speculative approaches to security practices also invite pragmatic questions as well.

This book argues that the digital humanities must include security planning as a key component in conducting research online. In a generations long project of digitizing and preserving the past and contemporary cultural legacy, the digital humanities will enjoy increasing attention online as well as an increased risk of security failures. There are practical procedural consequences to this: digital humanities projects must become adept at threat modeling and accounting for risk assessments in their research plans. There are consequences to attracting public and political attention online: a small minority of adversaries will be motivated by extreme ideologies and a desire to create conflict, but the majority of threats will remain indiscriminate, automated, and difficult to anticipate. The risks to our shared online cultural legacy are serious because much of this data is unique and highly specialized. There has not yet been a catastrophic cyberattack against humanities research infrastructure, but it will happen inevitably.

Recent attacks have re-enforced the role of cybersecurity in several domains and have transformed institutions. These incidents might serve as a warning for how suddenly things can change. The 2009 Aurora Attacks, perpetrated by Chinese state-sponsored Elderwood Group, gained high-level access to many major corporations, including defense contractors, financial targets, and technology companies.[2] Aurora openly exposed the emerging Cold War footing between the Communist Party of China and the Western allied countries, which continue to center on corporate espionage. In the 2010 joint US and Israeli developed Stuxnet attack, Iranian nuclear weapons facilities were damaged by taking over industrial control systems that operated the uranium enrichment centrifuges used to make weapons grade nuclear material.[3] Stuxnet demonstrated the ability for a sufficiently patient nation-state to use a cyberattack against significant military targets without declaring war or firing a single bullet. In November of 2014, Sony Pictures was attacked in response to the upcoming film *The Interview* that depicted a plot to assassinate North Korean leader Kim Jong-un. After breaching Sony Pictures systems, North Korean state-sponsored hackers threatened to dump corporate data to embarrass the company and harass them into releasing a less graphic version of the film.[4] In 2015 and 2016, the US Democratic National Committee was attacked by multiple Russian state-sponsored groups, whose data was then released on WikiLeaks to embarrass the Democratic Party as well as the Presidential nominee, Hilary Clinton.[5] The hack and leak operation would prove detrimental to the Democrats, helping to elect Donald Trump to the White House. Cyberattacks like these appear to be escalating, which the 2020 SolarWinds attack suggests, after confirming that as many as eleven US federal government agencies were hacked.[6] Microsoft describes the hack as "the largest and most sophisticated attack the world has ever seen," and it included targets such as the Department of State, Department of Homeland Security's Cybersecurity and Infrastructure Security Agency, and The Pentagon.[7] Regardless of the level of access attained, that is a breathtaking list of targets to attack simultaneously. In the recent evolution of cyberattacks, there have been significant attacks on corporate, military, cultural, as well as political institutions. Simply put, each of these attacks has reshaped previous assumptions in a fundamental way. It is remarkable that computer hacking could fight wars, upend elections, or change the ending of a film. It should perhaps come as no surprise when a cultural or educational institution suffers a significant disruption resulting from a cyberattack.[8]

Hacks are culturally oriented and politically active. The political impact of data dumps and leaks are filtered through social media in a way that either amplifies their effect or diminishes their impact. Data leaks are powerful in a political sense, but these events shape cultural attitudes as well. They can influence public perceptions, ideological frameworks, and personal opinions in remarkable ways. But, as with most things, these hacks cut both ways. As a feature of our increasingly public exposure online, digital humanities must include security planning as a key component in conducting research. The digital humanities will enjoy increasing attention online as well as an increased risk of security breaches. There are practical procedural consequences that require sustained analysis of threat and risk to both humans and technology. Digital humanities projects must now embrace security best practices in the ways we plan, conduct, and communicate research.

There is evidence that cultural institutions are already facing increasing threats, primarily in the form of ransomware and data theft.[9] Often, these attacks risk being lumped into the same category as public institutional or municipal government attacks that have been an increasingly prevalent trend.[10] While municipal government hacks are very costly and disruptive, cultural and educational institutions house rare and historically significant data that could be impossible or very difficult to restore in the event of an attack. This situation is made worse by the lack of funding available to repair or rebuild digital projects. If a ransomware attack leaves unique cultural data encrypted or otherwise damaged, a portion of our shared cultural legacy is lost. University- and college-based humanities researchers face threats beyond the perpetual crises of budget short falls, although some risks are made worse by these contextual factors. Many of the risks emerge from digital humanities practitioners who regularly publish data online, develop web applications, or engage the public directly through social media. Digital humanities projects tend to be public facing and engage with cultural issues or histories that are politically charged precisely because they are poorly understood. The symptoms of political division and extremism regularly include trolling and threats on social media, so it is probable that prominent digital humanities projects will be targeted due to their visibility. Additionally, the mere presence of research materials on the internet exposes data and applications to indiscriminate attacks that are merely attempting to profit from a poorly managed or insecure web application.

There is vanity in fearing any and all possible security issues, however. Assuming that the humanities are "under attack" overstates the current level of risk. It is absolutely necessary not to assume a false sense of importance, if only because pride is an easy human exploit. Instead, humanists and cultural workers need to threat model their institutional security alongside their IT departments or appropriate government agencies. It makes good sense to follow a standard practice described by the US National Institute of Standards and Technology Cybersecurity framework.[11] A threat model that contains an asset audit and risk assessment should be part of designing a research proposal and developing a project charter. Project charters are agreements used by large teams to define the rules and practices governing their collaboration.[12] It is common to define expectations of work as well as the terms of employment and credit allocation among partners. Digital humanities projects should use such a document to train team members and work to define things like access control rules, with attention to password management, granting and revoking privileged access, and physical security of hardware. Projects must allocate grant funds to monitor and update both infrastructure and software by aligning development, security, and operations of public facing software. When an incident occurs, the project leads should be ready to respond and mitigate an attack and implement a recovery phase to improve and secure infrastructure.

Project teams must first evaluate and understand their shared assets. By understanding what about a project is valuable, teams will be able to define what needs to be protected. In defining the assets that are valuable and necessary to conduct research, humanists will be able to define the broader public value of their research and protect research objects held in public trust. An asset is something a knowledge stakeholder values and wants to protect. Whether these knowledge stakeholders are the producers, users, or subjects of humanistic research, researchers are bound to protect the resources and information produced. Other information like emails, contacts, messages, locations, and files may be important now, on a daily basis, or may be useful in the far future. Humanist research objects are highly varied, making risk assessments similarly varied. The assets of the humanities might be more tangible things like artifacts, art, or paper documents. If a team is digitizing archival materials, those materials may possess some intrinsic value that must also be protected on behalf of the owners.

It is common to assume that data or software are the primary assets, but humanities research must also account for the physical and online security of project partners and participants. If the research has human subjects, like with an oral history project or survey data, researchers must first pass some version of an Institutional Review Board (IRB) evaluation in research ethics.[13] Data protection and integrity guidelines must protect participant data to conduct research in good faith and, in some cases, protect the privacy and safety of participants. If the research conducted with human subjects is vulnerable to politically motivated reprisals for their participation, such as deportation, imprisonment, harassment, or threats to bodily injury or death, data protection measures simply cannot be an afterthought.

It is important to anonymize research data as much as possible, and consider deleting location-based metadata from images and videos. In general, keep data for only as long as necessary and delete data using a method that renders it irretrievable. These are difficult decisions for digital archives, where data retention policies focus on improving access to more information. Research ethics should demand *research security policies* to include robust data protection that account for chain of custody controls, biometric authentication, as well as a protocol for immediate deletion if the data is at risk of misuse. In assessing a threat and potential risk, it is important to understand the intentions of your known adversaries, whether a potential attack is targeted or not. In politicized contexts, teams are likely aware of who potential adversaries will be because they are simply opposed to the research itself. Other adversaries could include individuals, criminal groups, government agencies, or even corporations, depending on the nature of your research.

A risk assessment must also consider the consequences of failing to protect project assets. Risk assessments are fluid and require constant reappraisal: Are you at risk of losing valuable work? Is it replaceable? Could it be co-opted? Corrupted? Or misused? Could your work become part of a disinformation campaign? Distorted, decontextualized, and used on the web to feed more social media churn? Can people be hurt? Can cultural artifacts be lost or damaged? Are the risks acceptable or can they be adequately mitigated? In assessing risk, the likelihood of a threat occurring will change over time. Perhaps threats will pass shortly, or maybe political climate means your work will be under constant scrutiny. It is always important to consider the capability of an adversary, who may simply not be able to effectively disrupt the research.

Some threats must be treated seriously, but others might be just too difficult to mitigate. Is it reasonable to avoid Google or Facebook data collection? It is not likely without massive regulatory reform and strict enforcement of data sovereignty laws. Consider the cost and effort required to combat such threats, and take steps against those threats that are both serious risk to the project and preventable. Humanist researchers working in vulnerable fields should adopt and review security processes throughout the entire research life cycle. A security minded research design process will require an entire team to think about moments when security decisions are made and when trust is granted or shared. Who makes decisions when crossing trust boundaries? Are those decisions made by humans or machines? When are trust boundaries crossed? How is trust established, shared, and used? These are not simple questions nor will they be consistent between teams.

The effort required to secure projects will be added to the workload of already busy teams. Long-term data storage of a hundred years or more means that data preservation is also a security issue. Long-term security processes along with regular updates mean that security protocols must be handed down over time. The exchange of passwords and key material can cause difficulties when managed over this time scale. This is a startling prospect when we would assume, with little effort, that a book might last one hundred years or more. Archival longevity in digital spaces is a real problem, which the sciences have begun to address.[14] In the digital humanities, long-term archiving is less clear particularly when handling applications with long lists of software dependencies. The LOCKSS (Lots of Copies to Keep Stuff Safe) protocol is important from a security point of view if data is destroyed.[15] What happens if your data is tampered with? Made subtly unusable? How will the team leads approve using those copies to restore the canonical digital copy for posterity? Assuming that humanities archives, collections, and software will be likely aggregated in the future—either through acquisition, sharing, adoption, or technological change—how will security policies and procedures be passed on to ensure continued access? Free and Open Source Software might include a security certificate that communicates project security practices and protocols, to help ensure data is not used by surveillance capitalists to further track and surveil citizens. There may be a potential to share Open Access data on the condition that those same security practices are followed, like a Creative Commons license, to help ensure project longevity and availability.[16] Provided the threat model remains consistent with these already evolving security practices, a project could require users or inheritors of the data to adopt privacy and surveillance policies that preserve the integrity of the data for the long term.

Yet the rapid pace of change of security issues is also an opportunity for students to maintain an evolving threat model for projects. Adapting to new threats or software vulnerabilities throughout the research design process would help normalize the critical suspicion that is so helpful in keeping systems secure. If significant security vulnerabilities exist for a particular software, programming language, and all related technologies, researchers might also just choose tooling and deployment approaches with fewer potential problems. Students involved in this security minded research will learn about software supply chains, cryptography, and network protocols, by doing cybersecurity work in the humanities. There is a real potential for humanities students, with well-developed critical sensibilities and excellent written communication abilities, to work in the cybersecurity industry in documentation and analysis. These students would be well positioned to engage directly in activism. With a good understanding of defensive approaches, students in the humanities might also be able to collect compromising information or explore the security of websites of interest. Civil disobedience might require citizens to disrupt the normal functioning of public society to call attention to injustice. Activism is an important activity in public life, but protests are not meant to be convenient. Students might want to be something like a "gray hat" hacker, ethically oriented in their approach but also not always asking for permission. Digital humanists should be as engaged in making things and writing, while ready to break things when necessary.

In a broader sense, digital humanities will be contributing to the security awareness of more active and engaged citizens. Citizens who are more suspicious of content online will be ready to identify politically motivated disinformation and misinformation during elections. Increased cybersecurity literacy is a way of mitigating those human exploits that threaten civil society and a functioning democracy. Without this active approach, the sheer pervasiveness of surveillance and risks online could spread even greater apathy. Citizens robbed of agency and autonomy will grow embittered and fatalistic about the role of technology and democracy in their lives. This learned helplessness assumes laws and cultural norms of life online are inevitable. We risk succumbing to a life of merely responding to the messages, wherein our lives merely pulse in time with a profit-generating algorithm. We become both consumer and producer of content with no ownership, control, or privacy rights. And in a bitter twist, this apathy will still leave many utterly dependent on surveillance capitalism and social media for feelings of validation, respect, and happiness.

By studying speculative fiction, literature and technology work together to both imagine pessimistic futures and prepare readers to advocate for the regulation of real world technologies. The dystopian visions of cyberpunk—of an ecologically ruined planet, urban decay, retreating or incapable government, powerful corporations, and crime filled cyberspace—are a warning. Cyberpunk also grants us a vision of renewed agency and the ability to speak truth to power through code. Cyberspace is the virtual world of information and experience that grants hacker heroes a chance to fight back. Our internet is not so different. As Phineas Fisher remarked after taking responsibility for the attack on the infamous Italian based hacker-for-hire corporation, HackingTeam: "That's all it takes to take down a company and stop their human rights abuses. That's the beauty and asymmetry of hacking: with 100 hours of work, one person can undo years of work by a multi-million dollar company. Hacking gives the underdog a chance to fight and win."[17] HackingTeam was then well known for providing services to many countries with very poor human rights records, including the Lebanese Army, Sudan, Bahrain, and many others. In Fisher, a fictional hacker seems to have stepped out of a cyberpunk novel into reality. They are a very romantic vision of a brilliant, anonymous individual willing to risk prison time in the name of justice and peace. As reported in an ArsTechnica piece from the time, DanTentler, CEO of Phobos Group, described Fisher's work in the following way: "They are kind of a ninja. It's pretty rare you find exploitation, reverse engineering, exploit development, lateral movement, networking/routing, and exfiltration all in the same person."[18] Cyberninjas are, certainly, pretty cool.

With that said, the HackingTeam attack and data breach was absolutely illegal. After a long investigation, the Italian authorities are still incapable of determining who committed the attack.[19] In the balance of global human rights issues or breaking the law, it might be an easy choice, but we have to admit that the ethics of this kind of hack are not completely clear. Phineas Fisher would go on to hack and leak internal government communications of the Turkish government for their repression of Kurdish independence.[20] Blending hacktivism on the global stage, where the actions of an individual can be misapprehended as the hostile actions of another nation, poses particular risks. While a hack and leak of governmental emails are unlikely to rile tensions to the point of conflict, there may be a line crossed in the future in which hacktivism is regarded as direct nation-state backed hostile action and provokes an international incident. Hacking is not a crime; it's research. But is there a place for this kind of ethical hacking in the humanities?

I am reminded of a quote from the beginning of Brian Knappenberger's documentary *The Internet's Own Boy: The story of Aaron Swartz* from 2014. The documentary collects the story of Aaron Swartz, a gifted programmer and open data advocate. Swartz was involved in so many high-profile projects including Reddit, Markdown, RSS, and the Creative Commons. When he was caught downloading JSTOR data from an MIT library, the FBI harassed him to such a degree that he took his own life in 2013 rather than go to jail. At the beginning of the film, Knappenberger quotes Henry David Thoreau's *Civil Disobedience*: "Unjust laws exist; shall we be content to obey them, or shall we endeavor to amend them, and obey them until we have succeeded, or shall we transgress them at once?"[21] It seems that Knappenberger is suggesting that Aaron Swartz transgressed them at once. You can watch *The*

Internet's Own Boy, for free, on the Internet Archive.[22] Disobedience to unjust systems will require breaking the unjust rules that support those systems. Supporting our colleagues who make this jump from academia to activist will require a renewed solidarity with those seeking to gather and protect our historical and cultural record. The historical and cultural record is online, and our web experience is increasingly dominated by paywalls and surveillance capitalist corporations eager to harvest our data. This is an untenable state. Our history and culture is now bound up in corporations that could care less about the humanities. Without reclaiming cultural data, we risk the first part of the twenty-first century becoming a digital dark age. We risk a digital dark age not because the data doesn't exist. We risk losing our cultural heritage because we do not own it. We may be left with no choice but to take it back, at least as individuals.[23]

More recently, Fisher has championed a "Hack Back" program that promises aspiring hackers 100,000 US dollars if they successfully hack capitalist institutions, such as a bank.[24] In an effort to fight economic inequality, Fisher encouraged new hacktivists to develop their skills and hack back for social change and to embarrass the excessive hording of wealth by global elite.[25] Fisher recalls the oldest drives of hacking in their call to hack back. Hacktivism in this case is a pedagogical call: hack to learn, don't learn to hack. Start small, and learn as you go. Not all hacks need to steal and donate money, it is possible to leak compromising data on a site like Distributed Denial of Secrets, for example.[26] Anyone is able to leak data, with or without the editorial consent of a major news outlet. By contrast, The Panama Papers leak had a limited effect because of the lack of public access to data and the way it was filtered through large news media corporations.[27] The effect of this media oversight served to protect the identities of tax avoiding global plutocrats for fear of charges of libel. The scandal generated by these leaks only serves to feed the bogus capitalistic process of profiting from, and ultimately suppressing, real social, economic, and cultural change.

The answer is simple for Fisher: "I only saw the injustice in this world, felt love for all beings, and expressed that love in the best way I could, through the tools I know how to use." Fisher's "Hack Back" campaign sought radical wealth redistribution by stealing from known tax havens for the global super rich and redistributing it to the poorest on the globe. They are vague about how and where the money went exactly, not wanting to implicate charities in crimes for "receiving expropriated funds." The global nature of the internet has allowed for this redistribution of wealth, wherein the concentration of wealth is distributed across a decentralized network. The HackingTeam attack is easy to understand as a protest. An active measure of civil disobedience, where the illegality of the act exposes further injustices. The HackingTeam attack was a hack against hackers. The illegality of the attack showed how unethical it is to then sell similar crimes in the form of software exploits.

The Hack Back campaign sought to reward hackers with expropriated funds from the very institutions that support capitalism, in an incentivized feedback loop of theft funding more theft. There is a reflexive, ironic, quality to this kind of hacktivist critique. Hacking frees capital, while prosecution of hacking keeps the rich rich. Fisher is well aware of the way capitalism disincentivizes the risks needed to hack back and incentivizes conformity and corporate service:

> Hackers working for social change have limited themselves to developing security and privacy tools, DDoS, performing vandalism and leaks. Wherever you go, there are radical projects for a social change in a complete state of precariousness, and there would be much that they could do with some expropriated money. At least for the working class, bank robbery is something socially accepted, and those who do are seen as heroes of the people. In the digital age, robbing a bank is a non-violent, less risky act, and the reward is greater than ever.[28]

They are working to give hacktivists the cultural and economic incentive to take action. The Hack Back document is one part manifesto and one part hacker tutorial, complete with Powershell scripts and exploits in C# and. NET. In documenting their exploit chain along with a cogent argument about economic inequality, Fisher is defining a new form of critique. The exploit chain they provide is a logical argument, complete with guidance on public engagement and activism. In these terms, Fisher can be thought of as a gray hat humanist. They are neither wholly criminal nor entirely altruistic, but they are committed to change. They seek justice and equity by thoroughly reading the political, cultural, and technological forces at work and seeking to disrupt it through critical acts of logic and argument. It is hardly surprising that the logic and arguments Fisher uses are described in code. In this way, they deserve the last word:

```
  _____

/The story is ours\
\ and it is done by hackers! /
  ----------------------

    \
     \ ^__^
     (oo)_____
     ((__)\       )\/\
     _)/  ||----w |
     (.)/   ||    ||
      `'
```

Everyone together, now and forever![29]

Notes

1   Victoria Blake, "Introduction," in *Cyberpunk: Stories of Hardware, Software, Wetware, Evolution and Revolution*, ed. Victoria Blake (New York: Underland Press, 2013), 13.

2   David Drummond, "A New Approach to China," *Googleblog.blogspot. com*, January 12, 2010, https://googleblog.blogspot.com/2010/01/new-approach-to-china.html; George Kurtz, "Operation Aurora Hit Google, Others," *Blogs.mcafee.com*, January 14, 2010, https://web.archive.org/web/20120911141122/http://blogs.mcafee.com/corporate/cto/operation-aurora-hit-google-others.

3   Ellen Nakashima and Joby Warrick, "Stuxnet Was the Work of U.S. and Israeli Experts, Officials Say," *Washingtonpost.com*, June 2, 2012, https://web.archive.org/web/20120911141122/http://blogs.mcafee.com/corporate/cto/operation-aurora-hit-google-others.

4   David E. Sanger and Nicole Perlroth, "U.S. Said to Find North Korea Ordered Cyberattack on Sony," *Nytimes.com*, December 17, 2014, https://www.nytimes.com/2014/12/18/world/asia/us-links-north-korea-to-sony-hacking.html.

5   Ellen Nakashima, "Russian Government Hackers Penetrated DNC, Stole Opposition Research on Trump," *Washingtonpost.com*, June 14, 2016, https://www.washingtonpost.com/world/national-security/russian-government-hackers-penetrated-dnc-stole-opposition-research-on-trump/2016/06/14/cf006cb4-316e-11e6-8ff7-7b6c1998b7a0_story.html.

6   Brad Smith, "A Moment of Reckoning: The Need for a Strong and Global Cybersecurity Response," *Blogs.microsoft.com*, December 17, 2020, https://blogs.microsoft.com/on-the-issues/2020/12/17/cyberattacks-cybersecurity-solarwinds-fireeye/.

7   Liam Tung, "Microsoft: SolarWinds Attack Took More Than 1,000 Engineers to Create," *Zdnet.com*, February 15, 2021, https://www.zdnet.com/article/microsoft-solarwinds-attack-took-more-than-1000-engineers-to-create/.

8   See https://us-cert.cisa.gov/resources/academia and https://www.educause.edu/focus-areas-and-initiatives/policy-and-security/cybersecurity-program.

9   Nancy Kenney, "Smithsonian Confirms That Its Donor Data Was Potentially Breached in Ransomware Attack," *Theartnewspaper.com*, September 2, 2020, https://www.theartnewspaper.com/news/smithsonian-confirms-that-its-donor-data-was-potentially-breached-in-ransomware-attack.

10 Mark Stone, "Municipal Cyberattacks Put Us All at Risk: What Can We Learn From Previous Attacks?," *Securityintelligence.com*, February 21, 2020, https://securityintelligence.com/articles/municipal-cyberattacks-put-us-all-at-risk-what-can-we-learn-from-previous-attacks/.

11 See https://www.nist.gov/cyberframework.

12 There are any number of project charters available online. They often outline the project scope, deliverables and outcomes, audience, roles and responsibilities, timelines, communications practices, credit allocation, attribution, and ownership, as well as deadlines. Security practices like using

passphrases and multifactor authentication, network security, handling RSA/GPG key material, privileged user responsibilities, as well as security minded communication practices.

13 Nearly every educational institution has data security policies, but there is little consistency and standard protections are vague. See https://www.educause.edu/focus-areas-and-initiatives/policy-and-security/cybersecurity-program/resources/information-security-guide/about-the-guide.

14 See https://www.nsf.gov/pubs/2004/nsf04592/nsf04592.htm?org=NSF.

15 See https://www.lockss.org/.

16 See https://creativecommons.org/.

17 J.M. Porup, "How Hacking Team Got hacked," *Arstechnica.com*, April 19, 2016, https://arstechnica.com/information-technology/2016/04/how-hacking-team-got-hacked-phineas-phisher/. Phineas Fisher has appeared in the online press under various names, but in a recent interview with Phineas Fisher, appearing as a sock puppet, they have spelled the pseudonym's surname Fisher.

18 Ibid. I have silently corrected this citation to reflect Phineas Fisher's choice of pronouns as they/them.

19 Lorenzo Franceschi-Bicchierai, "Hacking Team Hacker Phineas Fisher Has Gotten Away With It," *Vice.com*, December 11, 2018, https://www.vice.com/en/article/3k9zzk/hacking-team-hacker-phineas-fisher-has-gotten-away-with-it.

20 Lorenzo Franceschi-Bicchierai, "Notorious Hacker 'Phineas Fisher' Says He Hacked The Turkish Government," *Vice.com*, July 20, 2016, https://www.vice.com/en/article/yp3n55/phineas-fisher-turkish-government-hack.

21 Henry David Thoreau, *Civil Disobedience and Other Essays* (New York: Dover, 1993), 7.

22 See https://archive.org/details/TheInternetsOwnBoyTheStoryOfAaronSwartz.

23 The sale of ProQuest to Clarivate for 5.4 billion US dollars is evidence of the scale of the problem and the forces at work. See https://finance.yahoo.com/news/clarivate-acquire-proquest-creating-leading-100000391.html.

24 Fisher's manifesto is available in the original Spanish here: https://unicornriot.ninja/wp-content/uploads/2019/11/hackback-announce-text.txt. A translation was also made available on Pastebin: https://pastebin.com/8rXhtqgr.

25 Joseph Cox, "Offshore Bank Targeted by Phineas Fisher Confirms It Was Hacked," *Vice.com*, November 18, 2019, https://www.vice.com/en/article/ne8p9b/offshore-bank-targeted-phineas-fisher-confirms-hack-cayman-national-bank.

26 See https://ddosecrets.com/wiki/Distributed_Denial_of_Secrets.

27 See https://panamapapers.org/.

28 See https://pastebin.com/8rXhtqgr.

29 Ibid.

Selected Bibliography

Appadurai, Arjun. "Introduction: Commodities and the Politics of Value." In *The Social Life of Things: Commodities in Cultural Perspective*. Edited by Arjun Appadurai, 3–63. Cambridge: Cambridge University Press, 1986.

Appadurai, Arjun. *Modernity at Large: Cultural Dimensions of Globalization*. Minneapolis: University of Minnesota Press, 1996.

Attebery, Brian. *Decoding Gender in Science Fiction*. New York: Routledge, 2002.

Balsamo, Anne. "Forms of Technological Embodiment: Reading the Body in Contemporary Culture." In *Cyberspace/Cyberbodies/Cyberpunk: Cultures of Technological Embodiment*. Edited by Mike Featherstone and Roger Burrows, 215–37. London: Sage Publications, 1995.

Bamford, James. *The Puzzle Palace: A Report on America's Most Secret Agency*. New York: Houghton Mifflin, 1982.

Baum, Joan. *The Calculating Passion of Ada Byron*. Hamden, CT: Archon Books, 1986.

Benjamin, Ruha. *Race After Technology: Abolitionist Tools for the New Jim Code*. Cambridge, UK: Polity, 2019.

Bennett, Jane. *Vibrant Matter: A Political Ecology of Things*. Durham, NC: Duke University Press, 2010.

Berners-Lee, Tim. *Weaving the Web: The Original Design and Ultimate Destiny for the World Wide Web*. New York: HarperCollins, 1999.

Berry, David M. *The Philosophy of Software: Code and Mediation in the Digital Age*. New York: Palgrave MacMillan, 2011.

Blake, Victoria. "Introduction." In *Cyberpunk: Stories of Hardware, Software, Wetware, Evolution and Revolution*. Edited by Victoria Blake, 9–13. New York: Underland Press, 2013.

Browne, Simone. *Dark Matters: On the Surveillance of Blackness*. Durham: Duke University Press, 2015.

Brunner, John. *Shockwave Rider*. New York: Ballentine Books, 1975.

Cadigan, Pat. *Synners*. New York: Bantam, 1991.

Cavallaro, Dani. *Cyberpunk and Cyberculture: Science Fiction and the Work of William Gibson*. London: The Athlone Press, 2000.

Clark, Dylan. "The Death and Life of Punk, The Last Subculture." In *The Post-Subcultures Reader*. Edited by David Muggleton and Rupert Weinzierl, 223–36. Oxford: Berg, 2003.

Clark, Dylan. "The Raw and the Rotten: Punk Cuisine." *Ethnology* 43, no. 1 (2004): 19–31.

Cline, Ernst. *Ready Player One*. New York: Ballentine Books, 2011.

Cline, Ernst. *Ready Player Two*. New York: Ballentine Books, 2020.

Chun, Wendy Hui Kyong. *Programmed Visions: Software and Memory*. Cambridge, MA: MIT Press, 2011.

Coleman, Gabriella. *Coding Freedom: The Ethics and Aesthetics of Hacking.* Princeton, NJ: Princeton University Press, 2013.

Coleman, Gabriella. *Hacker, Hoaxer, Whistleblower, Spy: The Many Faces of Anonymous.* New York: Verso, 2014.

Delany, Samuel. *Silent Interviews: On Language, Race, Sex, Science Fiction and Some Comics.* Hanover: Wesleyan University Press, 1994.

D'Ignazio, Catherine and Lauren F. Klein. *Data Feminism.* Cambridge, MA: MIT Press, 2020.

Doctorow, Cory. *Little Brother.* New York: Tor Books, 2008.

Doctorow, Cory. *Walkaway.* New York: Tor Books, 2017.

Doctorow, Cory. *Radicalized.* New York: Tor Books, 2019.

Doctorow, Cory. *Attack Surface.* New York: Tor Books, 2020.

Duarte, Marisa Elena. *Network Sovereignty: Building the Internet across Indian Country.* Seattle: University of Washington Press, 2017.

Dunne, Anthony and Fiona Raby. *Speculative Everything: Design Fiction and Social Dreaming.* Cambridge, MA: MIT Press, 2013.

Easley, David and Jon Kleinberg. *Networks, Crowds, and Markets: Reasoning about a Highly Connected World.* Cambridge: Cambridge University Press, 2010.

Farivar, Cyrus. *The Internet of Elsewhere: The Emergent Effects of a Wired World.* New Brunswick, NJ: Rutgers University Press, 2011.

Feathersone, Mike and Roger Burrows. "Cultures of Technological Embodiment: An Introduction." In *Cyberspace/Cyberbodies/Cyberpunk: Cultures of Technological Embodiment.* Edited by Mike Featherstone and Roger Burrows, 1–19. London: Sage Publications, 1995.

Finn, Ed and Kathryn Cramer. *Hieroglyph: Stories and Visions for a Better Future.* New York: William Morrow, 2015.

Jameson, Frederic. "Postmodernism, or, the Cultural Logic of Late Capitalism." *New Left Review* 146 (1984): 53–94.

Fanon, Frantz. *Black Skin, White Masks.* New York: Grove Press, 2008.

Ferguson, Niels Bruce Schneier, and Tadayoshi Kohno. *Cryptography Engineering: Design Principles and Practical Applications.* Indianapolis: Wiley Publishing, 2010.

Finn, Ed. *What Algorithms Want: Imagination in the Age of Computing.* Cambridge, MA: MIT Press, 2017.

Frum, David. *Trumpocracy: The Corruption of the American Republic.* New York: HarperCollins, 2018.

Fukuyama, Francis. *The End of History and the Last Man.* New York: The Free Press, 1992.

Galloway, Alexander R. and Eugene Thacker. *The Exploit: A Theory of Networks.* Minneapolis: University of Minnesota Press, 2007.

Gibson, William. *Neuromancer.* New York: Ace 1984.

Gibson, William. "Burning Chrome." In *Hackers,* Edited by Jack Dann and Gardner Dozois, 1–23. New York: Ace, 1996.

Gleick, James. *The Information: A History, a Theory, a Flood.* New York: Pantheon Books, 2011.

Golumbia, David. *The Cultural Logic of Computation.* Cambridge, Mass.: Harvard University Press, 2009.

Gottschall, Jonathan. *The Storytelling Animal: How Stories Make Us Human.* New York: Mariner Books, 2013.

Graham, Shawn. *Failing Gloriously and Other Essays*. Grand Forks: The Digital Press at the University of North Dakota, 2019.

Gray, Chris Hables, Heidi J. Figueroa-Sarriera, and Steven Mentor. *Modified: Living as a Cyborg*. New York: Routledge, 2021.

Greenberg, Andy. *Sandworm: A New Era of Cyberwar and the Hunt for the Kremlin's Most Dangerous Hackers*. New York: Doubleday, 2019.

Grimes, Roger A. *Cryptography Apocalypse: Preparing for the Day when Quantum Computing Breaks Today's Crypto*. New Jersey: John Wiley & Sons, 2020.

Haney II, William S. *Cyberculture, Cyborgs and Science Fiction: Consciousness and the Posthuman*. New York: Rodopi, 2006.

Haraway, Donna. *Simians, Cyborgs, and Women: The Reinvention of Nature*. New York: Routledge, 1991.

Hayles, N. Katherine. *How We Became Posthuman: Virtual Bodies in Cybernetics, Literature and Informatics*. Chicago: University of Chicago Press, 1999.

Himanen, Pekka. *The Hacker Ethic and the Spirit of the Information Age*. New York: Random House, 2001.

Igo, Sarah E. *The Known Citizen: A History of Privacy in Modern America*. Cambridge: Harvard University Press, 2018.

Isin, Engin and Evelyn Ruppert. *Being Digital Citizens*. London: Rowman & Littlefield, 2015.

Kahn, David. *The Codebreakers: The Story of Secret Writing*. New York: Macmillan, 1967.

Lanier, Jaron. *Ten Arguments for Deleting Your Social Media Accounts Right Now*. New York: Henry Holt and Co., 2018.

Lavigne, Carlen. *Cyberpunk Women, Feminism and Science Fiction: A Critical Study*. Jefferson: McFarland and Company, 2013.

Levy, Steven. *Hackers: Heroes of the Computer Revolution*. New York: O'Reilly, 1984.

Levy, Steven. *Crypto: How the Code Rebels Beat the Government—Saving Privacy in the Digital Age*. New York: Viking, 2001.

Liu, Alan. *The Laws of Cool: Knowledge Work and the Culture of Information*. Chicago: University of Chicago Press, 2004.

Lovink, Geert. *Dark Fiber: Tracking Critical Internet Culture*. Cambridge: MIT Press, 2002.

Lyotard, Jean-François. *The Postmodern Condition: A Report on Knowledge*. Translated by Geoff Bennington and Brian Massumi. Minneapolis: University of Minnesota Press, 1984.

Mason, Zachary. *Void Star*. New York: Farrar, Straus, and Giroux, 2017.

McGann, Jerome. *Radiant Textuality: Literature after the World Wide Web*. New York: Palgrave, 2001.

McIlwain, Charlton D. *Black Software: The Internet and Racial Justice, from the AfroNet to Black Lives Matter*. Oxford: Oxford University Press, 2020.

Moravec, Hans. *Robot: Mere Machine to Transcendent Mind*. Oxford: Oxford University Press, 1999.

Nakamura, Lisa. *Cybertypes: Race, Ethnicity, and Identity on the Internet*. New York: Routledge, 2002.

Nelson, Ted. *Computer Lib/Dream Machines*. Self-published, 1974. https://archive.org/details/computer-lib-dream-machines/.

Newitz, Annalee. *Autonomous*. New York: Tor, 2017.

Noble, Safiya Umoja. *Algorithms of Oppression: How Search Engines Reinforce Racism*. New York: New York University Press, 2018.

Older, Malka. *Informocracy*. New York: Tor Books, 2016.

Older, Malka. *Null States*. New York: Tor Books, 2017.

Older, Malka. *State Tectonics*. New York: Tor, 2018.

O'Neil, Cathy. *Weapons of Math Destruction: How Big Data Increases Inequality and Threatens Democracy*. New York: Crown Publishing, 2016.

Pariser, Eli. *The Filter Bubble: How the New Personalized Web Is Changing What We Read and How We Think*. New York: Penguin, 2012.

Pavel, Thomas G. *Fictional Worlds*. Cambridge, MA: Harvard University Press, 1989.

Poe, Edgar Allan. *The Gold-Bug and Other Tales*. New York: Dover, 1991.

Poletti, Anna and Julie Rak. *Identity Technologies: Constructing the Self Online*. Madison, WI: University of Wisconsin Press, 2014.

Postman, Matthew. *Technopoly: The Surrender of Culture to Technology*. New York: Vintage, 1992.

Raymond, Eric S. *The Cathedral and the Bazaar: Musings on Linux and Open Source by an Accidental Revolutionary*. Cambridge: O'Reilly, 1999.

Redfield, Marc. *Shibboleth: Judges, Derrida, Celan*. New York: Fordham University Press, 2020.

Schneier, Bruce. *Applied Cryptography: Protocols, Algorithms, and Source Code in C, second edition*. New York: John Wiley & Sons, 1996.

Schneier, Bruce. *Beyond Fear: Thinking Sensibly About Security in an Uncertain World*. New York: Copernicus, 2003.

Shell, Marc. *The Economy of Literature*. Baltimore: Johns Hopkins University Press, 1978.

Shillingsburg, Peter L. *From Gutenberg to Google: Electronic Representations of Literary Texts*. Cambridge: Cambridge University Press, 2006.

Silverman, Kenneth. *Edgar A. Poe: Mournful and Never-ending Remembrance*. New York: Harper Perennial, 1992.

Snowden, Edward. *Permanent Record*. New York: Metropolitan Books, 2019.

Stallman, Richard. *Free Software, Free Society: Selected Essays*. Boston: GNU Press, 2002.

Stephenson, Neal. *Snow Crash*. New York: Del Rey, 1992.

Stephenson, Neal. *Cryptonomicon*. New York: Avon, 1999.

Sterling, Bruce, ed. *Mirrorshades: The Cyberpunk Anthology*. New York: Ace, 1988.

Toffler, Alvin. *Future Shock*. New York: Random House, 1970.

Wagner, Pheobe and Christopher Wieland (eds.). *Sunvault: Stories of Solarpunk and Eco-Speculation*. Nashville: Upper Rubber Books, 2017.

Wark, Mackenzie. *The Hacker Manifesto*. Cambridge, MA: Harvard University Press, 2004.

Webb, Maureen. *Coding Democracy: How Hackers Are Disrupting Power, Surveillance, and Authoritarianism*. Cambridge, MA: MIT Press, 2020.

Wernimont, Jacqueline. *Numbered Lives: Life and Death in Quantum Media*. Cambridge, MA: MIT Press, 2018.

Williams, Walter Jon. *Hardwired*. New York: Tor Books, 1986.

Williams, Walter Jon. *Voice of the Whirlwind*. New York: Tor Books, 1987.

Williams, Walter Jon. *Solip: System*. Eugene: Axolotl Press, 1989.

Williams, Sam. *Free as in Freedom: Richard Stallman's Crusade for Free Software*. Sebastopol, CA: O'Reilly, 2002.

Wiener, Norbert. *Human Uses for Human Beings: Cybernetics and Society*. London: Free Association Books.

Youngquist, Paul. *Cyberfiction: After the Future*. New York: Palgrave Macmillan, 2010.

Zelle, John. *Python Programming: An Introduction to Computer Science*. Portland: Franklin, Beedle & Associates, 2017.

Zuboff, Shoshana. *The Age of Surveillance Capitalism: The fight for a Human Future at the New Frontier of Power*. New York: PublicAffairs, 2019.

Index

CPSIA information can be obtained
at www.ICGtesting.com
Printed in the USA
LVHW050241090723
751824LV00005B/222